THE OXFORD
HISTORY OF MUSIC

VOL. VI

THE ROMANTIC PERIOD

BY

EDWARD DANNREUTHER

Second Edition

NEW YORK
COOPER SQUARE PUBLISHERS, INC.
1973

Revised edition Published 1932 by Oxford University Press
Reprinted by Permission of Oxford University Press
Published 1973 by Cooper Square Publishers, Inc.
59 Fourth Avenue, New York, New York 10003
International Standard Book Number 0-8154-0474-3
Library of Congress Catalog Card Number 72-97076

Printed in the United States of America

NOTE

It is not fitting to speak here of the heavy loss which English Music has sustained in the death of Mr. Edward Dannreuther. To his long career of unselfish and devoted labour there have been paid elsewhere tributes which no words of mine could enhance. But, from respect to his memory, I would ask leave to offer a brief explanation of the circumstances under which this his last work is presented to the public.

The manuscript was finished and partly revised by the Autumn of 1904. All that remained was to complete the revision and to make a selection of the musical examples. During the winter Mr. Dannreuther was prevented by illness from continuing the work; and at his request, and under his instructions, I carried it on to the best of my ability. The volume as it stands embodies the results of his research and the verdicts of his critical judgement: but it did not receive the final touch of his hand.

There is one more point to which the attention of the reader may be directed. When the Oxford History was first planned it appeared advisable to end with Schumann, and to leave to some future historian the more controversial topics of our own time. This view it has been found necessary to modify, and the present volume contains reference to the principal works, of whatever date, which in origin or character can be directly attributed to the Romantic movement.

My cordial thanks are due to Mr. J. A. Fuller Maitland for his assistance in the correction of the proofs.

W. H. HADOW.

NOTE TO 'THE SECOND EDITION.

THE Oxford History of Music was originally planned as a series of six volumes, ending at the death of Schumann. It was then contemplated that a seventh volume should follow, dealing with the works of Wagner, Brahms, Dvořák and the other composers who flourished during the latter half of the nineteenth century.

It was clear that no exact line of demarcation could be drawn. History does not lend itself to precise chronological divisions, and is not violated if we extend Annian poetry to the Essay on Man or include in the Elizabethan Age the madrigals of Orlando Gibbons. While, therefore, Dannreuther was chiefly occupied with the two decades which followed the death of Schubert, he took full freedom to enlarge his boundaries, wherever such enlargement was justified by similarities of conception or treatment, and to comprise within them all works in which he could most directly trace the methods and influence of the Romantic School. Hence the amount of space devoted to Liszt who died in 1886, to Borodine who died in 1887, and to Tchaikovsky who died in 1893. Hence also the virtual restriction of Wagner to the romantic operas, the few and slender references to Brahms, and the omission of Dvořák, whom he rightly regarded as more suitable for a later volume.

This explains a certain irregularity of outline which is not, I venture to say, a defect in the volume but a natural consequence of its position in the general scheme. The sixth volume has its own unity of purpose ; a seventh is now being prepared, and will serve as its continuation and counterpart.

The opinions expressed in this book have been left untouched. In some instances we of the present day might readjust the proportion, in a few we might reconsider the verdict. But the whole work bears the impress of its author's personality, and garners the mature harvest of his life. He was a man of wide experience and encyclopædic knowledge, the friend and early champion of Wagner, the master of Hubert Parry, a pioneer of the new music and a steadfast supporter of the old. He died while the first edition of his volume was passing through the press, and bequeathed it as a monument of the devoted and unselfish labour with which, during the space of forty years, he had encouraged and advanced the cause of music in England.

PREFACE

An attempt is here made to show, with the aid of copious examples, analyses, and comments, how the course of Music has gradually changed since Beethoven's day. Not to disturb the impression of historical sequence each department is treated chronologically, but as the different classes of music are discussed separately the dates necessarily overlap. Musical quotations are in some instances rather long, because the reader, to be in a position to judge of the calibre and style of a passage, ought to have at least one complete sentence or period before him. They are compressed in so far as compression is consistent with perspicuity, and the original is always faithfully reproduced. In connexion with the description of the works that stand for the various phases of the Romantic movement, certain questions arising out of the attitude towards artistic problems taken by leading masters are discussed as they come into view; and it is the ever-varying aspect of such questions that forms both the link and the contrast between chapter and chapter, sometimes even between one paragraph and another.

A book so closely in touch with the actualities of present-day musical life must needs contain some controversial matter. It ought to be trustworthy as to facts, but it can hardly avoid the expression of disputable criticisms. These must be understood to represent merely the personal opinions of the writer.

EDWARD DANNREUTHER.

CONTENTS

THE ROMANTIC PERIOD

CHAPTER I

INTRODUCTION

MUSIC, polyphonic and harmonic, considered in relation to other departments of artistic endeavour, is somewhat late in its manifestations. It was not until the fifteenth and sixteenth centuries, when Counterpoint flourished in the Netherlands, England, and Italy, that the affinity between polyphony and Gothic architecture became apparent. The religious painting of the early Italian Renaissance hardly found a counterpart in music before Palestrina's time. Some aspects of the secular poetry and painting of the later Renaissance are reproduced in the Italian and English Madrigals and the Spanish, French, and English lute music of the seventeenth century. The spirit of Protestantism acquired its musical voice very gradually—first in Schütz, then in Bach and Handel. The elaborate courtesy and urbanity of the first half of the eighteenth century are, to a certain degree, reflected in the operas of Gluck and Mozart. Echoes of the worship of nature, the humanitarian enthusiasm, and the social upheaval of the second half of that century can be traced in the symphonic work of Beethoven, which properly belongs to the first quarter of the nineteenth. Even in the revival of Teutonic myth, and in the dreamland of Norse, Celtic, or Slavonic poetry, the relation of things poetic to things musical exhibits the same order : the songs of Tieck's *Schöne Magelone* had to wait for Brahms, the revival of old German stories of gods and heroes for Wagner. But as time goes on and new processes are discovered the intervals become shorter. The

rate of growth is accelerated, and musical art comes nearer to
the sister arts, to thought, and to life. Examined from this
point of view, the period of musical development here to be
discussed—the Romantic period, from Weber to Wagner, i. e.
from *Der Freischütz* to *Lohengrin* and *Tristan*, or from Weber's
overtures to the symphonic pieces of Berlioz and Liszt—is, on
the emotional side, seen to be imbued with the spirit of romantic
poetry and literature, whilst, on the technical side, it is a time
of transition from the formal to the characteristic, from the
'Singspiel' or the 'Opera seria' to the 'Opera caratteristica,'
and the Wagnerian Music-drama, from the Sonata to the
'Characterstück,' from the Symphony to the 'Poème symphonique.'

Romantic music is, in some sense, an offshoot of literature;
a reflex of poetry expressed in musical terms; a kind of
impressionism which tends to reject formality, and aims at
a direct rendering of its object; a desire to produce musical
effects suggested by natural phenomena; an art eager, sensitive,
impulsive, which seeks its ideal of beauty through emotional
expression. With Wagner it is *ancilla dramatis*—a powerful
rhetoric which, like scenery and action, is made subservient to
the purposes of the Theatre.

Literary Romanticism, about 1800, found a voice for the
thoughts and feelings which by natural reaction had begun to
invade the rationalistic world of the eighteenth century. It was
not so much a protest against classical work as against some
aspects of the reasoned taste in art that had sprung from the
spirit of rationalism. It gave voice to a keen love of the past,
especially of the religious aspect of past ages, and to a keen
passion for nature. The Christian ideals and the ideals of
Rousseau met in the sentimentality of Bernardin de St. Pierre,
Chateaubriand, de Senancourt, and many others who mistook
the *furore espressivo* for a symptom of strength. 'L'aspiration
du sublime,' says George Sand, 'était même une maladie du
temps—c'était quelque chose de fiévreux qui s'emparait de la

jeunesse.' In Germany as in France, a little later on, the growth of music proceeded on similar lines. German music followed the traces of German literature at an interval of a generation or so—whilst in France, more directly in accordance with the *École romantique*, music and literature came to be very nearly contemporaneous. On every side it is evident that music received, and in its peculiar way brought to efflorescence, modes of feeling which had their roots in literature.

Goethe claimed to have been the first to use the elusive term Romantic in contrast to Classical. 'The familiar conception of the classical and the romantic arose in my mind and in Schiller's. My maxims were in favour of the objective method of treatment. But Schiller preferred his own subjective method, and defended it in his essay on "Naïve and Sentimental Poetry." He showed that I was romantically inclined in spite of my desire to be otherwise, and that my *Iphigenie,* because of the preponderance of sentiment, was by no means so antique in feeling as I thought. Later on the brothers Schlegel took up the matter; and people now talk glibly of classicism and romanticism, to which fifty years ago no one gave a thought [1].' Romanticism in Germany reached its acme during the period of reaction and restoration following the Napoleonic wars, when the Germans, in their ardour for historical studies, developed the historical sense—a high degree of sympathy with modes of feeling long lost, a taste for conditions and characteristics of past ages and climes remote. The historical studies at the Universities induced a leaning towards criticism. A school of literary critics arose; innumerable translations were attempted (Homer, Shakespeare, Calderon, Cervantes), philologists worked at Sanscrit, Persian, Old Norse, and mediaeval German. Teutonic mythology was reconstructed; legends, fairy tales, remnants of folk-lore, popular ballads, and songs, were collected and compared.

[1] J. P. Eckermann, II. 137, *Gespräche mit Goethe*: three parts published in 1837. The preface to Part I is dated October 31, 1835.

Following in the wake of Thomson, J. J. Rousseau, and their own Goethe, German romanticists in prose and verse—such as Novalis, Tieck, Fr. and A. W. Schlegel, Eichendorf, Brentano, and later on Chamisso, Hoffmann, Fouquet, Jean Paul Richter, Uhland, Rückert, Platen, Lenau, Heine—attempted an emotional interpretation of nature. The prevailing sentimentalism, together with their special historical predilections, prompted the earlier of these writers to deal mainly with mediaeval legends, with magic superstition, with knight-errantry, and the worship of woman. Mythology and poetry, symbolical legend and art, they asserted, must be considered as óne and indivisible; 'the deepest want and deficiency of modern art lies in the fact that artists have no mythology to fall back upon[1].' And they insisted that only in the service of religion had art ever flourished—only in that service could it flourish. Some of them, like Tieck and A. W. Schlegel, inclined towards mediaeval Catholicism—the revival of which they greeted with the sympathy of poetical enthusiasts; others, like Fr. Schlegel and Novalis, accepted its doctrines in full; whilst contemporary German painters, such as Overbeck and Cornelius, under the same influence, busied themselves with an attempt to revive the forms of early Christian art. Goethe, with some disdain, spoke of the painters as 'Nazarenes,' and of the litterati as 'forced talents.' What he particularly disliked in the productions of the eccentric younger men was not so much the prevalent musical note in their verse, for in their schemes of verbal melody they often followed his example, as the quasi-musical mood underlying the things set forth—vague visions and states of feeling, dissolving views bathed in moonlight and made faintly vocal with the notes of the Aeolian harp.

The German writers of fantastic prose or verse (E. T. A. Hoffmann excepted) were but dilettanti in music—lovers of fine sound with little knowledge of the art. Yet it is of real interest

---

[1] Fr. Schlegel, *Gespräche über Poesie*, pp. 263, 274.

to note how persistently their instinct turned towards music as a possible fulfilment of their aims, and how much that is sane and good in their efforts has found expression in artistic music.

Premising that music, be it vocal or instrumental, is incapable of describing matters of fact, we may speak of the romantic element in music as poetical suggestion by musical means. The suggestiveness and witchery of certain fragments of impressionist music is best illustrated by citation from Weber and Wagner. Take a few typical examples : the last eighteen bars of the second act of *Die Meistersinger,* when the moonlight peers through the streets of old Nürnberg after the riot, the forest voices in *Siegfried,* the strange chords when Brünnhilde sinks to sleep. Weber, Wagner's great prototype in this respect, has such things in abundance—e.g. the introductions of the overtures to *Der Freischütz* and to *Oberon,* the intermezzo in the overture to *Euryanthe.* Effects of mystery—dreams of the past, with all the illusions of a dream—'The horns of Elfland faintly blowing'—a rustle of fairies, the chant of some nameless knight—dim memories and suggestions, *Mondbeglänzte Zaubernacht, Liebe denkt in süssen Tönen, Alles singt zu dieser Stunde.* Nor is the suggestiveness confined to snatches of Weber or Wagner. Entire pieces or strings of pieces by composers contemporary with both of them are imbued with it. Take, for further instance, Schubert's C major symphony ; compare the tones of the horn in the introductory 'Andante' and the 'Andante con moto' ; take the sound of the strings and oboe in Mendelssohn's overture *The Hebrides,* and of the horns in his Scotch symphony, or Schumann's trumpet effects in the overture to *Manfred,* his Song-cycle *Liederkreis von Eichendorf,* or certain of his pianoforte pieces such as the *Kreisleriana.* Everywhere there are musical echoes of nature, recollections of ' old unhappy far-off things ' ; appeals to sentiment and emotion which would lose half their force had they not already been anticipated by literature.

Of course musical romanticism in the nineteenth century, be it German, French, or Italian, was not a new departure. Premonitions of it are already discernible in Schütz, d'Anglebert, Froberger, Buxtehude, J. S. Bach, Beethoven, Dussek, Schubert, Spohr; also in the work of certain men who made their mark in Italy or in Paris—Gluck (parts of *Alceste*, particularly the superb recitative chorus and aria, ' Grands Dieux,' Act III, No. 3); Pergolesi (*Stabat Mater*); Spontini (*La Vestale*, notably the chorus of vestals in E♭); Méhul (*Uthal* and *Joseph en Égypte*); Boieldieu (*Jean de Paris* and *La Dame blanche*). No one can mistake the romantic sensibility expressed in Froberger's *Tombeaux* (' Laments '); in J. S. Bach's Prelude in E♭ minor [1], the Chromatic Fantasia, the recitative arioso *Ach Golgotha, unseliges Golgotha*, and *Am Abend da es kühle war*; in that Passion according to St. Matthew, in Dussek's *Élégie harmonique*; or in some of Beethoven's smaller pieces, such as *Adelaide, An die Hoffnung*, Op. 94, *In questa tomba oscura*; Liederkreis, *An die ferne Geliebte*, the first movement of the *Sonate pathétique*, the second movement of the Trio in D, Op. 70; and in many a song and instrumental piece of Schubert.

It is worthy of note that the touches of romantic sentiment in Schütz or in the works of some of Bach's precursors like Buxtehude and Böhm, as in J. S. Bach's own compositions, occur but sporadically, whilst the technical means employed to express them are in no way exceptional. The case is very different with the composers of the nineteenth century. Romantic sentiment with them is always present, and at the same time they exhibit a continuous striving to keep pace with the spiritual transmutation that is going on around them. Under some personal impulse, some suggestion without, always with a view to musical characterization, they are seen to be taking pains to elaborate this or that point, or trying to discover

---

[1] Compare it with Chopin's Étude in C♯ minor, or with the Preludes Nos. 2 and 4 in E minor.

more suitable technical means to attain this or that particular effect.

From Weber's time, about 1820, a new spirit was in the air and an increasingly rapid process of change and expansion resulted from its appearance. It can be traced from Spohr and Weber to Mendelssohn, Schumann, Gade, Sterndale-Bennett, Rubinstein, and Tchaikovsky; from Berlioz to Liszt; and from Schumann, Liszt, and Berlioz to the ingenious Neo-Russians such as Balakirev, Borodine, Cui, and Rimsky-Korsakov; and again from Wagner, Berlioz, and Liszt to Anton Bruckner, and, *mutatis mutandis*, to Richard Strauss. Taken altogether, the romantic movement—in so far at least as instrumental music and the orchestra is concerned—appears as an unconscious tendency towards the relaxation of the laws of structure in favour of characteristic details, an almost total rejection of organic design on self-contained lines, and, step by step, an approach to a sketchy sort of impressionism and a kind of scene-painting— a huge piling up of means for purposes of illustration. No doubt it was guilty of many excesses. It was often crude, often extravagant; sometimes apparently inspired by mere defiance and bravado. But, when all this has been said, it remains true that the net gain, the widening both of the range of knowledge and of the scope of emotion, which has resulted from the move- ment, is a possession the value of which cannot be overrated [1].

After Weber the change from the formal to the characteristic and the tendency towards programme music went on apace. The attitude of Mendelssohn and Schumann, regarding titles and descriptive indications generally, like that of Beethoven and the earlier masters, was the attitude of the specific musician. Up till about 1850, music on self-sufficing lines was by far the main concern from the professional point of view. With

---

[1] The reaction against vague impressionism or pictorial illustration came in Germany under Brahms, and in England under Parry, Stanford, and the other masters of the English Renaissance; and it seems to be coming in Russia. The stragglers, adherents of Berlioz and Liszt (their name is legion), hardly count.

Mendelssohn and Schumann, conscious poetical intentions, admittedly present in many instances, appear on the second or third plane—as it were by implication only—and do not directly touch the musical design. Every good overture or introduction to an opera has in the nature of things a sort of programme implied or avowed. The programme consists of the opera to follow—witness Beethoven's overture to *Fidelio* [1]. Mendelssohn held that any attempt to reduce definite combinations of tone and rhythm—that is to say, musical expression generally—to verbal expression or vice versa, must result in failure. Musical utterance, he maintained, is positive, and remains so whether or not a more general significance be attributed to it; whilst any verbal or pictorial allusion to the effects of music will be less definite than the music itself. To this it may be added that music contrived with intent to illustrate a ready-made programme may—by lucky chance, and in a way of its own —prove to be a satisfactory statement of essentials. But it is by no means sure to be so, and this was the point of view Wagner took regarding Liszt's symphonic programme music.

Not only in Germany, but all round, the spirit of Weber's opera led the romantic development. 'Questo è inventore,' as Jommelli said of Piccinni. Through the whole field of musical art Weber's temper prevailed. From *Der Freischütz* onwards, opera (apart from the *bel canto* of the Italians) is in a large measure derived from Weber, and many of the novel procedures in instrumental music rest on his method. Thus, on the one hand, the innovations and experiments in the treatment of operatic forms first suggested to Weber by theatrical considerations, constitute the starting-point of the changes that led to Meyerbeer's *Robert le Diable*, Marschner's *Vampyr* and *Hans Heiling*, and the earlier operas of Wagner [2]. And, on the other

---

[1] Spohr in his *Faust* has gone the length of explicitly acquainting the audience with what he wishes them to imagine.

[2] *Lohengrin* was the last of Wagner's works which he called a 'romantic opera.' His later application of Beethoven's symphonic music to his own ends as a musical dramatist—in *Der Ring des Nibelungen, Tristan und Isolde, Die Meistersinger*

hand, the orchestral pieces—the overtures and symphonies of Mendelssohn and his followers, as well as the orchestral pieces of Schumann, bear traces of Weber's spirit and practice. Besides, in several minor departments, such as music for the pianoforte, and part-songs for male voices, Weber stands in the position of a pioneer [1].

In France the immediate musical sequel to the romantic movement in literature was restricted to about a dozen works. Several grand operas belong to it: Auber's *La Muette de Portici*, Rossini's *Guillaume Tell*, Meyerbeer's *Robert le Diable*, Halévy's *La Juive*; as also the symphonies and overtures of Berlioz, his early opera semi-seria *Benvenuto Cellini*, and an 'Ode-symphonie,' *Le Désert*, by Berlioz' disciple Félicien David.

The representatives of the opéra comique—Boieldieu, Auber, Adam, Hérold—moved on the ordinary light French lines of Grétry, Monsigny, Dalayrac, Isouard, and kept far away from the glimmer of romance; whilst in the operas of Italian composers the influence of French literary and pictorial romanticism (Victor Hugo, Delacroix, Ary Scheffer) can be traced in a few cases only—in the sentimentality, for instance, of Bellini's *Norma*, *La Sonnambula*, and *I Puritani*, which had its source in Rousseau, through Chateaubriand and Madame de Staël, and in the violence of some of Verdi's early operas, *Ernani*, *Rigoletto*, both of which are founded on plays by Victor Hugo. The power of the romantic literature of the day is also manifest in certain early Russian, Polish, and Bohemian operas, such as Glinka's *La Vie pour le Tzar*, *Russlan et Ludmilla*, Sérof's *Judith*, Moniusko's *Halka*, and Smetana's *Prodana nevěsta* ('The Bartered Bride').

---

von Nürnberg, and *Parsifal*—is best considered apart; though in many ways, even in the latest phase of Wagner's art, *Parsifal*, the romantic impulse is felt to be present, and the master appears intimately connected with romanticism—both on the literary and the musical side.

[1] The entire German 'Männergesang' of the present day, with all its political significance, springs from Weber's initiative in such spirited little masterpieces as *Lützow's wilde Jagd* and *Gebet vor der Schlacht*.

Many an important development in orchestral music, apart from the stage, starts indirectly from Weber's overtures to *Freischütz, Euryanthe, Oberon*. Weber's vivid imagination and fiery impulse found complete expression in these typically romantic pieces. Less compact and strictly consistent on musical lines than Beethoven's overtures, they are, to a large extent, made up of extracts from or allusions to scenes of the operas to which they serve as introductions. But they are so well put together, the contrasting modes are so well arranged, that there is no suspicion of any shortcoming in design. Mendelssohn in his concert overtures improved on Weber's type, inasmuch as the thematic materials he worked with, figures, and melodies, are more homogeneous and suitable for development. The plaintive tone pervading *Fingal*, the translucent atmosphere of *Meeresstille*, the tender and delicately passionate romance of *Melusina*, have little in common with Weber's dramatic power; but Weber's instrumental technique is present, notably in the overture to *A Midsummer Night's Dream*, and many a subtle device of Weber's orchestration is adopted and put to ingenious use. In his symphonies, just as much as in his overtures, Mendelssohn aimed at the expression of distinct moods and definite ideas, but always on lines of purely musical design. In no instance did he venture beyond distinctive titles or inscriptions, and it is significant that he has hardly ever furnished sub-titles, or any other hints of his meaning, though he might just as well, for instance, have called the slow movement of the Italian symphony a 'Pilgrim's Procession' as the finale a 'Saltarello.' Schumann, the Romantic *par excellence* after Weber, was more inclined to give special titles to his musical poems. One of his symphonies, the first in Bb, was known to his friends as the Spring Symphony, and another, Eb, Op. 97, as the Rhenish. His overtures, *Manfred* and *Genoveva*, were intended to be close reproductions of the moods which underlie the subjects indicated or suggested by the titles. But with Schumann, as with Mendelssohn, the titles are never meant to furnish programmatic details which can in any way control the course of the music.

Nothing could better prove the strength of the impulse towards characterization than the fact that Spohr, who in most things was a follower of Mozart, should in his latter days have composed symphonies illustrating ideas more or less alien to music. The true initiator, however, the path-finder in the direction of musical illustration, was Berlioz. He and Liszt are the most conspicuous and thoroughgoing representatives of programme music, i.e. instrumental music expressly devised to illustrate in detail some play or poem or some succession of ideas or pictures.

In pieces such as the first and last movements of Berlioz' *Symphonie fantastique*, the first and last movements of his symphony *Harold en Italie*, Liszt's Poèmes symphoniques *Ce qu'on entend sur la montagne*, after a poem by Victor Hugo, and *Die Ideale*, after a poem by Schiller, the hearer is bewildered by a series of startling orchestral effects which are not explicable on any principle of musical design.

The use of the oratorio and the cantata for concert rather than church purposes—which in Germany began with Haydn's *Creation* and *Seasons*, and with Beethoven's setting of Goethe's *Meeresstille*—reached a climax when Mendelssohn produced his cantata *Die erste Walpurgisnacht* and the oratorios *St. Paul* and *Elijah*. Before that time Spohr, notably in *The Last Judgement*, had found the oratorio better suited to his powers than the opera or the symphony. Contemporaneously with Mendelssohn, Schumann made a new start with a secular oratorio (or rather a set of three cantatas) after Moore's rimed story 'Paradise and the Peri' in *Lalla Rookh*. Berlioz, too, attempted something resembling oratorio in the 'Trilogie sacrée' *L'Enfance du Christ*, and something like a dramatic cantata, or an 'opéra de concert,' in *La Damnation de Faust*. With his *Messe des Morts*, and the *Te Deum*, he aimed at the secularization of church music, purposely setting the words of the Catholic service on a grandiose scale and somewhat histrionically.

Liszt, in a more religious spirit, followed with the *Graner Fest-Messe* and *Ungarische Krönungs-Messe*, the *Thirteenth Psalm*, the oratorios *St. Elizabeth* and *Christus*.

A tendency to deviate from the lines of the sonata, akin to the tendency which brought about changes in the concert-overture and the symphony, can be traced in the concerto, the quartet, and other forms of concerted chamber music. To Schumann and his contemporaries it seemed difficult to produce string quartets true in spirit and technique, yet distinct from the classical models, unless they could venture upon some modifications of design in the direction of the ' Characterstück.' Schumann appears to have felt that the chances of making the most of his peculiar gifts were not entirely favourable on such lines. His three string quartets, written so rapidly that they may almost be described as improvisations, are of more account for beauty of detail than for any general mastery of design, and it is significant that after the single outburst which created them he turned, as though with a sense of relief, to the combination of pianoforte with stringed instruments by which the modern taste for warm colour and volume of sound can be gratified without fear of conflict between technical means and the end in view.

The tendency towards concise expression of emotion reached its zenith in some of the short lyrical pieces, both vocal and instrumental, by Schumann—and in a number of the solo pianoforte pieces by Chopin. Chopin and Schumann appear as the greatest lyrists among romantic composers of the century. In their best pieces for the pianoforte, both forsook the old ordinance of the sonata, and treated the pianoforte as the confidante of their personal feelings. Thus they found new ways and new patterns of expression, discovered abundance of novel and striking effects of sonorousness, and brought about a notable change in the spirit as well as in the technique of pianoforte playing. Some detailed account of these representative pieces, as well as of certain concertos for the violin, the pianoforte, and solo pieces by Weber, Mendelssohn, Schumann, Chopin, Liszt, and others, will be attempted later on—when it will also be convenient to touch upon the Lieder of Schumann, Mendelssohn, Robert Franz, Liszt, Wagner, the melodies of Berlioz, the Balladen of Loewe, and the church music of Samuel and Sebastian Wesley.

This sketch of the most important work produced during the period would be incomplete without a reference to the influence of the instrumental virtuosi who—from Paganini to Liszt, Thalberg, Ernst, Vieuxtemps, Wieniawski, Joachim—aroused the enthusiasm of the public, and to the good work done by some of the leading composers as critics and writers on music. About the beginning of the nineteenth century a change in the status and habits of certain classes of musicians took place. The 'Musicien de chambre' ('Kammermusicus') became the wandering virtuoso who appealed to the miscellaneous public with a show of manipulative skill. Composers of concerted and solo music had in consequence to reckon with an element of display [1] which soon came to be regarded as an important ingredient in the composition of instrumental pieces. The inclination to emphasize virtuosity in lieu of musical quality came to a head with the appearance of Paganini, who exhausted the. technical capabilities of the violin, and of Liszt and Thalberg, who did the same with the pianoforte. Inevitably one amongst the results was an undue preponderance of glitter and show and an inordinate display of gymnastics in finger, wrist, and arm. But at the same time there was brought about a result of which we are now reaping the benefit—that is to say, technical mastery, absolute command of all the capabilities of an instrument. To exhaust the technical possibilities in every direction was the task that executants of genius like Paganini and Liszt set themselves to accomplish; and the command they attained over every kind of executive difficulty was the most salient, if not the most valuable

---

[1] It was always there—witness Bach and the concertos of Mozart and Beethoven—but not prominently and pointedly so.

among the many factors which contributed to the style of their playing.

Dilettanti and literary men fond of music and eager to discuss it had not been wanting in the eighteenth century, from Mattheson, Marpurg, Rousseau, and Grimm onwards. But professional musicians with a taste for literature, themselves competent to act as writers and critics, were hardly known to exist in Germany before the time of Weber and in France before Berlioz. E. T. A. Hoffmann—lawyer and littérateur by profession, composer and conductor by choice—had written a number of fantastic articles about Mozart, Gluck, and Beethoven, showing a rare combination of poetical with practical insight, and gaining for himself the reputation of a prophet of romanticism. But Weber was really the first among professional musicians to put forth his opinions with the distinct object of instructing the public. He helped to start Meyerbeer, Marschner, Hoffmann, Fesca, and many others. In early days it appeared as though Schumann would be able to make better use of his rare gift of verbal expression than of his specifically musical gifts. Generously putting aside his own claims to recognition as a composer, Schumann, with comprehensive sympathy, acted for a number of years as the advocate of Chopin, Mendelssohn, Gade, Sterndale-Bennett, Heller, Liszt, Berlioz—and, finally, of Brahms. Thus he materially assisted in bringing about a change for the better in the relation between aspiring composers and the public. Liszt's enthusiasm was most helpful in the cause of Wagner. Berlioz furnished reports 'à travers chants' for some twenty-eight years. His peculiar view of music and its effects on the mind and body can in a manner be taken as embodying a romantic leader's profession of faith, and may fitly close this chapter of outlines. It is an exaggerated view, perhaps, but it fairly represents the spirit of the period [1].

'La musique, s'associant à des idées qu'elle a mille moyens

[1] *A travers chants*, p. 1.

de faire naître, augmente l'intensité de son action de toute la puissance de ce qu'on appelle la poésie . . . réunissant à la fois toutes ses forces sur l'oreille qu'elle charme, et qu'elle offense habilement, sur le système nerveux qu'elle surexcite, sur la circulation du sang qu'elle accélère, sur le cerveau qu'elle embrase, sur le cœur qu'elle gonfle et fait battre à coups redoublés, sur la pensée qu'elle agrandit démesurément et lance dans les régions de l'infini; elle agit dans la sphère qui lui est propre, c'est-à-dire sur des êtres chez lesquels le sens musical existe réellement.'

CHAPTER II

A GERMAN 'Singspiel' is a play of light texture in prose or verse copiously supplied with incidental music. A German 'Oper' is a musical play in which a minimum of dialogue is employed for the exposition of the situations, while music serves as the exponent of emotion. With the exception of Weber's *Euryanthe* and Schumann's *Genoveva*, German operas up to Wagner are merely enlarged 'Singspiele.'

The increase in the function and the efficacy of music in connexion with the actor's art; the widening of its scope, as it gradually rises from the position of a merely incidental embellishment in a play, to melodrama, where it accompanies, illustrates, and enforces the action; and again, the rise from melodrama to the aria and operatic scena—where it serves as the principal means of expression—are well seen by the comparison of certain German dramatic pieces wherein incidental music plays a part or contributes to the dénouement—for example, Schiller's *Turandot* and A. P. Wolff's *Preciosa*—with Weber's music. In *Turandot*, a play in Chinese garb, adapted from Gozzi's *Il Re Turandotte*, Weber's music is incidental only, consisting of orchestral pieces—an overture, marches, &c. In *Preciosa*, a romantic play in four acts, the music answers the purpose of embellishment as well as direct expression and characterization. Some of the dance tunes, choruses, and portions of the melodrama, might be omitted without loss to the action; but Preciosa's solo dance in the first 'Ballo,' and particularly her song 'Einsam bin ich nicht alleine,' are essential to the part. It is worthy of note that this song

illustrates the character and contributes to the portrayal of
Preciosa as much as ' Meine Ruh' ist hin' illustrates the
character of Gretchen in Goethe's *Faust*, or 'Freudvoll und
leidvoll' and ' Die Trommel gerühret' portray Clärchen in
Egmont.

The triumph of romanticism in operatic music begins with
Weber's success *Der Freischütz* (1821)[1]. In the story of this
opera the motives contrast greatly with the rather stilted pathos
of the older opera seria and with the equally conventional
comicalities of the opera buffa. Certain romantic elements,
such as the mystery of the forest, the interference of demoniacal
powers in the life of men, the redemption of a man's soul
through a woman's devotion, appealed powerfully to the
instincts of the German people and assisted in establishing
Weber's work in the position of a national favourite.

After the failure of Napoleon's invasion of Russia, Weber
had come to the fore as the musical exponent of German
aspirations for independence with his setting for male voices
of some of the fighting songs from Körner's *Leyer und
Schwert*, such as 'Lützow's wilde Jagd,' 'Gebet vor der
Schlacht,' 'Du Schwert an meiner Linken.' His melodies
stimulated the national enthusiasm, and Germany hailed *Der
Freischütz* as the first artistic expression of its patriotic sentiment[2]. It is the most German of operas ; the music, in some
respects, is the very quintessence of contemporary German
popular melody. The workmanship throughout is conscientious
and sincere. Never before, unless it be in the second act of
Beethoven's *Fidelio*, has so intimate a connexion between the
orchestra and the stage been attempted. Weber's fine feeling
for effect and his extraordinary sense of instrumental colour
served to define and contrast the scenes and situations, and to
intensify the emotional expression. 'The various characters

---

[1] Weber was born in 1786, he died in 1826.

[2] ' Die verschiedensten Richtungen des politischen Lebens trafen hier in einem
gemeinsamen Punkt zusammen : von einem Ende Deutschlands zum anderen wurde
Der Freischütz gehört, gesungen, getanzt.' *Wagner-Schriften*, i, p. 266.

are perfectly identified with the music they have to sing. Caspar, the reckless meddler in dangerous magic, was easily drawn; but the heroine Agathe and the lighter spirited Aennchen both also keep their musical identity quite well, even when they are singing together. The scenes are separate, but the final transition to the continuous music of later times is happily illustrated in such a case as Agathe's famous scena, in which a great variety of moods and changes of rhythm and speed and melody are all closely welded into a complete and well-designed unity[1].' Perhaps the most remarkable section of the whole work is the melodramatic Finale of the second act, the scene of the casting of the magic bullets. Here Weber found splendid opportunity for the suggestive and descriptive power of his music. The orchestral effects are as novel and telling to-day as they were at the first performance: 'For such things must be heard,' as Beethoven said of them. They told on contemporary musicians, hostile or friendly, just as they tell to-day[2].

In his scenas and melodramas Weber represents the environment, as well as the emotions, of the characters. 'His music conveys a pictorial and a psychological impression simultaneously[3],' as in Max's scena and aria 'Durch die Wälder, durch die Auen' (*Freischütz*), in the cavatina 'Glöcklein im Thale' (*Euryanthe*), wherein the musical phraseology is equally well adapted to every phase of emotion that passes through Euryanthe's mind as to her woodland surroundings, and more distinctly still in Agathe's scena in *Der Freischütz*, 'Wie nahte

[1] C. Hubert H. Parry, *The Evolution of the Art of Music*, p. 316.

[2] A telling effect familiar to every concert-goer, the long-drawn melody for the clarinet in the overture, is thus described by Berlioz: 'Cette longue mélodie gémissante, jetée par la clarinette au travers du *tremolo* de l'orchestre, comme une plainte lointaine dispersée par les vents dans les profondeurs des bois, cela frappe droit au cœur; et, pour moi du moins, ce chant virginal qui semble exhaler vers le ciel un timide reproche, pendant qu'une sombre harmonie frémit et menace au-dessous de lui, est une des oppositions les plus neuves, les plus poétiques et les plus belles qu'ait produit en musique l'art moderne.'

[3] W. H. Hadow, Lecture delivered at the Royal Institution, 1902.

mir der Schlummer,' in Rezia's scena in *Oberon*, ' Ocean, thou
mighty monster,' and in the great melodrama already mentioned
which forms the Finale of the second act of *Der Freischütz*.

The mere names of Weber's operas and Singspiele suffice to
show the wealth of opportunity for the display of colour which
the romantic subjects afforded him.   Thus *Silvana* (1812)—an
improvement on *Das Waldmädchen* (1800)—and *Der Freischütz*
(1821), serve to exhibit German forest legends. *Preciosa* (1821) is
based on a Spanish novel of Cervantes. *Euryanthe* (1823), based
on an old French story, illustrates feudalism. *Turandot* (1808),
Abu Hassan (1811), and *Oberon* (1826), represent the East.

The novelty and peculiarity of Weber's method in opera
consist in the close and persistent attention to characterization
and the use of special devices of orchestration for particular
purposes, so that the musical speech of one character shall be
palpably distinct from that of another.   Weber attains his
object by the use of instrumental tone-quality, i. e. ' colour ' ;
also by the use of folk-songs and dances, or of melodic and
rhythmic traits belonging to them, i. e. local colour.   It must
not, however, be supposed that devices to obtain particular
descriptive effects by suggestion were a new thing in Weber's
time.   Such devices were by no means rare in the older classical
opera, but they were employed there in single and separate
pieces only—as when Gluck introduced the choruses of
Scythians in *Iphigénie en Tauride*, when Mozart employed the
so-called Turkish music in the *Entführung aus dem Serail*, or
when he made use of a Spanish fandango in the second act of
Le Nozze di Figaro.   But Weber, in *Der Freischütz*, and still
more in *Euryanthe*, kept up the colour once adopted throughout
an entire scene, or an entire act.   And he managed to do this
by the use of striking melodic curves, figures, rhythms, and such
peculiarities of instrumentation as are suggested by the particulars of the action and the environment.

The vigorous rhythms, characteristic figures, and ingenious
orchestral contrivances which go to make up Weber's design also

assist in the presentation of certain scenes and generally in the portrayal of the characters. 'That fellow stands like a house,' Beethoven said of Caspar in *Der Freischütz*. Caspar is depicted as a burly peasant, with an uncanny touch of evil; and indeed Weber's originality in the invention and the use of striking vocal phrases and instrumental effects to depict special characters is surprising[1]. Weber's strong feeling for 'local colour' had its concomitant in a love of folk-songs and dances. Adopting a method entirely different from that of Beethoven, who occasionally takes a hint from a folk-tune or embodies fragments of folk-song or dance as a builder might have used curious bits of stone, Weber introduces popular melodies just as he may have heard them sung or played in the fields or streets, or found them in books, e. g. the Gipsy march in *Preciosa*, the Peasants' march or the waltz in *Der Freischütz*, or the Chinese tune in *Turandot*, which he found in J. J. Rousseau's *Dictionnaire de la musique*. His own peculiar type of melody, closely akin to the contemporary German Volkslied, is based upon the major scale and often consists solely of a statement of the notes of that scale resting on chords, of the tonic or of the dominant or subdominant chords. Apart from this native type, which is Weber's personal note and prevails in those of his works that count most, his fondness for exotic tunes—Bohemian, Spanish, Polish, Hungarian, and even Turkish or Chinese—is in all cases typically romantic. Thus Weber, together with Schubert, is the initiator of those picturesque touches of exotic tonality or instrumentation, and of that tendency towards nationalism in melody, rhythm, and even harmony, which is now so prominent a feature in music.

The German tradition of spoken dialogue is still maintained in *Der Freischütz*. Once only, in *Euryanthe*[2] (1823), Weber

---

[1] The first part of Caspar's drinking song consists of a succession of three-bar phrases, the second part of a succession of four-bar phrases. In *Oberon* there are several cases where the melodic outlines show the juxtaposition of four bars or five. Compare the first part of the subject in Brahms' variations *Ueber ein eigenes Thema*, Op. 21.

[2] *Euryanthe*, grosse heroisch-romantische Oper 'in drei Aufzügen' (literally,

discarded it and trusted to music alone, or rather to music in close connexion with poetry, mimetics, and scenic accessories. ' The proper effect of my new work,' he wrote in 1824 (letter to the Musik-Verein of Breslau), ' can only be expected from the united efforts of the sister arts.' The ideal towards which his instincts led him was that of the musical drama as subsequently realized by Wagner in *Lohengrin*. He intended to make the design of the several musical movements conform to the course of the action, and the details were to spring directly from the verse with as little repetition as possible of single words or lines. But his intuition of the theatrical concentration necessary to present his effects was not equal to his genius for musical expression. He made a mistake in the choice of subject. His imagination was captivated by the glamour of romantic incidents displayed in an old French story of a lady's constancy, a version of which he had read in Count Tressan's *Bibliothèque des romans*[1]. But he disregarded, or at least underrated, the want of true interest in the leading motives. He was not far wrong in his belief that the principal personages concerned in the ' Histoire ' were sufficiently distinct to serve as types for musical characterization. His librettist, Frau von Chezy, published a translation of the original text in F. Schlegel's *Sammlung romantischer Dichtungen des Mittelalters*, 1804, and a revised version 1823, as *Geschichte der tugendsamen Euryanthe*. But she failed to produce an intelligible play from the materials at her disposal. As the opera now stands [2] the difficulty from the point of view of the stage lies in the fact that the plot rests on the existence of a certain secret, constantly referred to but

---

Grand heroic-romantic opera in three rises of the curtain). First performed at Vienna in 1823 ; first heard in London in 1833, and again in 1882.

[1] ' Histoire de Gérard de Nevers et de la belle et vertueuse Euryante de Savoye, sa mie '—a tale probably known to Boccaccio in its original verse form, ' Roman de la Violette,' by Gilbert de Montreil (*Decamerone*, second day, ninth tale), and again in Boccaccio's version known to Shakespeare (*Cymbeline*).

[2] According to Frau von Chezy it was rewritten eleven times. It has been revised again, Vienna, 1904, seventeen pages of the pianoforte score cancelled, some cuts sanctioned by Weber restored. It seems a hopeless case.

not clearly explained. Weber, when he had already written the greater part of the music, came to realize this source of trouble. Apparently in despair, and at the last moment, he adopted an expedient. In the course of the overture, at the Largo played by the strings *pianissimo possibile*, the curtain is directed to rise upon a tableau vivant showing Adolar and Euryanthe, the hero and heroine, at the tomb of Emma, Adolar's sister—who, at the death of her own betrothed, is supposed to have sucked poison from a ring—and who now, to the weird sound of the music, tries to inform Adolar and Euryanthe in dumb show that 'her soul will never find rest until the fatal ring is bathed in tears of innocence.' This absurdity exhibits the crux of Romanticism in music, that is to say the gap between the end in view and the means to attain it.

Is it surprising that a work which commands the admiration of musicians when they read it, leaves them dissatisfied when it is acted, sung, or played? The excellence of the musical material is incontestable; the score contains finer individual passages than any other work of Weber's, the exigencies of musical design do not hamper the action, the style is noble, broad, consistently German ; and yet *Euryanthe* has failed.

Wagner, loth to charge Weber with a lack of discernment in stage effects, attributed the indifferent success to a want of balance between the musical and the dramatic factors. ' Critics,' he said, ' have not thoroughly sifted the heterogeneous elements which meet and contradict one another in this work, nor have they tried to show that the composer's inability to combine them into a harmonious total was the true cause of failure. Never since opera began has there been a work like this, in which the contradictions of the entire operatic *genre* have been so methodically exposed, by a composer so gifted, genuine, and high-minded. These contradictions are, absolute self-contained melody as an end *per se*, and dramatic expression which shall be true throughout. Assuredly the one or the other, the melody or the drama, must give way. Rossini sacrificed the drama: Weber tried to

restore it by the power of his expressive melody, and had finally
to acknowledge the impossibility of the task [1].'

Viewed from the standpoint of *Lohengrin*, where scenic
arrangement, verse, and music are justly combined, Wagner's
contention cannot be denied, though it is more a defence of his
own position than an appreciation of Weber's work. The words
of the historian Ambros [2] are more to the point : ' The libretto
of Weber's greatest work *Euryanthe* is a romantic product; and
it is greatly to Weber's credit that he succeeded in giving flesh
and blood to these moonlit phantoms of Provençal knights and
ladies. The rôle of Eglantine in his hands becomes a demoniacal figure such as had not yet been depicted in music. The
part of Ortrud in Wagner's *Lohengrin* is modelled upon that
of Eglantine, even to the wild burst of triumph at the end of
both operas. Similarly the rôle of Telramund in *Lohengrin*
rests on that of Lysiart. *Euryanthe* is truly an epoch-making
work. The roots of Wagner's art, as we have it in *Der fliegende
Holländer*, *Tannhäuser*, and *Lohengrin*, spring from this score
of *Euryanthe*, which is also the source of much of Marschner's
operas and of some part of Meyerbeer's operatic writing.'
Weber's fairy opera *Oberon*, on the lines of an enlarged Singspiel after the manner of *Der Freischütz*, was written to order
for Covent Garden under Kemble's management in the year of
Weber's death, 1826. It proved a popular success in London
and abroad, but failed to hold the stage. Well aware of the
puerility of the book, Weber expressed his intention of having
it recast, and of rewriting the music, ' so that it shall deserve
to be called an opera.' The fame of *Oberon* now rests on the
delightful fairy choruses, the superb overture, and the great
aria ' Ocean, thou mighty monster.'

The nature of the stories of Spohr's [3] principal operas (*Faust*,
1815–8, *Zelmira und Azor*, 1718–22, *Jessonda*, 1823, and *Die*

---

[1] Wagner, *Oper und Drama*, iii, p. 361.
[2] A. W. Ambros, *Culturhistorische Bilder aus dem Musikleben der Gegenwart*, p. 45.
[3] Spohr was born in 1784, he died in 1859.

Kreuzfahrer, 1844), together with a certain plaintive sensitiveness, i. e. chromatics in the inner parts, which is the personal note that pervades Spohr's music, has induced German writers to present him as one of the originators of musical romanticism, and by reason of the early date of his *Faust* (he began the work in 1813), as the precursor of Weber in romantic opera[1]. A study of his scores does not, however, bear this out. It is a far cry from romantic elements in a libretto to true romanticism in music. Spohr's predilections and, what is more important, his musical method, are distinctly Mozartian—to say classical would perhaps be saying too much. The formal finish of his pieces and the easy mastery of orchestral effect fascinated contemporary musicians. But nothing can be further from the drastic verve and vivid suggestiveness of Weber's musical speech than the languor of Spohr's melody and his fondness for square rhythms and square structure[2].

It would have been nearer the mark to represent E. T. A. Hoffmann[3], with his opera *Undine* (1816), after de la Motte-Fouqué's *Märchen*, as a precursor of Weber. But though Hoffmann acted for a number of years as a professional musician and writer on musical subjects, he never rose above the level of a highly gifted dilettante. His opera did not and could not gain a firm footing on the stage, it was far too tentative. Weber introduced it to the public of Prague. The story of *Undine* is

---

[1] The overture to *Faust* has a kind of programme which Spohr caused to be printed at the head of the libretto: 'The tone pictures of the Allegro vivace, Largo grave, and Tempo primo are meant to suggest to the auditor the changing moods and conditions of Faust's inner life.'

[2] The chromatic and enharmonic intervals in the inner parts, of which Spohr was so inordinately fond, may once and again have furnished hints to Schumann or Wagner. But it is abundantly evident that the chromatics of romantic music, as we find them in Schumann, Chopin, Wagner, are really, in so far at least as harmony is concerned, derived from J. S. Bach and his sons, and only to a very limited extent from Mozart, or Haydn, or Spohr. Compare introduction to Mozart's quartet in C and Haydn's orchestral pieces, 'Chaos' in the *Creation*, and 'Summer' in the *Seasons*.

[3] Hoffmann, 1776–1822, wrote several singspiele, three operas, a mass, a requiem, a symphony, several overtures and sonatas, some chamber music, and a number of smaller vocal and instrumental pieces.

that of a water-nymph, who has no soul, but who acquires one
through her love for a knight. Together with the birth of the soul,
she also receives knowledge of human distress and pain ; her husband breaks his faith, and she kills him with a kiss. The music
to *Undine*, though performed twenty-one times in all (1816-7),
has not been published, but manuscript copies of the score,
preserved at Berlin, bear out Weber's appreciation of it : ' The
work is one of the most ingenious of recent years . . . and so
consistent that details disappear and the interest is absorbed by
the composition as a whole . . . the composer avoids emphasizing any particular piece to the detriment of another, he is
careful not to hamper the action and always strives for true
dramatic expression. The part of Kühleborn stands out as that
of the most prominent character, by reason of the particular
cast of melody and instrumentation which persistently accompanies his uncanny appearance [1].'

Weber objected to certain weak points in Hoffmann's music,
such as his love of short phrases and figures which lack variety,
monotonous employment of violoncellos and violas, amateurish
use of sequences of diminished sevenths, and of cadences
which are abrupt and occur too often in the same shape.
On the whole, it may be said that the characters and
situations in Hoffmann's opera are well depicted. The declamation, in the airs and the comparatively few recitatives, is
remarkably direct and spirited. The overture and the short
instrumental pieces which serve as introductions to the second
and third acts—rather poor and somewhat incoherent—are
made up of scraps and hints of things to come. The orchestration, particularly of the vocal pieces, shows an acute sense of
instrumental colouring and considerable knowledge of effect.
The following extract from *Undine* may be taken as fairly
representative [2] :—

---

[1] Compare ' Caspar ' and ' Samiel ' in *Der Freischütz*.
[2] Compare the excellent article on Hoffmann by Vianna da Motta, the quotations
in *Bayreuther Blätter*, 1898, and *Die Musik*, p. 1666.

Marschner[1] had the tact to select subjects fit for theatrical presentation and favourable to the display of his peculiar musical gifts, which lay in the direction of jovial popular humour, combined with a striking and, from a theatrical point of view, very effective combination of sentiment with a feeling of awe and horror. Friar Tuck, in *Der Templer und die Jüdin*, is a good example of the former quality; and the latter—Marschner's idiosyncrasy—is exhibited, in a more or less prominent manner, by each of the heroes of his three best operas—*Der Vampyr* (1828)[2], *Templer und Jüdin* (1829), and *Hans Heiling* (1833).

As early as 1820, Weber had credited an opera of Marschner's, *Heinrich der Vierte und D'Aubigné*, with 'vivid original invention and careful workmanship.' Schumann, twenty years later, summed up his impression of *Der Templer und die Jüdin* thus: 'the music is occasionally restless : the instrumentation not sufficiently discriminate. There is a good deal of clever melody, considerable dramatic talent—sundry echoes of Weber. A gem not entirely cleared from its rough covering.'

Wagner used to point to certain portions of the Templar's long scena, No. 12, Act II, particularly the passage where the rapid triplets of the wind instruments depict a feverish state of excitement, as remarkably spontaneous and original examples of emotional expression :—

[1] Heinrich Marschner (1795–1861) became Weber's assistant as conductor of German opera at Dresden in 1824, and for a number of years subsequently acted as conductor at Hanover.

[2] The sixtieth performance of *Der Vampyr* took place in London, 1829. The libretto is based on a little known fragment of a novel by Byron, *Augusta Darvel* (first published together with *Mazeppa*), which Byron began in 1816 at Geneva, when Mary Shelley wrote *Frankenstein*.

Hans Heiling, an opera based on one of the many legends in which a goblin in disguise woos a maiden, appears to be the immediate precursor of Wagner's *Holländer* as regards both the play and the music.   In like manner the opening of its prologue, when the hero departs from the subterraneous abode of the Queen of the Goblins, contains the germ of the scene in the first act of *Tannhäuser,* which culminates in Tannhäuser's flight from the Venusberg.

Wagner's admiration for Marschner, though sincere and warmly expressed both in public and private, was yet by no means unqualified.   He strongly objected to certain banalities which now and then disfigure Marschner's melody and to his rather slovenly declamation.   He also drew the line between ' the mellifluous choral sing-song ' of some of the concerted pieces for male voices, which Marschner in his operas and in separate publications addressed to the populace, and the noble and touching choruses which have dramatic significance, such as those in the Finale to the second act of *Der Templer.*

Marschner's operas, later in date than those mentioned, and sundry miscellaneous pieces of vocal and instrumental chamber music of no particular importance, never gained a hearing outside Germany ; and even there the repute of his three typically romantic operas is distinctly on the wane.   But the fact that they form a link between Weber and Wagner's early operas secures for them a permanent place in the history of the German operatic stage.

Schumann [1], with his introspective ways and his devotion to personal ideals, was the least theatrically minded musician that it is possible to conceive.   A man totally devoid of mimetic gift and as far removed from the theatre as an educated German can well be, he had but scant acquaintance with the aspects of opera from the standpoint of the audience, and knew next to nothing about its conditions as they appear to actors and singers. Beyond listening to an opera once in a while, he does not seem

[1] Schumann was born in 1810, he died in 1856.

ever to have come in contact with the operatic stage and its
belongings; nor did he trouble to make a special study of
the conditions of success, when the desire to produce an opera
took hold of him. The 'Theaterbüchlein'—little theatre-book,
printed at the end of his collected writings—records impressions
of some fifteen operas heard at Dresden during the years 1847–
50. His words show him to have been keenly responsive to
certain musical points, such as details of instrumentation, the
treatment of the voice in connexion with particular instruments,
the use of the chorus. But the histrionic side, the peculiar
position and function of music in combination with stage
action, does not appear to have occupied much of his attention.
While seeking a suitable subject for an opera, he examined and
rejected the stories of the *Nibelungenlied*, the contest of
Minnesänger at the Wartburg, *Die Braut von Messina*, *Abélard
et Héloïse*, *Faust*, *Sakuntala*, Byron's *Corsair* and *Sardana-
palus*, Moore's *Veiled Prophet of Khorassan*, and many others,
amongst which was a sketch of his own, after E. T. A. Hoffmann's
Doge und Dogaressa. In the end his choice fell on the
legend of St. Genevieve—perhaps of all the subjects that came
under consideration the least amenable to effective treatment as
an opera. Apart from its popularity as a favourite story like
that of Patient Grissel, *Genoveva* seems to have attracted him
as bearing a certain affinity to the story of Weber's *Euryanthe*
(both stories tell of maligned innocence, banishment, and
ultimate rehabilitation), and perhaps also because his ambition
was stimulated by the prospect of producing something like
a match for Weber's work. The construction of a libretto
seemed to be easy, since the legend of Genoveva had already
been treated in dramatic form, for reading purposes by Tieck,
and for performance by 'Maler Müller' (the poet of Schubert's
'Die Schöne Müllerin'), Raupach, and Hebbel. Tieck's tragedy[1],
written in alternating rimed verse and prose, is a long shape-

---

[1] *Leben und Tod der heiligen Genoveva*, ein Trauerspiel von Ludwig Tieck,
1799; *Genoveva*, eine Tragödie in fünf Akten von Friedrich Hebbel, 1843.

less, pious, and rather insipid expansion of the old Volksbuch, *Geschichte von der heiligen Genoveva*. Hebbel's is an extravagant acting play in blank verse, with a touch of brutality in the treatment. Starting with such material, Robert Reinick, painter, poet, and a friend of the composer, sketched a scenario, but failed, after repeated attempts, to satisfy Schumann, who then, in vain, applied to Hebbel for assistance. Finally, following as he thought the example of Lortzing and Wagner [1], Schumann himself undertook the task of arranging a libretto. He managed, with very indifferent success, to contrive an amalgamation of the two plays. In accordance with Hebbel rather than with Tieck, he chose to eliminate most of the legendary features, which lend a charm to the mediaeval story. Thus certain telling traits, delicately developed in Tieck's version—Genoveva's long sojourn in the wilderness, the friendship of her little son with the doe and the beasts and birds, even that most musical incident, the chance meeting with her husband and the recognition and reconciliation—are rejected; and their place is taken by certain ugly scenes from Hebbel's play, which exhibit the insults and brutalities Genoveva suffers at the hands of her domestics. 'Do not expect to find the old sentimental Genoveva [2];' 'I rather believe it is a piece of actual life, as a dramatic poem should be.' Golo, the traitor squire, who, with Tieck, wavers inconstantly between wickedness and contrition, is presented as a cowardly sensualist and scoundrel. Genoveva's husband Siegfried, and Margaretha the witch-wife, are little better than lay figures. The final scene of the second act, where the rabble of servants—who a moment before might have sworn to Genoveva's innocence—force their way to her apartment, is as repulsive as the murder of the old Seneschal Drago, Genoveva's supposed paramour. Part of the third act is occupied by a series of pictures shown in a magic mirror whilst an invisible

---

[1] *Genoveva*, 1849-50, was completed two years after the first performance of *Tannhäuser*.

[2] Schumann: Letter to Dorn, 1849.

D

chorus comments in the background. The fourth act contains a repetition of the tiresome incidents which make up the close of Weber's *Euryanthe*—a visit to the wild wood, an attempt to murder, a rescue, and the usual jubilant Finale. ' When Schumann consulted me about the libretto of his opera [1],' says Wagner, ' I failed to induce him to alter the ineptitudes of the third act, especially the magic pictures : he lost his temper and appeared to believe my warnings were meant to mar his best efforts.'

It is evident that Schumann had no just conception of the magnifying or dwarfing effect of stage presentation. He did not perceive that a particular incident, though sufficiently interesting in narrative, may yet appear puerile or artistically impossible from a histrionic point of view ; and that to read about brutality is one thing, to see it presented on the stage, with the details emphasized by music, is a very different matter altogether [2].

Schumann adopted Weber's method of connecting the scenes and fusing the words and the music into one single and coherent act, as in *Euryanthe*, but he fell far short of Weber's grip and brilliancy. In *Genoveva* the composer's power of invention appears to be on the wane. The daring originality, the force and passion of the younger Schumann is gone. The opera contains no spoken dialogue, and nothing resembling plain recitative, which might perhaps have acted as a foil to the lyrism that pervades the whole. Neither in general design nor in detail does the music spring direct from the dramatic situation. Throughout there is a lack of actuality of vivid contrast and telling colour. The composer occupies the position of an annotator. He stands outside the story, and puts forth his own musical comments on the situation which it portrays. Rarely, if ever, does he rise to the height of his opportunity and succeed in making the

---

[1] *Wagner-Schriften*, x. pp. 222, 223.

[2] Liszt's verdict on Schumann's work was generous. Writing to a friend in 1855, when he was rehearsing *Genoveva* at Weimar, he says : ' I prefer certain faults to certain virtues—the mistakes of clever people to the effects of mediocrity. In this sense there are failures which are better than many a success.'

characters speak their own language. He cannot paint *affresco*, as in the salient points of an operatic scena he should. The wealth of clever detail in melody, harmony, and at times even the orchestration, is no doubt interesting ; but it must be added that in performance the majority of these subtleties do not make the impression of being in perfect accordance with the action. They are too minute, and therefore do not produce the effect intended [1].

[1] On its first performance at Leipzig, 1850, Schumann himself conducting, *Genoveva* was coldly received. Subsequent performances at Dresden, Vienna, Weimar, Leipzig—and also a revival in English, carefully prepared by the pupils of the Royal College of Music under Sir Charles Stanford in 1893—one and all resulted in a lukewarm *succès d'estime*.

CHAPTER III

ROMANTIC OPERA IN PARIS

IN France, as compared with Germany, the powerful romantic movement in literature was less in accord with the national taste in music. A leaning towards romanticism in music was mainly confined to those members of literary and artistic coteries, amateurs for the most part, who felt the influence of Byron, Scott, Moore, or Goethe, and to some extent of Beethoven. Parisian musical romanticism was but a reflex of the ferment in French literature. It came to the fore at the Opéra, where everything is sung in French; whilst the so-called opéra comique, where the entertainment consists of light music alternating with spoken dialogue, was hardly touched by it. At the Opéra, the way was opened, in 1828, by the *Muette de Portici* (*Masaniello*) of Scribe and Auber [1]. This work, romantic, extravagant, revolutionary in spirit, is rich in captivating tunes, full of clever instrumental effects, and remarkable for the novel use of massing the chorus, so as to permit them to take a prominent share in the action. ' So lively an opera had not yet been seen [2].' It was the first realistic drama in five acts, with all the attributes of a tragedy, particularly a tragic end. I well remember hearing that the latter circumstance made an especial sensation. Hitherto operatic stories (in Germany at least) had ended comfortably—no German composer could venture to send people home in a sad mood. When Spontini came to Dresden to conduct

---

[1] Scribe, 1791–1861, produced, or at least lent his name to, 422 pieces—47 plays, 28 grand operas, 95 comic operas, 244 vaudevilles, and 8 ballets. Auber was born in 1782, he died in 1871.

[2] Wagner, *Erinnerungen an Auber*, ix. 55 (1871).

La Vestale, he waxed wroth when he found that, after Julia had been happily saved from death, we intended to let the opera conclude with the scene in the cemetery. He would not permit such a thing. The scenario had to be changed, the Bower of Roses with the Temple of Venus had to appear, the priest and priestesses of Love had to lead the happy pair to the altar: ' Chantez, dansez ' . . . impossible that things should be otherwise. . . . But all this conventional business suddenly came to a stop when *La Muette* appeared. Here was a grand opera, a tragedy in five acts, completely set to music ; without a trace of stiffness, of empty pathos, of so-called classical dignity, warm enough to burn, heady enough to intoxicate. German musicians confessed themselves bewildered by the new prodigy, and, after some acrimonious discussion of its merits and defects, finally cut the knot by referring it to the influence of Rossini. This judgement, like many others in the history of Music, has been reversed on appeal. No doubt Rossini was in a sense the father of modern operatic melody, yet even he was unable to produce or rival the particular quality that gave such dramatic power and effect to this music of Auber's ; moreover, the fates denied, not only to Rossini, but to other Italians and Frenchmen, and even to Auber himself, a chance to continue in the path of *La Muette* [1].

Before we speak of Rossini's romantic masterpiece *Guillaume Tell* [2] it may be well to touch on his career in Italy, and to trace through early years of conflict the preparation for his triumphs in London and Paris. In tʰ ᐧ main a self-made man, he studied Mozart's operas, Haydn's and Mozart's symphonies, and tried to score some of their quartets. He rapidly acquired facility, though not complete mastership. At first he composed for the lesser Italian theatres, rapidly producing serious or comic operas, which lived, at best for a couple of seasons, and at worst for

[1] Performances of *La Muette* have repeatedly furnished an excuse for political demonstrations.

[2] Rossini was born in 1792, he died in 1868.

a single day. Then, in 1813, he achieved his first great
successes with *Tancredi*, an opera seria, and *L' Italiana in
Algeri*, an opera buffa. The latter, a forerunner of *Il Barbiere
di Siviglia*, was a surprising display of comical gaiety and verve
with a savour of Cimarosa's *Il Matrimonio segreto*, but still
with a distinct note of its own [1]. These were followed by
Elisabetta, regina d' Inghilterra (Naples, 1815) and *Il Barbiere*
(Rome, 1816) on a subject already treated by Paisiello, after
which came *La Cenerentola* and *La Gazza ladra* (1817), *Mosè
in Egitto* (1818), and, in 1819, *La Donna del Lago*, after Scott's
The Lady of the Lake. The failure of *Semiramide*—one of his
most ambitious works—at Venice, in 1823, prompted him to
go to London, where he laid the foundations of his fortune, and
in the following year to Paris, where the authorities appointed
him Director of the Opéra with a salary of 20,000 francs and
a share in whatever *tantièmes* he might be entitled to in case he
chose to write a new work or rewrite an old one. At first he
adopted the latter plan and rewrote two of his best Italian
scores—*Maometto II*, which at the Opéra became *Le Siège de
Corinthe* (1826), and *Mosè in Egitto*, which was called *Moïse*.
A third piece, *Le Comte d'Ory*, a pretty comic opera (1828),
was a *pasticcio* of old and new fragments. Finally, he crowned
the edifice with *Guillaume Tell*.

In the transformation of older work the influence of French
theatrical art and French taste in music is felt ; and there is no
doubt that Rossini was bent on making the most of his talents.
He added and changed a good deal, especially with regard to
instrumentation, rendered the declamation more precise, the
accents more incisive, and revised the entire workmanship with
a fuller comprehension of the requirements of the stage.

A grand opera, Italian in all essentials, yet French in aspect,
elaborate in style and rich in melody, *Guillaume Tell* (1829)
came upon the world as a surprise. Certain qualities always

---

[1] The once popular sentimental tune from *Tancredi*, ' Di tanti palpiti,' now serves
for the professional song of the tailors in the third act of Wagner's *Meistersinger*.

rare with Italian composers, and particularly rare with Rossini
—characterization in great things and in small, the orchestra in
touch with the action, careful declamation, appropriate local
colour[1]—combined to form a masterpiece for which neither school
was entirely prepared. Up to the time of *Guillaume Tell*
Rossini had mainly addressed himself to hearers who had
a sense of musical verve and movement, as for instance in
Il Barbiere di Siviglia. In *Guillaume Tell* he chose to speak
seriously to the *élite* of the public and of professional musicians.
He aimed at perfection of musical style under cosmopolitan conditions, and attempted a fusion of the good qualities of Italian,
French, and German masters in opera. The workmanship in
the score of *Guillaume Tell* is good throughout, the melody spontaneous, the harmony often refined in a very original manner ;
the treatment of the solo and chorus voices and the orchestra
masterly. The overture ranks high amongst overtures of the
potpourri sort, and is only excluded from the first place by the
bustling vulgarity of its close. The power and originality of
the principal pieces is best shown in the scene of the conspiracy
and the taking of the oath at the Rütli ; also in the duet between
Tell and Arnold, in Matilda's recitative and romanza at the
beginning of the second act; in the dainty ballet tunes and the
Tyrolienne of Act III ; the quartet in Act I ; and the storm in
Act IV. The solo parts exhibit a wealth of device for the
display of fine emotional singing ; and nowhere does Rossini's
affluence of vocal melody fail him. It may be that such tune-
ful facility as is his rests on the traditional musical speech of
the earlier Italian composers such as Piccinni, Paisiello, Cimarosa,
and in some measure on that of Mozart; but the melodies
themselves, even if at times they exhibit touches of superficial
emotionalism or border on triviality, have a stamp of their own
and possess a peculiar sensuous charm. *Guillaume Tell* exhibits
full measure of the scenic display that especially belongs to the

---

[1] Local colour so perfect was not again seen or heard in opera till 1875, when
Bizet's *Carmen* was produced.

Parisian opera—grand choral masses, a large corps de ballet, sumptuous pageantry, dazzling effects of light and colour, &c.—and the skilful rhetoric of the libretto has given rise to many a novel and telling detail in the musical setting.

To illustrate the power of Rossini's temperament when it touches upon a strong theatrical situation no better example exists than the Terzetto in Act II between Arnold, Tell, and Walter—tenor, baritone, and bass. The scene shows Arnold (the son of a patriot leader, connected with the governing party by his love for the governor's sister) at the moment when he is informed of the ruthless slaying of his father; and the music reflects the conflict of his emotions.

drò, mai più lo ri-ve-drò, no, no, mai più non lo ri - ve-drò

tale, si la ben - - da strap-pò

pò, si la ben - - da strap-pò

There is in this piece direct presentation of feeling—very effective from the actor's point of view—and a considerable degree of musical originality. It will be found worth while to compare it with certain celebrated operatic ensembles of a later period, such as the quartet in Bellini's *I Puritani*, the sextet in Donizetti's *Lucia*, the quartet in Verdi's *Rigoletto*, or even with the superb quintet in Wagner's *Meistersinger*, the middle portion of which is musically, if not emotionally, cast in a similar mould.

As time advances it appears evident that Rossini made a mistake in not demanding more than a mere picturesque book of words from his librettist, Étienne de Jouy[1]. *Guillaume Tell* contains little that resembles a plot. The interest in the story wanes after the second act, and the succession of pretty scenes does not make amends. In performance, the order of things produces a sense of *diminuendo*—there is a gradual falling off from the scene of the morning sun on Alpine summits, after the nocturnal meeting of the conspirators, to the storm on the lake, the leap from the little boat, and the shooting at the apple. In Germany, where Schiller's *Wilhelm Tell* had

[1] Writer of the libretti to Spontini's *La Vestale* and *Olympie*, and mentioned in Byron's *Letters*, vol. vi. p. 230, as the author of the tragedies *Scylla* and *L'Hermite*.

familiarized people with the peculiar order of scenes[1], this drawback was hardly noticed, and the opera, accepted on its musical merits alone, became a great favourite.

It is characteristic of Rossini that he does not indulge in experiments. There is always a personal note about his work, be it trivial or passionate—the intuition of a great personality. Something resembling a distinct personal note is also felt to be present in the work of his principal successors, Bellini, Donizetti, and Verdi, notably Bellini, but in a far less marked degree. The successors too had something of their own to say, and, under prevailing theatrical conditions, did say it, often in a convincing way. No one can justly assert that Bellini, Donizetti, and Verdi derived directly from Rossini. Did they openly imitate his ways or copy his mannerisms? Bellini never attempted such a thing; Donizetti, an Italian eclectic aspiring to cosmopolitan sway, here and there followed him; Verdi, late in life, worked on totally different lines[2]. The kinship is the kinship of tradition. The ways of Italian opera persist, though the lines of its development may deviate— there is the spirit of continuance in its treatment of the theatre and in its entire absence of introspection. Together with Donizetti (*Lucia di Lammermoor*), Bellini forms the link in the growth of opera from Rossini's exuberant force and the consummate *savoir-faire* of his later years to the more earnest and consciously cosmopolitan art of Verdi. In France, however, soon after the appearance of *Guillaume Tell*, people began to hint at defects which they could not describe—they felt that there was something wanting or something amiss. The fact that Rossini's individual art had gained much by its contact with the French stage was gracefully acknowledged. ' But '— it was asked in artistic circles—' if the maestro's masterpiece does not entirely fulfil the promise of romanticism, cannot

---

[1] The order is not that of a play, but rather of an epic poem, the plan for which Goethe communicated to Schiller.

[2] Compare his *Otello* with Rossini's.

some other musician be discovered who will reproduce the fantastic or demonic side of it, and create a truly romantic opera ? '

This other musician was soon found, and proved to be Jacob Meyer Beer, better known as Giacomo Meyerbeer[1]. The wild side of romanticism ran riot in Scribe and Meyerbeer's *Robert le Diable*, 1831. In this work the most strenuous theatrical and musical means are employed to bring about contrasting effects. All the elements of romantic and operatic excitement are made to serve the same purpose : characters and situations as extravagant as possible, demons and men in conflict, plain-chant and ballet-tunes intermixed, church-pageantry transported to the stage, prayer alternating with bacchanalian song, simple tunes interlarded with gruesome melodramatic chords, and the most ethereal effects of instrumentation in conjunction with vulgar noise. On the dramatist's side there is an exhibition of extremes ; on the musician's an accumulation of Italian, French, and German devices grossly exaggerated ; and the total is contrived with little regard for consistency of style, and with hardly a trace of artistic conscience. ' Meyerbeer's object was to make the mere externals tell. He did not care in the least whether his details were commonplace or not. His scores look elaborate and full of work, but the details are the commonest arpeggios, familiar and hackneyed types of accompaniment, scales, and obvious rhythms. Musically it is a huge pile of commonplaces, infinitely ingenious, and barren. There is but little cohesion between the scenes, and no attempt at consistency with the situation in style and expression. No doubt Meyerbeer had a great sense of general effect. The music glitters and roars and warbles in well-disposed contrasts, but the inner life is wanting. It is the same with the treatment of his characters. They metaphorically strut and pose and gesticulate, but express next to nothing ; they

---

[1] Meyerbeer was born in 1791, six years before Schubert and eighteen years before Mendelssohn ; he died in 1864.

get into frenzies, but are for the most part incapable of human passion. The element of wholesome musical sincerity is wanting in him, but the power of astonishing and bewildering is almost unlimited [1].'

When Scribe shifted the slides of the lantern to replace the romantic phantasmagoria of *Robert le Diable* by the quasi-historical pictures of *Les Huguenots* (1836) and *Le Prophète* (1849), his method remained unchanged. He continued to exhibit the same mixture of operatic contrasts of ecclesiastical display and voluptuous ballet, of passion torn to tatters, and violent death. Nor was Meyerbeer's musical procedure modified in any important way. There is in both these later operas some increase of means—such as enlarged choral masses, greater swarms of figurantes, a fuller and even noisier orchestra. There is also some gain in the choice and variety of instrumental colour, some advance in the precision and energy of the declamation ; but hardly anything deserving the name of musical polyphony either vocal or orchestral, and what little there is of it savours of banality. Of invention, novelty in the contrivance of melody, harmony, rhythm, there is very little that in any way surpasses the average quality of the musical materials in *Robert le Diable*. It may interest students to see how this condition of things struck a great contemporary between 1836 and 1850. After protesting against certain frivolous tendencies in the book of *Les Huguenots*, Robert Schumann wrote of the music as follows : ' It would take volumes to comment on the music. Each bar has been considered and reconsidered by the composer, and something might be said about it. To astonish and to amuse is Meyerbeer's object, and he succeeds with the vulgar. As for the ubiquitous chorale, " Ein' feste Burg," about which French journals rave, I confess that if a clever pupil were to submit counterpoint of that sort to me I would beg of him not to do worse in future. How studiously shallow, how carefully superficial

---

[1] C. Hubert H. Parry, *The Evolution of the Art of Music*, p. 315.

is all this obtrusive screaming of "Ein' feste Burg" at the groundlings! A great fuss has also been made about the "Benediction of the Swords" in the fourth act. I admit that the piece has a good deal of dramatic force, that it contains several clever and striking traits, and that the chorus is particularly effective and makes a great show. The situation, the stage accessories, and the instrumentation support one another; and since the terrible, and the horrible, are Meyerbeer's predilection, he has done his share of the work with enthusiasm. But, if we examine the particular melody closely, is it other than a bedizened *marseillaise*? And does it really take much artistic wisdom to produce a strong effect by such means and in such a place? I do not blame the use of every possible means of effect in the right place—but people ought not to cry aloud and marvel if a dozen trombones, trumpets, and ophicleides, together with a hundred men singing in unison, are audible at some distance. A special refinement of Meyerbeer's must not be forgotten here. He knows the public too well not to perceive that too much noise might produce apathy. And how cleverly he gets over this. Directly following upon such rattling movements as the "Benediction of the Swords," he inserts entire airs with the accompaniment of a single instrument—as if to say, "Behold, ye people, how much I can do with so little." Certainly some degree of *esprit* cannot in this instance be denied him [1]. It would be an easy task to point out traces of the style of Rossini, Mozart, Hérold, Weber, Bellini, and even of Spohr. Meyerbeer's

---

[1] The telling effect of contrast Schumann here alludes to really belongs to Weber, who in *Euryanthe*, Act II, after the violent duet between the evil characters Lysiart and Eglantine, introduces Adolar's aria 'Wehen mir Lüfte Ruh'' with a long delicate ritornello. Compare the similar situation in Wagner's *Lohengrin*, Act II, where, after the duet of rage and hate between Ortrud and Telramund, Elsa's appearance on the balcony is accompanied by a lovely melody played upon the clarinet. With Meyerbeer the trick, for such it becomes in his hands, is first employed in *Robert le Diable*, Act III, when Bertram rushes into the cave amid a most violent orchestral uproar, which is immediately followed by the soft ritornello of Alice's 'Romanza.'

exclusive speciality, however, consists in that famous ambiguous rhythm which appears in nearly all the themes of the opera [1].

'I had already begun to note the passages in which it occurs, but I soon grew weary of the task. Ill-will and envy could alone deny the presence of many better things, even of some truly grand and noble points. Thus Marcel's battle-song is telling, the song of the page is lovely, the greater part of the third act, with its scenes of common life, is interesting. The first part of the duet between Marcel and Valentine is both interesting and characteristic, and so is the sextet. The chorus of derision has a comic effect. The "Benediction of the Swords" is comparatively original; but, above all, the duet between Raoul and Valentine, which follows it, is distinguished by fluency of thought and musicianly treatment. Yet how can all this atone for the vulgarity, grotesqueness, ambiguity, and anti-musical quality of the whole? Thanks to Heaven, we have reached an end— things cannot come to a worse plight.'

Schumann did not cry aloud over *Le Prophète*. He recorded the first performance at Dresden thus :—

'*Prophet von Giac. Meyerbeer.*
(Den 2. Febr. 1850.)'

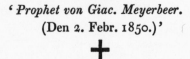

If it be permissible to view and estimate the value of Meyerbeer's work from the standpoint of Wagner's achievements, Schumann's strictures, taken together with Sir Hubert Parry's weighty words, may be taken to represent the verdict—severe, perhaps, but not unjust [2].

[1]

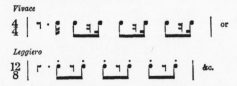

[2] Meyerbeer's early works—after some failures such as the setting of the 98th Psalm, an oratorio *Gott und die Natur*, 1811, the operas *Jephthas Tochter* and

Meyerbeer's manner is more or less apparent in the operas of Halévy and Hérold, and even rouses echoes in the works of Gounod, Bizet, Massenet, Ambroise Thomas, and Saint-Saëns. It is felt in Mercadante's *Il Giuramento*, Donizetti's *Lucrezia Borgia*, *Dom Sebastien*, *La Favorita*; in Verdi's *Rigoletto*, *La Forza del destino*, *Don Carlos*, and *Aïda*. There are touches of it in Wagner's *Rienzi*, and still more in Goldmark's *Königin von Saba* and *Merlin*.

Ludovic Halévy[1] stands to Meyerbeer not so much in the position of a disciple as in that of a partial imitator, and in some sense a rival. In *La Juive* (1835), Scribe, the librettist, produced a very striking lyric tragedy, and one peculiarly fit for Halévy's talent. At its best, Halévy's music is distinguished by a certain gloomy sublimity. It is often full of dramatic animation, and rarely, if ever, sinks to the depths of Meyerbeer's bathos. The musical movements of *La Juive*, connected by means of recitative, are for the most part of large dimensions, deftly put together, well written for the voices, well scored, and remarkable for the skilful use of the wood-wind instruments—such as corni di bassetto, corni inglesi, bassoons, oboes, and clarinets, in combination with modern brass. *L'Éclair* (1835), the only other one of Halévy's many operas (upwards of thirty in all) that was altogether a success, forms a strange contrast to this sumptuous theatrical display. There is nothing in the short libretto of *L'Éclair* that can be called a plot; and the music is for two tenors

---

Abimelek oder die beiden Kalifen, 1813 (Munich and Vienna), all of which were written while he was still in a state of pupilage (Weber and Meyerbeer studied under the Abbé Vogler, Browning's Vogler, about 1810–12)—consist of a number of Italian operas: *Romilda e Constanza*, Padua, 1818; *Semiramide riconosciuta*, Turin, 1819; *Emma di Resburgo*, Venice, 1819; *Margherita d'Angiù*, *L'Esule di Granata*, Milan, 1820 and 1822; and *Il Crociato in Egitto*, Venice, 1824, which was repeated in Paris, 1826. The later operas are :—*Das Feldlager in Schlesien*, 1842, given in Vienna as *Vielka*, 1844, and rewritten for Paris as *L'Étoile du Nord*, 1854; *Le Pardon de Ploërmel* (*Dinorah*), a so-called opéra comique, Paris, 1859; and the grand opera *L'Africaine*, which, though posthumous, really belongs to the time of *Le Prophète*. *L'Africaine* was first performed in Paris, 1865, one year after the composer's death.

[1] Born 1799, died 1862.

and two sopranos without chorus[1]. In connexion with *La Muette* and *Robert le Diable*, Adam's *Le Postillon de Longjumeau* (1836), and Hérold's *Zampa* (1831), together with his *Pré aux clercs* (1832), may be mentioned [2].

Benvenuto Cellini, Berlioz' [3] first opera, was produced at the Académie Royale in 1838, as an excuse for a ballet, and withdrawn after the third performance. Though meant for an ' opera semiseria ' the work was presented as an opera proper. Originally it consisted of two acts only, each divided into two tableaux. The two acts were turned into four, when Liszt in 1852 conducted the work at Weimar. Subsequently, by dint of omissions, and with Berlioz' consent, the four acts were reduced to three, in which latter form Berlioz himself (1853) conducted it in London, and Bülow revived it at Hanover in 1878. It was never a success. Reasons sufficient to account for the persistent failure may perhaps be found in the nature of the subject, which, though lively enough and far from commonplace, does not offer many interesting situations. But the peculiar character of Berlioz' music, the rarity of genuine pathos in the melody, and a continuous striving after novelty of rhythmical effect have had quite as much to do with the disappointing general impression as any defects in the subject or faults in the construction of the book. The music throughout is clever but artificial. For the most part it is anything rather than dramatic. In rapid movements the variety and bizarre originality of the rhythms together with the dazzling instrumentation produce a sense of haste and restless excitement, and in slow movements the phraseology

---

[1] Probably *Le Guitarrero* and *La Reine de Chypre* would now be completely forgotten, were it not for the fact that the *partitions de piano* of both are among the journeyman tasks Wagner executed for publishers during his first stay in Paris. He speaks in warm terms of the quartet ' En cet instant suprême,' at the end of the fifth act, and remarks that in the first two acts there are instances of miscalculated effects, when the composer expects clarinets and oboes to do the work of horns and valve-trumpets. This early experience of Wagner's led him, later on, to suggest certain emendations in the scoring of the Scherzo of Beethoven's 9th symphony, which, it must be said, are not wanted.

[2] The latter piece, one of the most popular of light operas, was given for the thousandth time in 1871, and is still occasionally to be heard in Paris.

[3] Berlioz was born in 1803, he died in 1869.

fails to convince for lack of warmth and fluency. Always ingenious, Berlioz, offers a superabundance of clever devices in rhythm and orchestration. He seems to be addressing himself to an audience of experts, and consequently 'il faut de l'esprit pour lui en trouver'; that is to say, just the kind of musical *esprit* with which even the experts in his day were but scantily furnished. The result is best described in his own words:— 'On fit à l'ouverture un succès exagéré, et l'on siffla tout le reste avec un ensemble et une énergie admirable.' Considerable wit and finesse are shown in the whispering duet, Act I, and in the bantering aria of Scaramoglio. There is instrumental humour in the carnival scene which forms the finale of Act II. By the side of such pieces are movements, the scene of the oath for instance, that properly belong to the grand opera. Berlioz described his own score as containing 'une variété d'idées, une verve impétueuse, et un éclat de coloris musical que je ne retrouverai peut-être jamais et qui méritaient un meilleur sort' (*Mémoires*, p. 214). The following quotations may serve to illustrate the validity of his claim :—

som - mets de la mon - ta - gne,

som - mets de la mon - ta - gne,

Allegro con fuoco e marcato assai

CHORUS. ♪ = 184

Tenors.

Basses.

Si la terre aux beaux jours se cou - ron - ne . . . . . de

ger - bes, de fruits et de fleurs, . . en ses flancs l'hom -

Auber's principal contribution to the répertoire of grand
opéra, as has been stated, was *La Muette (Masaniello)*. All his
life long he wrote for the Opéra-Comique, and produced (mostly
in conjunction with Scribe) upwards of forty light operas and
operettas—ephemera all of them—always bright and amusing,
frankly written for the market and addressed to the bourgeoisie.
—'Que voulez-vous? C'est le genre,' answered Auber, when
Wagner expressed his astonishment at certain banalities.—At
the Opéra-Comique, Scribe and Auber met on equal terms. Both
show *esprit*, grace, theatrical instinct, at times even passion—but
the one, in Heine's phrase, lacks poesy, the other lacks music.
Apart from the French stage, *Fra Diavolo* (1830), *Le Domino
Noir*, *Le Philtre* (1831), and the little masterpiece *Le Maçon*
(1825) are the best known. The latter had a great run in
Germany as *Maurer und Schlosser*. 'C'est de la futilité
indestructible.'

CHAPTER IV

ITALIAN OPERA

OF the Italian composers who made their mark in Paris and London after Rossini's *Guillaume Tell*, the most conspicuous are Vicenzo Bellini[1] with his *La Sonnambula* (1831), *Norma* (1832), and *I Puritani* (1834), and Gaetano Donizetti[2] with his *Lucrezia Borgia* (1833), *Lucia di Lammermoor* (1835), and *La Favorita* (1840). None of these productions, though they are their composers' best, will stand close scrutiny as a whole, but each contains one or two pieces that, from a vocal and a theatrical point of view, possess high and genuine merit. Thus the quartet and chorus 'A te, o cara,' in *I Puritani*, the sextet in *Lucia*, and above all, the Finale to the second act of *Norma*, are in their way masterpieces. They exhibit a minimum of musical elaboration, yet there is much more contained in them than mere sentimental cantilena. In each the vocal expression rises to genuine pathos and passion.

Bellini, the favourite of the public and of the great vocal virtuosi such as Pasta, Grisi, Rubini, Lablache, met with scant justice at the hands of professional musicians, especially in Germany. ' Bellini's melody is of a monotonous type, it depends on the *bel canto* for its effect.' ' His cadences are weak, the choruses noisy and trivial, the orchestration childish.' Strictures of this sort may be true enough in the main, but the emotional quality of the pieces already mentioned, and of many a single recitative, aria, or scena besides, makes up for much that is poor or defective in Bellini's work as a whole[3]. In *La Sonnambula*, the idyllic

[1] 1802–35. [2] 1797–1848.
[3] Note, however, the wide divergence of Wagner's estimate of Bellini's abilities

mood of a slight ' Liederspiel,' a song-play, for such the little
opera virtually is, does not suffer much from the preponderance
of vocal fireworks that form part of the arias, whilst in *Norma*
(the best of Italian tragic operas before Verdi's *Otello*) the prevailing elevation of sentiment is sufficiently well sustained, in
spite of occasional banalities in the shape of noisy tunes in
choral unison, long drawn-out sequences of thirds, and the like [1].
In the middle of his career Bellini [2] had the good fortune to meet
the man who for his special purposes proved to be an ideal
librettist, Felice Romani—a person of considerable literary
attainment, of sufficient stage experience and of a rare instinct
for that peculiar compromise between stage action and song of
which in the time of Rossini and Bellini the traditions still
survived from the early days of the operatic spectacle in Italy.
Romani skilfully contrived the book of *Norma* (1831) after a
little known French play by Soumet, and that of *La Sonnambula* (also 1831) after a now forgotten vaudeville ballet by
Scribe [3]. In these model libretti, Romani provided Bellini with
the outlines, skilfully drawn and precisely adapted for musical
colouring : dramatic situations easily understood, and demanding few stage accessories for their proper presentation, but carefully arranged and graduated for the lyrical utterance of passion :
headlong words for rapid recitativos, telling scenas, culminating
in some cluster of verses apt for emotional cantilena. All the

from that of other contemporary German critics. Compare Wagner's account of
I Capuletti e Montecchi, 1834.

It cannot be overlooked that critics accustomed to the weakness of most contemporary German translations of operatic libretti, and, what is worse, accustomed to
the lax methods of the German operatic singers of the time, were not in a position
to appraise the value of lyrical effusions, such as those of Rossini in parts of
Otello, or of Bellini in parts of *Norma* or *I Puritani*.

[1] Earlier operas of Bellini that deserve passing record are *Il Pirata* (1827), *La
Straniera* (1829), *I Capuletti e Montecchi* (1830). His first opera, *Adelson e Salvina*,
written and produced at the Naples Conservatoire, was never published. A manuscript copy of it is preserved in the British Museum.

[2] He died at the age of 33.

[3] Count Pepoli, who wrote the book for *I Puritani*, followed Romani's lead,
though with far less success.

rest was left to the composer—who again, on his part, knew exactly how to adapt his knowledge and sense of vocal effect to the altogether exceptional gifts and attainments of the great singers for whom he wrote. Of the two composers, Bellini was the more delicately gifted and original, whilst Donizetti was the better trained. The dates of Donizetti's best known operas are: *Anna Bolena*, 1830; *Marino Falieri*, 1833; *Lucrezia Borgia*, 1833; *Lucia di Lammermoor*, 1835; *La Figlia del Reggimento*, 1840; *La Favorita*, 1840—in all, he produced sixty-six operas before his career was cut short by mental disease. Together with Donizetti, Bellini—the sentimentalist—forms the link between the gaiety and verve of Rossini and the more strenuous art of Verdi. Bellini has well expressed not only the genuine feeling, but also the prevailing sentimentality of his time. As a master of elegiac melody, he indicates his claim by one fact which outweighs a host of disparaging remarks—the fact that Chopin, the modern melodist *par excellence*, paid him the homage of conscious or unconscious imitation. For some of Chopin's most telling cantilena, no matter how subtle and refined it may appear as he presents it, is essentially the cantilena of Bellini[1].

About seven years after Bellini's untimely death, Giuseppe Verdi[2] began to attract attention with his *Nabucodonosor* (1842), *I Lombardi alla prima crociata* (1843), *Ernani* (1844), after Victor Hugo's *Hernani*, and particularly *Rigoletto* (1851), after Hugo's *Le Roi s'amuse*[3]. In his first operas, such as *I Lombardi*, he exhibits an audacious temperament and powerful theatrical instincts rather than high musical attainments, but already in *Rigoletto*, *Il Trovatore*, and *La Traviata*,

---

[1] See *post*, p. 254. [2] Verdi was born in 1814, he died in 1901.

[3] *Macbeth*, after Shakespeare, had been produced in 1847; *I due Foscari* in 1844 and *Il Corsaro* in 1848, both after Byron; *Giovanna d'Arco* in 1845; *I Masnadieri* (*Die Räuber*) in 1847; *Luisa Miller* (*Cabale und Liebe*) in 1849 and *Don Carlos* in 1867, after Schiller; *Les Vêpres Siciliennes*, in imitation of Meyerbeer's *Les Huguenots*, in 1855; *Un Ballo in maschera* in 1859—the libretto is identical with that of Auber's *Le Bal masqué*—and *La Forza del destino* in 1862, the latter after a Spanish play by the Duc de Rivas.

the accomplished musician is evident, whilst the marked
racial and theatrical qualities remain unimpaired. *Rigoletto*,
the *chef-d'œuvre* of Verdi's first period—his seventeenth opera
—was at least equalled in popularity by the success of *Il
Trovatore* and *La Traviata*, both of which were brought out in
1855. The subjects as well as the construction of the libretti
of these operas are each in its way typical of the curious conception of operatic romance that prevailed among fashionable
circles in Paris, Venice, Rome, and Milan about the middle of
the nineteenth century. The music runs on the cosmopolitan
lines which Verdi affected in those emotional days. His musical
gifts and predilections were exactly fitted to reflect the extravagant tragical situations of *Ernani* and *Rigoletto*, the lay-
figure and gipsies, monks, knights, and ladies of *Il Trovatore*,
the story of a consumptive courtesan and her ultimate purification
by love and death in *La Traviata*[1]. The great vogue of
I Lombardi, *Nabucodonosor*, *Ernani*, and especially *Rigoletto*,
with its appeal to the revolutionary spirit, is partly explained
by the political circumstances of the time. The romantic
movement, which elsewhere on the continent told in favour of
reaction, became in Italy the handmaid of revolution. By a
curious accident the letters of Verdi's name were adopted by
the Italian populace as an emblem connected with the liberation
of Italy—'Viva Verdi!' really meant 'Viva Vittorio Emanuele
Re D' Italia!' And it is certain that Verdi himself, when dealing
with operatic situations that happen to have a problematic social
significance—situations such as could be turned to account for
political purposes—was very much in earnest, and consciously
made the most of them. Of his perfect sincerity in such
matters there can be no doubt—witness the fine scena in the
first act of *Rigoletto*, 'Pari siamo. Io ho la lingua; egli ha il

---

[1] The libretto of *La Traviata* is based on Dumas fils' *La Dame aux Camélias.*
'Musical art,' it has been well said in this connexion, 'cannot depict the repulsive
without some glimmer of beauty. It penetrates and idealizes the elements of
corruption, and transmutes the terrible reality of the drama into a melancholy
dream.' Hanslick, *Die moderne Oper*, i. 232.

pugnale,' and other such semi-personal utterances. *Rigoletto* was originally called *La Maledizione*. The censorship objected to King Francis I being cursed by a court fool, as is the case in Victor Hugo's play. Eventually the monarch was turned into a duke of Mantua, and the opera appeared under the fool's name *Rigoletto*.

Musically it is interesting to compare the famous quartet in *Rigoletto* with its model, the quartet in Bellini's *I Puritani*, and to note the advance the former shows in the direction of *la musica caratteristica*, towards which Verdi came to lean more and more in course of time. The change for the better with regard to the independence of the vocal part-writing, the individualization of the characters, together with a wider range of harmony, may be slight in this particular case, but it is remarkable all the same. In so far as the outlines of form are concerned the two quartets are closely alike in the cast of the melody, the changes of harmonic centres, the culmination of vocal effects towards the close, and in the contrivance of the coda. The general resemblance may be easily detected by a comparison of the following quotations :—

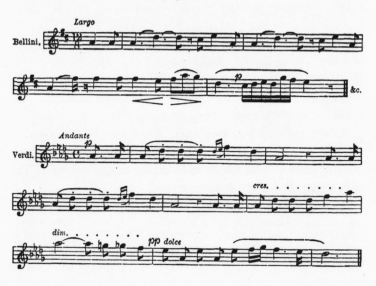

Verdi at first derived his manner and style from Mercadante and Bellini; then he felt the influence of Donizetti (*Lucrezia Borgia, Don Pasquale*), later on, and in an increasing degree, that of Meyerbeer. The role of Azucena in *Il Trovatore*, for instance, is but that of Fidès from *Le Prophète* translated into Romany. Then came the influence of Halévy (*La Juive*). Finally, he was swayed in a curious manner by Wagner (*Tannhäuser, Lohengrin*).

During the first twenty years of his career Verdi produced twenty-three operas. In the following period of twenty-seven years, only three—*Aïda, Otello, Falstaff*. Fully up to middle age the trend of his genius was evidently more inclined to theatrical than to musical ideals. Exceptionally gifted for the naturalistic expression of passion—it was partly a gift for finding emotional vocal melodies in the manner of Bellini, partly in that of Meyerbeer for combining such melodies with sharply accentuated rhythmical figures—he was able, by the aid of very simple choral and orchestral devices, to produce telling theatrical effects. Thus his music, as it were by fits and starts, is now operatically effective, now sentimentally weak or vulgar, now blatant with theatrical pathos, now genuinely original and dramatic.

At the age of 57 Verdi wrote *Aïda* for Cairo (1871-2), and produced it at the European centres as a pendant to Meyerbeer's *L'Africaine*. Then in his seventy-third year came *Otello*, first performed at La Scala, Milan, in 1887, the book by Arrigo Boïto after Shakespeare; and, finally, *Falstaff*, first performed in 1893, the book again by Boïto after the *Merry Wives of Windsor*.

Verdi's efforts to keep pace with the movement towards characterization in opera became more and more apparent from the date of *Rigoletto* onwards, and gradually brought about changes in his manner and considerable improvement in his technique. *Aïda* contains much that is mere pageant music or picturesque illustration of scenic evolutions, but also several scenes of emotional power and impressiveness. *Otello* very distinctly—and, to a greater extent still, *Falstaff*—shows a change in method. The master seems to have reversed his artistic direction, and to have adopted a more intellectual speculative 'Wagnerian' gait. That Verdi did assimilate some minor points in the method of Wagner is certain. Yet any one familiar with the scores of both masters will readily distinguish between the perhaps equally futile designations 'Maestro' and 'Meister.' In Verdi there is hardly a trace of Wagner's peculiar orchestral polyphony or variety and richness of tone-colour. Verdi, it is true, employs the representative phrase, the 'Leitmotiv,' but not in Wagner's many-sided, contrapuntal way, and only in so far as the device is helpful in clearing up special points in the action. Moreover the character of Verdi's representative phrases is as distinctly his own, that is to say Italian, as that of Wagner is Teutonic.

Comparison of Rossini's *Tragedia lirica*, *Otello* (1816) with the *Otello* of Verdi throws a vivid light on the changes brought about by the spirit of romanticism and the example of Wagner. Rossini's *Tragedia* has many traces of the older *opera seria*. Verdi's is an *opera caratteristica* of a very pronounced type. With Rossini there is but a faint shadow of Shakespeare's tragedy, and the music might, for the most part, be sung in solfeggio. With Verdi the librettist adheres closely to Shakespeare's text, whilst the composer strives to develop his powers of dramatic realization, and to find proper accents, passionate or tragic or comical, to tally with the characters and situations. It is a matter of give-and-take between dramatist and musician; Boïto's book inspires the composer to a new mode of utterance, and a good performance of *Otello* leaves the impression of a tragic drama dissolved in music. In certain particulars, however, the older *Otello* holds its own, and the points are not altogether in favour of Verdi and *la musica caratteristica*. In Desdemona's 'willow' song, for example, Rossini's melody is simple and beautiful; Verdi's slightly bizarre, though most effective in its place [1].　A note of warning, ' Wagner in the air,' was uttered in Italy after the production of *Otello*; it became a cry of alarm after *Falstaff*; but Verdi even here remains true to himself and the traditions of his country.　In no case has he traversed the Italian doctrine that vocal melody of some sort is the main concern, even when the music takes the place of rapid dialogue or passionate soliloquy.　His melody, in *Falstaff*, is more inclined towards recitative than cantilena ; and its power, though its presence is felt throughout, is but rarely condensed to actual song.　In one instance only—Fenton's little arioso ' Bocca bacciata '—there is something like the lilt of the younger Verdi's tunes.　For the most part the music has the character of a lively conversation, with here and there some bits of energetic declamation or emotional cantabile.　Boïto's libretto to the *Merry Wives* would be quite effective as a play without music.　Few lines in it appear to be written with a direct view to formal solo or concerted pieces.　But whenever Verdi chooses to make use of an opportunity to write ' in form ' —as for instance in the ensemble ' È un ribaldo, un furbo, un ladro,' in the second part of Act I, the duets ' Labbra di foco,' and ' Dal labbro il canto estasiato vola,' Acts II and III, and the fugal finale ' Tutto il mondo è burla,'—the result proves fine in effect, distinctly artistic and perspicuous, though less striking and impressive than earlier pieces, excepting, of course, the comical vocal fugue at the end, which is perfect in its way.

Falstaff is perhaps less remarkable than *Otello* in point of musical invention.　But the sardonic vivacity of its humour is surprising.　There is not a page in *Falstaff* which does not exhibit touches of musical as well as verbal wit of the most entrancing kind.　'Such scenes as the assignation made by Falstaff with Dame Quickly, with its playful iteration of the notes associated with the words " Dalle due alle tre," the whole

---

[1] There is in Verdi's setting a touch of artificiality, recalling the song ' Le roi de Thulé ' in Berlioz' *Damnation de Faust*. The prominent part played by the corno inglese, i. e. bass oboe, also recalls Berlioz.

scene of the buck-basket, the fat knight's soliloquy after his immersion in the Thames, and above all the working up of the final scene, are monuments of humorous power [1].'

In *Aïda*, *Otello*, and *Falstaff* the robust naturalistic expression of passion, so characteristic of the early operas, appears less crude, the declamation less violent and more carefully balanced ; the outlines of the melody more sinuous, the harmony and modulation richer and bolder, the instrumentation less coarse and commonplace, whilst the telling quality of the music, the sum total of its effect in combination with proper stage management (provided always that the later operas are performed at theatres of more reasonable dimensions than La Scala of Milan or Covent Garden), can hardly be said to fall short of what it was at the outset, that is to say, in such popular works as *Rigoletto*, *Il Trovatore*, and *La Traviata*. Allowing for the curious cosmopolitanism in his choice of subjects and the eclecticism in their musical treatment, the occasional crudity and frequent vacillation in his style, together with the not uncommon cases of perhaps unconscious borrowing of other men's devices, it is none the less evident that the operas of Verdi represent a forward movement in several branches of the musico-histrionic art, and that his music, taken altogether, is the result of self-developed Italianism, and the expression of a strong Italian individuality.

[1] Mr. J. A. Fuller Maitland.

CHAPTER V

THE FURTHER DEVELOPMENT OF ROMANTIC OPERA

AFTER Weber and Marschner the progress of operatic art did not move so rapidly in Germany as might have been expected. It is true the spirit of romantic opera had already entered the mind of Wagner, to await there its most complete embodiment in *Lohengrin*. But it was not till past the middle of the century that any of Wagner's works came to be an appreciable factor in musical life [1].

In the meantime the operas of lesser musicians, such as Konradin Kreutzer, Reissiger, Lortzing, Flotow and Nicolai, gained some degree of popular favour. It is enough to mention Kreutzer's *Nachtlager von Granada* (1834) [2], Reissiger's *Felsenmühle*, Flotow's *Martha* (1847), Lortzing's (1801–51) *Czar und Zimmermann* (1837), *Der Wildschütz* (1842), and Nicolai's *Die lustigen Weiber von Windsor* (1849). Lortzing, an experienced actor singer and conductor, wrote his own libretti, which, with considerable skill, he adapted from already existing plays. His practical knowledge of stage effect to some extent made up for the rather commonplace character of his music. Compared with the power of Marschner's work, Lortzing's is but that of a gifted dilettante, who was able to make good use of his experience in the theatre. With the aid of his lively tunes and his actor's *chic*, Lortzing managed somehow to express the provincial humours of the period (about 1840–50) in a manner

---

[1] The first performance of *Lohengrin* took place under Liszt, at Weimar, in 1850.

[2] Konradin Kreutzer, 1780–1849. Some of his choral songs for male voices, such as 'Die Kapelle,' 'Der Tag des Herrn,' 'Märznacht,' are models in their way, and had an immense vogue.

sufficiently artistic to ensure a widespread popularity in
Northern Germany. His successor in popular favour was
Flotow, another quasi-amateur, whose *Martha* made the round
of Europe; but Flotow's melody is at once more commonplace
and more sentimental, and the neatness of style, to which his
vogue was mainly due, does little more than borrow a few
epigrams from the current phraseology of French *opéra
comique.*

Nicolai, an excellent all-round musician, conductor and
singing-master, who had produced operas in Italy and church
music in Germany, put forth the ripe fruits of his experience
in *Die lustigen Weiber von Windsor,* ' komisch-phantastische
Oper in 3 Akten,' which was brought out shortly before his
death, at Berlin in 1849, and was received with acclamation.
The bright and spontaneous good humour that pervades the
music chimes with the gaiety of Shakespeare's play. The airs
and rapid conversational ensemble pieces are connected by
short snatches of dialogue, after the manner of Auber's *Le
Maçon.* Nicolai makes no attempt at close characterization,
such as Weber, for instance, achieved in the duet between
Agathe and Aennchen in *Der Freischütz* ; his Merry Wives,
indeed, might exchange their tunes throughout, as they actually
do, when, in an amusing duet, they compare Falstaff's letters.
But the humours of Falstaff, Mrs. Ford, Dr. Caius, are kept
sufficiently distinct. The finales of both the first and the
second acts are well contrived and effective. The declamation
is good and the treatment of the voice admirable. But it is
not till the third act, during the fairy scene in Windsor Forest,
that the limitations of Nicolai's talent become apparent. Here
his routine proves insufficient, and the music, pretty and brisk
as it is, lacks the touch of poesy.

It was said that Lesueur, Berlioz' master at the Paris
Conservatoire, put so much dramatic life into his church music
that there was none left for his operas. In an analogous way
it may be said that Berlioz' dramatic vein was nearly exhausted

by his symphonies when he began to write *Les Troyens*, which he intended to be his magnum opus for the stage.

The words and music to the ' Poème lyrique en deux parties ' *Les Troyens*: I. *La Prise de Troie*, opéra en trois actes, II. *Les Troyens à Carthage*, opéra en cinq actes avec un prologue, were completed in 1858. An opéra comique, *Béatrice et Bénédict*, after Shakespeare's *Much Ado about Nothing*, followed in 1862. As at first intended, *Les Troyens*, like any other grand opera, was to occupy one evening only; and *Béatrice et Bénédict* was planned as a musical comedy, a 'Lever de rideau,' in one act. Both works were repeatedly revised, unduly expanded, and spoilt. ' On peut dire de lui (Berlioz), comme de son héroïque homonyme, qu'il a péri sur les murs de Troie [1].' *Les Troyens*, although intended as an equivalent to Wagner's *Der Ring des Nibelungen*, is simply an opera upon an unusually large scale, bearing no sort of resemblance to the Wagnerian music-drama [2]. From the stage-manager's point of view, the disposition of *Les Troyens* (Berlioz' own) is unsatisfactory, and there are but few cases where the music supports and furthers the action or makes amends for defects in dramatic construction or scenic arrangements. Even the dance tunes, such as those of the Combat de geste [3], the Pantomime avec chœurs in *La Prise de Troie*, the Pantomime in the second act, the airs de danse in the third act of *Les Troyens à Carthage*, have a touch of artificiality. *La Prise de Troie* is a ponderous prelude to the main work. In the opera proper, *Les Troyens à Carthage*, the dramatic interest lies solely in the departure of Aeneas, and in the scene of Dido's death. The style of some of the airs and scenes and of the short choruses recalls the manner sometimes of Gluck, sometimes of Spontini. The best pieces in *La Prise de Troie* are a spirited choral ensemble,

---

[1] Gounod, Preface to Berlioz' *Lettres intimes*.

[2] Part I, *La Prise de Troie*, was inadequately performed in Paris at the Théâtre Lyrique, and withdrawn after twenty repetitions. A German version of both parts of *Les Troyens* was produced at Carlsruhe in 1897.

[3] Compare Wagner's *Rienzi*, Act II.

a fine Octet and chorus, ' Châtiment effroyable, mystérieuse horreur,' a touching prayer, 'Puissante Cybèle,' for female voices, Cassandra's air (in the manner of Spontini) ' Malheureux roi,' and a 'Marche tyrienne,' which occurs again in *Les Troyens à Carthage*, ' dans le mode triomphal ' and ' dans le mode triste.' In *Les Troyens à Carthage*, the more remarkable numbers are the introductory Lamento and the ensembles belonging to Act I, including the fine Chant national ' Gloire à Didon,' the ambitious and curious Chasse royale et Orage, called a *symphonie descriptive avec chœurs*, which forms the second act, the Quintet ' O pudeur,' and the Septet 'Tout n'est que paix et charme autour de nous,' the love duet, Dido and Aeneas (a *rifacimento* of the moonlight scene in *The Merchant of Venice*), the delicate ' Chanson du jeune matelot,' the noble fragment of a duet, Act V, ' Va, ma sœur, l'implorer,' Aeneas' air ' Ah, quand viendra l'instant suprême?' Dido's solo ' Je vais mourir,' and 'Énée, Énée, ah, mon âme te suit,' and some portions of the picturesque choral music which illustrates the funeral ceremonies.

Béatrice et Bénédict is a light opera, the texture of which, shot with strands of comedy and romance, was woven in the loom of *Benvenuto Cellini*. The influence of the earlier and more robust work is noticeable in many solo numbers and ensembles ; such for instance as Bénédict's rondo ' Ah ! je vais l'aimer,' the trio ' Me marier, Dieu me pardonne,' and the whimsical duet ' L'amour est un flambeau.' One of the strangest numbers is an 'Épithalame grotesque ' written in Berlioz' rather heavy-handed counterpoint, sung, according to the stage-direction, in tones of extravagant emphasis, and repeated with a farcical accompaniment of oboes and bassoons. Like the ' Amen ' chorus in *Faust* it is an obvious satire on academic methods, the purport of which hardly atones for its ugliness. But the opera contains two numbers which are fresh and spontaneous :—the Sicilienne which serves as entr'acte, and the duet ' Vous soupirez, Madame,' which in Act I occupies the place of the finale. The latter in particular is a shapely and beautiful composition, which in style and feeling forms a worthy pendant to the shepherd's chorus in the *Enfance du Christ*.

The music of Charles Gounod [1], an eclectic in the good sense of the word, shows traces of Mozart, Weber, Meyerbeer, Halévy, Auber, Schumann, and early Wagner. But Gounod so completely absorbed and assimilated the results of a close study of these masters as to place himself in a position to produce something that is new in effect if not new in substance. The distinctive personal note of his music consists in the expression of tender sentiment and longing—as in certain parts of *Faust et Marguerite* and *Roméo et Juliette*. It is worthy of remark that his lovers, Faust and Marguerite, Roméo and Juliette, Vincent and Mireille, Philémon and Baucis, all seem to make love to the same tune. Gounod rarely reaches the heights of passion. He contrives, however, to reflect the changes of light emotion—in *Mireille* for instance, or in *Philémon et Baucis*, and *Le Médecin malgré lui*. Based upon just declamation, as it was practised in the days of Lully and Gluck, the accents of Gounod's melody never contradict those of the words. The refinement of his style is peculiarly French, and he shows a consummate knowledge of orchestration for stage purposes. His first opera, *Sapho* (1851), was a failure, and so was *La Nonne sanglante*, in 1854. Success came with *Le Médecin malgré lui*, from Molière's comedy, which appeared in 1858, and particularly in 1859 with *Faust et Marguerite*, from the first part of Goethe's *Faust*, which, after a short period of suspense, brought him fame and position. Gounod professed to hold his own religious music—the oratorios *La Rédemption* (1882), *Mors et Vita* (1885), and sundry songs of a pious character—in higher esteem than his theatrical works; yet his talent was essentially imitative, histrionic, and his best work belongs to the operatic stage [2].

---

[1] 1818–93.

[2] After *Faust et Marguerite* Gounod produced *Philémon et Baucis* (1860), and *La Reine de Saba* (1862), both at the Grand-Opéra ; *Mireille* (1864), and *Roméo et Juliette*

Ambroise Thomas [1], an eclectic like Gounod, but of a somewhat weaker type, and more inclined towards the methods of Meyerbeer, made his mark in 1866 with *Mignon*, after Goethe's *Wilhelm Meister*; *Hamlet* followed in 1868, and *Françoise de Rimini* in 1882. But the next French opera of world-wide fame after Gounod's *Faust et Marguerite* was Bizet's *Carmen*, produced at Paris in 1875. Bizet [2] had already won some reputation with *The Fair Maid of Perth* (1867), *Djamileh* (1872), and with his brilliant incidental music to Alphonse Daudet's *Arlésienne* (1872), but it is into this, the latest and greatest of his compositions, that he put his best work. Despite a touch of *diablerie* which Georges Bizet's music shares with Mérimée's story, or perhaps because of that very touch, *Carmen* made a distinct and strong impression. The public was fascinated by the sensuous and picturesque dances and songs, and the murder in the Bull Ring; musicians were fascinated by the novelty of the Spanish gipsy measures, the subtle cleverness of the melodic, rhythmical, and harmonic devices, and by the strange realistic effects of instrumental local colour. In *Carmen* (as in Weber's *Preciosa*) the music is always in accord with the action, yet never crude or vulgar. Every note sung by the chief personages seems to belong to them by natural right. The music is singularly free from reminiscences of the classical composers; throughout it savours of Spanish and Provençal folk-songs and dances. Its beauties are too well known to need quotation, yet we may mention the Séguedille et Duo, the Habanera, the Chanson Bohème, and the dance with which Carmen fascinates at once her lover and her audience. Among composers of lesser account Edouard Lalo (1823–92) produced a considerable impression with his opéra comique *Le Roi d'Ys*, and Léo Delibes (1836–91) with *Le Roi l'a dit* and *Lakmé*.

(1867), both at the Théâtre-Lyrique; *Cinq Mars* (1877) ; *Polyeucte* (1878); *Le Tribut de Zamora* (1881)—again at the Grand-Opéra.

[1] 1811–96.
[2] 1838–75.

For a decade or so, during the Second Empire (1860–70), Jacques Offenbach[1] influenced, and in a manner controlled, public taste in France and elsewhere on the Continent, in a manner disproportionate to the musical value of his productions. Offenbach's opéra bouffe, which eclipsed the genuine opéra comique, was a perfect echo of the cynical caprice of the third Napoleon's time—theatrical extravagance paired with farce—satire with vulgarity—a theatrical *journal pour rire*, the stress laid upon the comic licence of the stage business and the licence emphasized by the music of a Meyerbeer *en miniature*.

Yet Offenbach had an individual gift of melody, his harmony at times was refined, his instrumentation often ingenious, though the means were simple. From the comedian's point of view the facility and rapidity of his invention was remarkable. His satirical vein never failed. Perhaps the operettas *Orphée aux enfers* and *La Chanson de Fortunio* represented him to best advantage. In the once celebrated *La Grande-Duchesse de Gérolstein* he appears at his worst. He returned to his first manner before his death in *Les Contes d'Hoffmann*.

Two German comic operas demand notice here: Peter Cornelius'[2] *Der Barbier von Bagdad,* produced at Weimar in 1858, and Hermann Goetz'[3] *Der Widerspenstigen Zähmung,* after Shakespeare's *Taming of the Shrew,* produced at Mannheim in 1875. Cornelius' work shows the influence of Berlioz' *Benvenuto Cellini*; Goetz' of Schumann generally, and, far away, of Wagner's *Meistersinger.* Both operas are *genre* pictures full of delicate details, but at times the music is too frail for stage effect. Goetz was not a man of theatrical instincts and had hardly come in contact with the theatre when he began to compose his opera. He had previously produced chamber music, pianoforte pieces, and songs. His sense of comedy lacked power, and, though he never actually lost sight of the stage action, yet, like his model Schumann, he deliberately chose to lay his chief stress on musical detail. After the performance at

[1] 1822–80.   [2] 1830–74.   [3] 1843–76.

Mannheim, *Der Widerspenstigen Zähmung* was warmly received at Vienna in 1875, and it is still occasionally given.

Wagner's *Meistersinger* apart, the book of Cornelius' *Barbier von Bagdad* is, from a literary point of view, far and away the best comic libretto in German. There is nothing to approach it in any other language, unless it be Boïto's libretto to Verdi's *Falstaff*—which has the great advantage of livelier stage action. In *Der Barbier von Bagdad*, Cornelius sometimes employs *parlando* recitative, and even the patter song, upon an elaborated orchestral background and with astonishing result—as for instance in the fifth scene : 'O wüsstest du, Verehrter, was ich für ein Gelehrter.' The various movements are formally complete, as is the case in Berlioz' *Benvenuto*, and Cornelius tried hard to resist Wagnerian influences—to which, however, in his last opera, *Der Cid*, and the unfinished *Gunlöd* he finally succumbed. Compared with Goetz, Cornelius' originality and fertility of invention is very striking.

Opera, more or less on the lines of racial and national characteristics, began in Russia with Glinka's [1] *La Vie pour le Tsar* (1836), *Russlan et Ludmilla* (1842) (the text after a romance in verse by Pushkin), and Serov's *Judith*, produced in 1863 ; in Poland with Moniuszko's *Halka* (1858); in Bohemia with Smetana's *Prodana nevesta* (The Bartered Bride) (1866); in Hungary with Erkel's *Hunyady Lazlo* (1844).

The operas of Glinka and Smetana are distinguished by their musical value apart from their position as national representatives. Glinka, Russian by birth, chose to adopt the characteristics of North-eastern European folk-song, both in the vocal and instrumental part of his operas. In *La Vie pour le Tsar*, Russian and Polish elements are combined [2]. In his incidental music to a

---

[1] Glinka was born in 1804, he died in 1857. His *mémoires* were published in 1870.

[2] In its strongest moments the music to *La Vie pour le Tsar* appears as a kind of scene painting, very bold and effective. That of *Russlan et Ludmilla* is of a fantastic, semi-oriental character, and differs so greatly from the first opera that one might guess at another composer. *La Vie pour le Tsar* has been given hundreds of times, and its popularity shows no signs of abating.

tragedy, *Le Prince Kholmsky*, by Koukolnik, there are reminiscences of Hebrew melodies. His technique, vocal and instrumental, is that of a master with a faint touch of dilettantism, trained in Italy and Germany. The melody, apart from Russian influence, is reminiscent of South-western Europe; the orchestration, too, has a Southern touch—French, Italian, or Spanish—it is always simple, often very effective, but occasionally thin. A song such as the following, from *La Vie pour le Tsar*, represents him well.

- çut . . . . . a - lors son . . . . . su - - prê - me sou-

- pir, son . . . son su - prê - - me sou - pir.

Certain orchestral pieces of Glinka's deserve mention : *Jotc Aragonese,* described as a ' Capriccio brillante,' a Fantaisie sui des thèmes espagnols, 'Souvenir d'une nuit d'été à Madrid, ' and *La Kamarinskaja,* which last is the true ancestor of Russian instrumental music. It consists of an orchestral fantasia on two Russian folk-tunes, a wedding song and a dancing song, rich in novel contrapuntal devices and orchestral contrivances of con- siderable originality [1].

Alexander Serov [2], critic, librettist, amateur composer, in early life came under the influence of Glinka, and later on under that of Wagner. His first opera, *Judith,* hesitating and inadequate in point of style, though written when he was upwards of forty, is

---

[1] National elements, Russian, Spanish, Italian, Polish, are always present in Glinka's songs—some eighty in number. He accepts existing dance-rhythms and takes no pains to modify or improve upon them, as Chopin did in his *Mazurkas* and *Polonaises.* The list of Glinka's works includes pianoforte pieces, chamber music, vocal quartets, choruses. [2] 1820–71.

laid out on the lines of Meyerbeer and scored in the manner of
Wagner's *Rienzi*. It was produced in 1863 and met with an
extraordinary and lasting popular success in Russia. His
second attempt at opera, *Rogneda*, contains, according to
Tchaikovsky, 'certain oases in the desert, of which the music
will pass muster.' In 1867 Serov tried something faintly
resembling a Wagnerian music drama in Russian, on a Russian
subject, and with the aid of Russian folk-tunes, thus following
in the wake of Glinka. He founded his libretto on Ostrovsky's
rather sordid play, *The Power of Evil*, but did not live to finish
the music, of which the orchestration was completed by Soloviev
—an arrangement that still keeps the stage [1].

Smetana's most famous opera, *The Bartered Bride*, like
Nicolai's *Merry Wives of Windsor*, is an enlarged Singspiel
of the family of Mozart. There are traces and touches of
Beethoven's *Fidelio* and Cherubini's *Les Deux Journées*. The
music throughout is fresh and bright, the melody refined, the
ensembles masterly, and there is a great deal of amusing inter-
play and episode. Six other operas by Smetana have been
performed. His cycle of Six Poèmes symphoniques, entitled
My Country, shows considerable cleverness and some originality.

Moniuszko's *Halka* is the favourite Polish opera. The
original two acts were first performed at Wilna in 1854.
With two further acts interpolated, it was heard at Warsaw in
1858, and repeated there for the five hundredth time in 1900.
The interpolations weaken the total effect, but the charm of
the tunes keeps the work afloat. It is admirably written for
the voices and admirably scored. Moniuszko put forth a
total of fifteen Polish operas, several Masses, cantatas, and a
number of songs.

The achievements of English composers during the first half
of the nineteenth century, the instrumental music of Sterndale

---

[1] Liszt (*Letters to Madame de Wittgenstein*, iii. p. 38) mentions some candid advice
on the subject of Serov's opera *Judith* : '. . . que je lui ai conseillé de traiter comme
Judith avait fait d'Holopherne ! Imaginez que Serov se figure qu'il est le Wagner
russe ! '

Bennett and the church music of the Wesleys excepted, were by no means imposing. Judged by quality, the operas of Balfe and Wallace, such as Balfe's still popular *Bohemian Girl* (1843), or Wallace's *Maritana* (1845) and *Lurline* (1860), are not inferior to the lighter operatic ware produced in France and Italy for the delectation of middle-class audiences—but, then as now, musicians must have found them weak and insufficient. Both Balfe and Wallace had a facile gift of melody. Expert vocalists and instrumentalists (Balfe was a famous singer, and Wallace has the reputation of having been a virtuoso upon the violin), they understood the requirements of popular operatic performers, and were sufficiently experienced as musicians to handle a small orchestra and a small chorus with ease and skill.

The operettas of Burnand and Gilbert, the librettists, and Sullivan the composer—from *Box and Cox*, and *Trial by Jury*, to *The Gondoliers, The Yeomen of the Guard*, and *The Mikado* —are the leading English contributions to the devolution of opéra comique to the opéra bouffe. These amusing pieces were hailed with delight by all English-speaking people, chiefly on account of the fresh air and healthy laughter that pervades their humorous extravagance. When Sullivan appeared with his music to Shakespeare's *Tempest*, Balfe and Wallace were near the end of their careers. Sullivan, a gifted and accomplished musician, had acquired the mannerisms of Mendelssohn, and felt the simple charm of Schubert; he came by degrees to emulate the *savoir-faire* of Auber, and to approach the satire of Offenbach. His first essays in operetta, *Box and Cox* (1867), and *Trial by Jury* (1875) (both libretti by Burnand), were avowedly due to Offenbach's example, but from the outset they were free from the grotesque eccentricities of their French models. There is a distinct personal note about Sullivan's lighter operatic tunes; amiable, tender, slightly ironical, always graceful and artistic. His lucid sense of humour stood him in good stead. In agreement with the Merry Andrew in the prologue to Goethe's *Faust*, he seems to have said to himself :—

'Posterity! Don't name the word to me! if *I* should choose to teach posterity, where would you get contemporary fun?' Technically Sullivan was a master all round; a good vocalist, and well acquainted with every instrument used in the orchestra, or in military bands. In the matter of orchestration he was completely at his ease, and at once found the simplest and best means of attaining his end. His melodic vein flowed readily and copiously; it was never deep nor passionate, yet at its best sufficiently capable of expressing emotion. His declamation was easy and natural: the words and the tune seemed to spring from the same source. His own favourite among the operettas was *The Yeomen of the Guard* (1888), probably because of the touching dramatic story. *Ivanhoe*, a serious effort in opera, can hardly be said to have fallen flat since there were one hundred and six consecutive performances in London only, but it failed to compel assent.

CHAPTER VI

OVERTURES AND SYMPHONIES

WEBER'S music, both vocal and instrumental, owes its character indirectly to the romantic nature of the legends and scenes which he employed as a basis of his works. His innate tendency—which in later years became a conscious aim—was to achieve a complete rendering of the emotional essence of a dramatic situation in terms of music, be it instrumental or vocal. Thus his Concertstück is essentially a 'Dramatic Concerto,' and the three overtures to his mature operas are the finest Dramatic Fantasias extant, reproducing, in a concentrated form, the sentiment of the scenes and situations which are to ensue.

Apart from the stage, romantic effects in instrumental music arose from a desire to reproduce impressions derived either from imaginative literature, or directly from natural phenomena —to express the prevailing emotion, the mood of some particular poem or story, or of some particular aspect of nature.

The latter may be illustrated by Mendelssohn's[1] famous overture *The Hebrides (Fingal)*, written in 1830.

The music here conveys a sense of distance, of solitude, and of moving water. Further on, there are suggestions and effects as of storm, or of wind-shaken surges, of shifting gleam and cloud, of the sea-mew's plaintive cry, and the shimmer of northern seas. Most hearers will confess to having received some such impressions—even if they do not happen to possess Heine's or Schumann's gift of evolving pictures from musical sounds,

[1] Mendelssohn was born in 1809, he died in 1847.

and are not aware that the work was conceived amid the rugged
scenery of Staffa and the adjacent islands.

'Mendelssohn,' Wagner said [1], 'was a landscape painter of the first order,' and this overture is his masterpiece. Note the extraordinary beauty of the passage where the oboe rises above the other instruments with a wail as of sea winds over the sea:

[1] Grove's *Dictionary of Music*, article Wagner.

It must not, however, be supposed that this piece is merely made up of a series of more or less picturesque devices of orchestration, or that it is in any way meant to be an example of programme music. It is pure instrumental music on musical lines [1].

Its originality consists in the nature of the fresh and characteristic subjects, especially the first subject—and in the masterly treatment of the orchestra. Mendelssohn's other overtures— *A Midsummer Night's Dream* (1826), *Meeresstille und glückliche Fahrt* (1828), and *Zum Märchen von der schönen Melusine* (1833)—are to a certain extent reflections of literature. In *Meeresstille* the composer is guided by the poet's order of ideas —Goethe's pictures of a calm at sea and a prosperous voyage. In *Melusina*, Tieck's version of the old French story prompts the music, which seems to depict, alternately, the beauteous water-nymph turned human, her pathetic distress on discovery, and the return to her former condition. Here again, the music is meant to tell its own tale in purely musical terms and on purely musical lines. The title contains all that the composer deemed needful to guide the audience [2].

Mendelssohn's nearest approach to the rôle of musical illustrator is contained in the Scherzo of an early work, the octet for strings (1825), and the instrumental introduction to the cantata, *Die erste Walpurgisnacht*. Originally the Scherzo in the octet was headed by a stanza from the ‘Intermezzo’ in Goethe's *Faust* :—

Orchester—*pianissimo.*

Wolkenzug und Nebelflor	Floating cloud and trailing mist
Erhellen sich von oben;	Bright'ning o'er us hover;
Luft im Laub, und Wind im Rohr,	Airs stir the brake, the rushes shake,
Und alles ist zerstoben.	And all their pomp is over.

---

[1] The materials are arranged in accordance with the usual scheme of harmonic distribution—the outlines of the sonata form: I. Exposition, first subject in B minor, second subject in the relative major D. II. The working-out section, wherein fresh harmonic centres are touched upon. III. Recapitulation, with both subjects in the principal key.

[2] Mendelssohn's aversion to anything resembling a detailed programme came out very clearly in his sarcastic answer to a question as to the ‘meaning’ of *Melusina* : ‘Hm—does my music hint at a mésalliance ? ’

The Introduction to *Die erste Walpurgisnacht* describes :—1. 'Das schlechte Wetter,' and 2. 'Der Uebergang zum Frühling.'

The germs of the overture to *A MidsummerNight's Dream* can be traced to a reading of Shakespeare's play in Schlegel and Tieck's translation, when Mendelssohn was still in his teens. The score was finished in 1826, before he had completed his eighteenth year. It is easy to see how impressions of certain scenes took shape in the young man's mind, and how, with Weber's overtures for a model, he fused and welded them together so as to form a consistent whole. The music seems to convey suggestions of Titania asleep, revels of fairies, a dance of clowns with the bray of 'Bottom translated,' the lovers' hide and seek, and the nuptial festivities. Technically the overture is a carefully planned and carefully finished piece of work. The orchestration is remarkable for its clearness and practical efficiency. Every fantastic effect is produced with perfect ease. The spirit, however, is Weber's from the first note to the last, and in this important respect this overture is inferior to *The Hebrides*, and perhaps even to *Melusina*. The rest of the *Midsummer Night's Dream* music is of later date. In 1843 Mendelssohn was asked to write incidental pieces for a performance of the comedy at Berlin. The orchestral numbers—Scherzo, Elfinmarsch, Intermezzo (Hermione seeking Lysander), Notturno, Wedding march, a comic Funeral march and a Clowns' dance—show the master at his very best.

There is no need to dwell on the other overtures—*Ruy Blas, Athalie*, the overture for a Military band, published as Op. 24, and the so-called Trumpet overture in C—for, apart from the technical merits which they possess in common with all Mendelssohn's orchestral pieces, they have not sufficient spontaneity and weight to make their gradual disappearance a matter for much regret.

Schumann wrote a number of overtures, of which *Manfred* (1848) and *Genoveva* (1847–8) are the only two that really represent his powers. The rest, such as *Faust, Julius Caesar,*

Die Braut von Messina, Hermann und Dorothea, belong to that unfortunate period of feverish productiveness which preceded his final collapse (1850-4); all more or less ineffectual, they leave an impression of weariness and vain effort.

The overture to *Manfred* stands forth among Schumann's works even more conspicuously than *The Hebrides* among Mendelssohn's. In some degree Schumann's tone-poem suggests the atmosphere of Byron's *Manfred,* though it can hardly be called Byronic in spirit; a generic name, such as Brahms chose for his ' Tragic ' overture, would suit it better. With the *Manfred* overture, a piece sombre in tone, deeply felt and very personal, Schumann came nearer to the inner fane of music than Mendelssohn with *The Hebrides,* or with *Meeresstille* or *Melusina.* Though perfectly original in matter and sentiment, the method of construction employed in *Manfred* recalls that of Beethoven's third period. The subjects are strong and novel in style. The passionate melody, the vehement rhythm, the keen chromatic progressions and poignant dissonances, combine to produce an effect of restless longing and fierce excitement, to which, in its particular kind, the history of music can afford no parallel.

Next to *Manfred* the overture to *Genoveva,* a shapely and spirited piece, full of refined melody, still holds its own in the concert-room.

Composers, after Beethoven, who desired to attempt the grand form of orchestral music, found the breaking of new ground a matter of considerable difficulty. Schumann shared Mendelssohn's reluctance to experiment in symphonic design. Both masters, however, introduced some novel features with a view to unity, such, for instance, as the use of the same subject in several movements and the more or less close con-nexion of one movement with another, as in Mendelssohn's symphony in A minor and in Schumann's symphonies in D minor and B flat.

Mendelssohn, in the so-called Scotch and Italian symphonies, depicts moods reflecting impressions which he received in Scotland and in Italy (1830–1). He also makes occasional use of certain characteristic traits of Scotch and Italian folk-music, apparently with a view to a musical picture of manners and local colour. In the symphony known as the ' Reformation,' in the symphony to the *Lobgesang,* and in the overture to *St. Paul* he appeals to religious sentiment and the associations of worship, by means of leading phrases, such as ' Alles was Odem hat, lobe den Herrn,' in the *Lobgesang,* or the ' Dresden Amen ' and the chorales ' Ein' feste Burg ist unser Gott,' in the ' Reformation ' symphony, and ' Sleepers wake,' in *St. Paul.*

Schumann, more introspective than Mendelssohn, more of a mystic and an intellectualist, and less open to external impressions, sought to express his personal desires—the glow of enthusiasm, the ardour of love, or joy, or sorrow [1]. Thus his four sym-phonies make a stronger appeal to the emotions, and stimulate the hearer in a more direct manner than those of Mendelssohn. They evince a greater power of invention in harmony, melody, and the rhythms and figures which constitute the thematic

---

[1] In every case the man and the musician always strove to speak simultaneously. ' Mensch und Musiker suchten sich immer gleichzeitig bei mir auszusprechen.'

material. There is more energy in the Allegros, deeper pathos in the slow movements.

The freshness and originality of Schumann's talent is fully apparent, even in his first symphony in B flat, Op. 38 [1]. Among his friends this work was known as the Spring Symphony ; and it is indeed full of the glory of spring and joyous youth. The Introduction starts with a stately phrase for horns and trumpets :

which is really the first subject of the Allegro :

it occurs again in a larger form at the close of the working-out section. After the recapitulation of the subjects the music breaks away into a new theme, a spring song which carries to a full climax the emotional fervour of the movement.

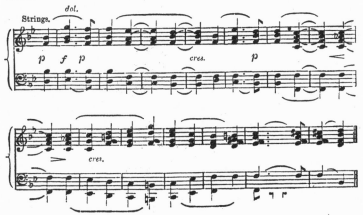

[1] First performed under Mendelssohn at the Gewandhaus, Leipzig, in 1845. At the same concert Mendelssohn's Violin Concerto was first heard.

Towards the end of the Larghetto, a gentle sensuous melody with variants recalling the early manner of Beethoven, the hearer is again surprised by the appearance of new melody. This time, however, it is not climax but anticipation. The new subject arises, ghostlike, to the sound of softly swelling trombones, and then, with a sudden forte, bursts forth as the Scherzo :

The Scherzo has two trios, the first of which consists of a curious device in groups of chords rather weak in effect, alternating between strings and winds in ²⁄₄ time. The same groups of chords are again introduced at the end of the movement, so as to serve as a kind of bridge to the Finale. Probably the construction of a suitable sequel to three movements of such exceptional calibre presented unforeseen difficulties. Schumann, serious by nature, when he wants to be jocose, is apt to become trivial. That he disliked triviality, so far as he saw it, seems proved by the fact of his employing the full orchestra, trombones

and all, to emphasize a concatenation of violent phrases, which
are meant to serve as a contrast to the somewhat flimsy leading
tunes of the Finale.

The result as a whole is hardly satisfactory. Incongruous
effects of this kind may be 'humorous,' or 'romantic,' or what
not—they are certainly eccentric. And the first leading tune
when it returns after a polite little cadenza for the horns and
the flute, comes dangerously near to a *Pas seul.*

With the symphony in D minor, No. 4[1], Schumann continued his efforts to attain unity. To this end, the leading phrase of the introduction to the first movement is repeated in the second —a 'Romanze'; the principal figure of the first Allegro is again employed to form a link between the close of the Scherzo and the beginning of the final Allegro; and all the movements are joined together so as to avoid a break. In spirit as well as in technical execution both the weak and the strong side of Schumann's talent are fully in evidence. The work contains bold, tender, and fantastic ideas presented in a very free and original manner, and, as in the second part of the first Allegro, often treated with remarkable skill. But both the first and last movements seem, at times, to suffer from a want of air and perspective.

The high-water mark of Schumann's symphonic music is reached in the symphony in C, Opus 61 (1846). Laid out on consistent lines, this work shows perfect unity of spirit, although there are fewer special devices to unify the movements than in the symphony in D minor. Some points in the Finale excepted, the entire work is strikingly original in topic, and the first three movements are admirably concise in form. As compared with the symphonies in B flat and D minor the efficiency of the orchestration is worthy of note. The sounds emitted by the various groups of instruments are characteristic and spontaneous in effect; and most of the themes give the impression that they were directly conceived in the actual form in which they reach the ear. The work opens with a solemn contrapuntal introduction, a broad theme for trumpets, horns and trombone, accompanied by a flowing counter-subject on the strings.

---

[1] This work is really the second symphony, having been sketched in 1841, soon after the first, though it was not completed till 1851. It was at first entitled 'Symphonische Phantasie,' and it appears, indeed, as a landmark on the border between the older symphony and the 'Poème symphonique.'

This in due course leads to an Allegro full of virile and impulsive energy. The breadth and conciseness of this movement are more noticeable than in any other of Schumann's orchestral compositions; the working-out section in particular has something of the grand style and the classic dignity. Next follows a vehement Scherzo with two well-contrasted trios, and then a slow movement of poignant pathos, remarkable alike for its closeness of texture and for several fine effects of instrumentation. Schumann's special power of vivid expression is well illustrated by his treatment here of the oboes and bassoons, and by the superb chain of trills for the violins which holds in unbroken unity the flying scales and arpeggios of the wood wind.

There is less of concentrated power in the Finale. The subjects are telling enough, but the persistent reiteration of a jerky rhythm—bars 13-46 and elsewhere—produces an impression as of a crowd of superlatives jostling one with another. The development section, in which part of the subject of the Adagio reappears both in an inverted form and *recte*, is ingenious, and the Coda, in which the phrase from the Introduction, quoted above, is interwoven with the other subjects, is as irresistible in movement as it is rich in texture. It cannot be denied, however, that the full effect is marred by want of balance and economy in the distribution of strongly emphasized points.

Taken as a whole this symphony, together with Schubert's symphony in the same key, ranks as the greatest achievement in symphonic form after Beethoven and before Brahms. It stamps Schumann as the most original of contemporary instrumental composers and, together with the *Manfred* overture, places him as the leading representative of the romantic spirit of his day.

Opus 97, in E flat, known as the Rhenish, written in 1850 and published as No. 3, in 1851, is the last and longest of Schumann's symphonies. It is also the least spontaneous and the most laboured. There are five movements. The personal note, that important element in Schumann's work, is not particularly

prominent, and the technique of the experienced artist can
hardly make amends for its absence. In the first movement
the process of elaboration is felt to be artificial, and the middle
portion of the last movement, for the same reason, appears dry
and dull. A so-called Scherzo in C major, ¾, molto moderato,
which in Schumann's words 'probably reflects a bit of life,'
has the lilt of a folk-song, and was at first called 'Morning
on the Rhine.' The most subtle and carefully written section
is an impressive contrapuntal movement in E flat minor, placed
between the Andante and the Finale. It was conceived at a
solemn ecclesiastical function held in Cologne Cathedral and
was originally headed 'Im Charakter der Begleitung einer
feierlichen Ceremonie'—'in the manner of music at a religious
ceremony.' The music of Schumann's later life is in more than
one respect touched with religious influence. In the days of
the *Myrthen*, of the Pianoforte quintet, of *Paradise and the
Peri*, he took the Romantic movement on its human side and
expressed in a heightened and intensified form the joys and
sorrows of customary human experience. But the second part
of Goethe's *Faust* opened to him a new world of thought and
feeling, and from thenceforward we find him striving towards
a deeper and more mystic utterance. It was not always with
success, for, with all its reticence, his natural temper was
human and sympathetic: when he attempted to scale the
remoter and more solitary heights he climbed with a vacillating
and uncertain tread, due partly to the unfamiliarity of his
surroundings, partly, no doubt, to the gradual encroachment
of disease. The craftsmanship would not always answer the
requirements of the thought: there is a want of that supreme
mastery which, in Bach or Beethoven, can embody the highest
truth without appearance of effort. Hence he shows at his
best when, as in the movement under discussion, he represents
the external pageantry of spiritual fervour:—the medium
through which it appeals to that romantic element in human
nature which even religion itself has not disdained to employ.

One of Schumann's lesser orchestral productions may fitly be mentioned here. It is a short Suite or Sinfonietta entitled 'Ouvertüre, Scherzo und Finale,' Op. 52, in E (1841–5),—a bright, slender, somewhat sketchy piece, with a touch of Cherubini in the Introduction and first Allegro.

The most notable weakness in Schumann's Symphonic work is his deficiency in orchestration. Now and then he succeeded in producing novel effects of great beauty, such as the weird sound of the chords for trumpets and trombones in the passage quoted above, from the overture to *Manfred*, or the thrilling tones of strings ending in the long chain of shakes in the Adagio of the second symphony. New and successful touches of instrumental colour are, however, rare with him. He shows but small sense of the possibilities of instrumental tone, and for want of intimate acquaintance with the peculiar qualities and capabilities of orchestral instruments either single or grouped, his musical ideas do not seem in the first instance to have presented themselves to his mental ear through the medium of the orchestra. His instrumentation, in consequence, falls short of Mendelssohn's habitual clearness and brilliancy, and even as compared with the instrumentation of lesser contemporary composers, German or French, it often appears inept, turgid, or dry. Occasionally, indeed, a page of his scoring looks and sounds like so many bars of rather clumsy pianoforte music writ large.

The finest of Mendelssohn's symphonies, the Scotch (1821–31 –42) and the Italian (1831), form a remarkable complement to Schumann. They certainly have more of the practical efficiency that comes of all-round ability, training and experience— especially in respect of copiousness and fluency of diction, and variety of instrumental colour. They are most carefully designed and finished down to the smallest details, and they have a picturesqueness and a poetical atmosphere of their own which leaves nothing to be desired in point of originality; yet they do not approach the emotional elevation of Schumann's work. The

convincing personal touches are absent; especially in the case of
the slow movements wherein Mendelssohn's habitual attitude of
reserve in the expression of deep emotion is most apparent.
Schumann's disposition always prompted him to deal directly
with passion, and strongly to emphasize the human element;
whereas Mendelssohn preferred to depict moods which are,
more or less directly, the results of external impressions. In
other words, Mendelssohn in his leading symphonies, and almost
as much in his best overtures, reveals himself as one who chooses
to express, in musical terms, the moods of a 'landscape' or
'*genre*' painter.   Thus the first sixteen bars of the Scotch symphony, which now act both as an introduction and as close to
the first Allegro, were written down as an *impression de voyage*
(1829) in the chapel of Holyrood Palace, 'open to the sky
and surrounded with grass and ivy, and everything ruined and
decayed.'   The subjects of the first Allegro (A minor, $\frac{6}{8}$), the
Scherzo (F major, $\frac{2}{4}$), and the Allegro maestoso which follows
the Allegro guerriero (A major, $\frac{6}{8}$), recall Highland scenery,
fighting legends, and the lilt of Scottish tunes.   The first subject
of the Scherzo is a happy transformation from minor to major
of 'Charlie is my darling.'   In the case of the Italian symphony
it is equally obvious that the most characteristic movements—
the Allegro, the Andante, and the Finale—are records of
musical moods suggested by things actually seen and heard.
The Andante con moto (D minor $\frac{4}{4}$) recalls the music of a
religious procession, a Pilgrim's March; and the final Saltarello,
named after two strains of a popular dance of the Romagna,
contains also a bit of a Neapolitan Tarantella.   Heine (1842), in
one of his half-serious moods, compared Felix Mendelssohn's
talent with the talent of Mademoiselle Rachel Felix, the
actress: 'Peculiar to both,' he says, 'is the fact that they are
seriously in earnest, they have a decided, almost an aggressive
predilection for classical models, they delight in the most ingenious calculations of delicate effects, they show singular cleverness and, finally, a total lack of *naïveté*.   But,' Heine adds, 'is

there such a thing in art as genuine originality without *naïveté*?
hitherto a case has not occurred.'

It seems a far cry from Mendelssohn to Wagner. But
Wagner's overture *Faust* distinctly belongs to the Central phase
of the Romantic development and is best discussed here.

Der Gott, der mir im Busen wohnt,
  Kann tief mein Innerstes erregen;
Der über allen meinen Kräften thront,
  Er kann nach aussen nichts bewegen;
Und so ist mir das Dasein eine Last,
  Der Tod erwünscht, das Leben mir
    verhasst.
	The God that dwells within my breast,
	  Can stir the inmost of my being,
	Holds all my power at His behest,
	  Yet naught without marks His decree-
	    ing;
	And so my whole existence is awry,
	  Life hateful, and my one desire to die.'

These are the lines from Goethe's *Faust* that serve for a
motto to Wagner's 'Eine Faust-Ouvertüre,' an orchestral piece
written at Paris, in 1840, and originally intended to be the first
movement of a *Faust*-symphony; it was entirely rewritten in
1854–5, and is now complete as it stands. The second part of
the projected symphony was to have depicted Gretchen. The
overture, as we have it, is concerned with Faust's moods alone.
It depicts Faust in solitude, with his day-dreams, his sadness,
and his despair. In spite of the motto, it would be wrong to
interpret this eminently independent and original work as a
piece of programme music. The designation 'Eine Ouvertüre'
is equivalent to Characterstück or Stimmungsbild—a picture of
a particular mental state or expression of feeling, as is the case
with certain overtures of Beethoven such as *Egmont, Coriolan,
Leonora*, No. 1. There is in Wagner's *Faust* no conflict or
discrepancy between externals and the innermost being of man;
the state of feeling is conveyed to the mind by purely musical
means, and the design depends upon purely musical devices.
There is nothing left to be gathered from a printed programme,
and there are no traces of a symbolical or histrionic kind. 'Eine
Faust-Ouvertüre' invites comparison with the *Coriolan* overture of Beethoven and the *Manfred* overture of Schumann.
Faust's moods are as vividly expressed by Wagner, as the
essentials of Coriolanus's character, and the emotional influences

that touch upon it, are depicted by Beethoven; and Wagner's music reflects Faust's passion more closely perhaps than Schumann's music reflects the passion of Manfred. In the striking originality of the Coda and in the conciseness and perspicuity throughout, Wagner's *Faust* forms a parallel to Beethoven's *Coriolan*. The instrumentation is as efficient and telling as Beethoven's, and already foreshadows Wagner's later practice of grouping the instruments in accordance with delicate affinities of timbre.

The slow introduction is a model of condensation, and as it were a presage or anticipation of the Allegro. It contains some of the leading subjects and figures *in nuce*:

Nothing could be more characteristic of Wagner than this bleak and rugged theme. Its incisive rhythm, its tragic intensity, its challenging defiance of conventional melodic beauty, all may find a hundred parallels in his later compositions.

The opening themes of the Allegro are as follows:—

The second subject, presumably suggested by the lines :

Ein unbegreiflich holdes Sehnen	A sweet uncomprehended yearning
Trieb mich durch Wald und Wiesen	Drove forth my feet through woods
hinzugehn,	and meadows free,
Und unter tausend heissen Thränen	And while a thousand tears were burning
Fühlt' ich mir eine Welt entstehn.	I felt a world arise for me.

consists of a broad melody in F major, typically instrumental by reason of its great width of range.   A marvel in the beauty of its instrumental colour, it is at first intoned by a group of wood wind and horns, and then repeated in A major by the strings.

Through a series of transitions of a type fully developed in *Tristan und Isolde* it approaches the third subject, also in F, which during some sixty bars of ingenious modulation gradually comes to a crisis, and prepares for the development section commencing thus :

and finally leading to a climax of force and power. The conclusion consists of a condensed recapitulation, and a long-drawn-out Coda, *pianissimo*.

'In instrumental music I am a réactionnaire, a conservative,' said Wagner in 1877. 'I dislike everything that requires a verbal explanation beyond the actual sounds.' Together with the *Huldigungsmarsch*, the *Kaisermarsch*, and that miracle of rare device, the *Siegfried-Idyll*, this overture, so consistent in design and execution, is a practical illustration of his views.

CHAPTER VII

PROGRAMME MUSIC

BERLIOZ and Liszt were not content with the novel possibilities opened up by the infusion of the romantic spirit into the established forms. They desired, rather, to bring about some sort of direct alliance of instrumental music with poetry. To effect this they chose to make use of the means of musical expression for purposes of illustration. Thus they came to lay stress upon the conjunction of music with some particular poem or some special order of ideas, and, in the construction of their pieces, to rely directly on suggestions received from literary or other non-musical sources. The result was the production of a curious hybrid which has been called Programme music, i.e. music posing as an unsatisfactory kind of poetry [1].

In the case of Berlioz' symphonies, the programme forms an important part of the artistic scheme and the music is hardly intelligible without it. His symphonies comprise the *Symphonie fantastique* (1828–30), and its sequel, *Lélio, ou le retour à la vie — monodrame lyrique* (1832); *Harold en Italie* (1834); and the Symphonie dramatique, *Roméo et Juliette* (1839).

In Berlioz' overtures, such as *Waverley, Les Francs-Juges, Rob Roy, Roi Lear, Le Corsaire, Le Carneval romain*, the mere names ought to be sufficient to define the nature of the appeal to the hearer's imagination. But in a large part of the *Symphonie*

---

[1] Lesueur (1763–1837), Berlioz' composition master at the Conservatoire of Paris, in his pamphlet *Exposé d'une musique imitative et particulière*, so early as 1786 pointed at imitation as the true aim of music, and his compositions were written in accordance with a ‘plan raisonné,’ which plan or programme was printed for the benefit of the audience. In this respect there appears to be a ‘filiation artistique’ between Lesueur and his pupil.

fantastique, notably the Finale, the music is sheer nonsense unless the hearer has knowledge of the programme; yet even if he has full knowledge, the heterogeneous factors interfere with one another, and leave an annoying sense of incoherence and incongruity. The same may be said of parts of such movements as the 'Orgie des Brigands,' which forms the finale of *Harold en Italie*, or the 'Invocation et Réveil de Juliette,' and the middle portion of the 'scène d'amour,' which forms the central movement of *Roméo et Juliette*.

Berlioz, who claimed to have 'taken up music where Beethoven laid it down,' deserves respect for the power and persistence of his efforts. About his originality there can be no contention. His aim was always high, his ambition unbounded. Whether he succeeded in expressing what he meant to express, as Beethoven almost invariably did, is another matter. After more than half a century of controversy, it is by no means easy to estimate the value or to gauge the genuineness of his claims. None, however, need take him at his own valuation or at that of his partisan Liszt. The problems involved are:—Were his conceptions formed in harmony with the conditions of musical art? Did his methods of composition do justice to his conception? Is his style convincing? And the answers, even if they are mainly in the negative, may now be given with some hope of general acceptance. The whole question hinges on the special nature of Berlioz' gifts and attainments, and on their particular limitations. He was a man of excitable temperament and vivid imagination, a great master of instrumental effect, an adept in the use of colour and rhythm, a melodist of limited scope and power, a poor harmonist, and an equally poor contrapuntist. His instinct for form and just proportion was defective, his judgement wanting in balance.

His disposition was in reality more poetically imaginative than musical. He was inclined to emphasize the histrionic side of art and to indulge in extravagance. His ideals of beauty and style in music appear to have been narrowly personal, and he chose at times to embody them in a bizarre and eccentric manner. He was familiar with the principal operas of Gluck and Spontini; and with those of Weber, in so far at least as they can be appreciated without a knowledge of German. On the other hand, the assistance he derived from the example of the masters of self-dependent instrumental music was comparatively small. His acquaintance with the bulk of their work, Beethoven excepted, was little more than casual, his knowledge of Bach practically *nil*. The view that he took of Haydn and Mozart is best stated in his own words :—' When I hear Mozart I am troubled with a slight nightmare, when I hear Haydn I am troubled with a big one.' It is undeniable that in spite of his sympathy with Beethoven's symphonies, quartets and sonatas, he was unable fully to grasp and value the principles of design which underlie them and to appreciate the many subtle devices by which Beethoven contrives to give them life and unity.

Berlioz' failure to combine his many excitable impulses into an organic whole, caused him to feel the need of a ' programme ' which should explain the intention of his music. The programme, as employed by him, serves on the one hand to disguise a lack of constructive power, and on the other hand assists in the attempt to express literary and theatrical ideas in terms of orchestral colour and rhythm. It follows that those sections of his instrumental works in which design is of the greatest importance, that is to say, the principal Allegros and the Finales of the symphonies, exhibit his peculiar powers in the least favourable light.

The programme of his first important instrumental production, the *Symphonie fantastique* (1830), informs us that the work is intended to depict an ' épisode de la vie d'un artiste,' and goes on to state how a young musician is affected by ' le vague des passions,' which causes the image of a beloved maiden always to appear to him accompanied by a musical phrase, a Leitmotif, ' comme une double idée fixe.' At a ball, the young man in an exalted mood stands and gazes upon the scene, but the 'idée fixe,' both maiden and tune, continues to trouble him. Of an evening, in the country, he hears two shepherds piping to one another from afar; he reflects that the maiden might be false to him: 'Bruit éloigné de tonnerre . . . solitude . . . silence . . .' Having acquired the certitude that his sentiments are misunderstood, he takes a dose of opium. He dreams he has murdered the beloved and has been condemned to death, but is yet in a position to witness the execution: 'Marche au supplice'; at the end of which 'l'idée fixe' appears again, but is cut short by the fall of the axe.—Finale: Visions of a witches' sabbath—'howls, laughter, cries of pain, wailings,'—the melody appears yet again, now turned into a vulgar dance tune—'Demoniacal orgies, death bells, the *Dies irae* and *Ronde du Sabbat* combined amid wild yells,' and so forth.

The outlines of the customary movements of a symphony are shadowed forth in this curious scheme. I. 'Rêveries—passions,' Largo and Allegro. II. 'Un Bal,' a dance movement. III. 'Scène aux champs,' Adagio. IV. 'Vision—*a.* Marche du supplice; *b.* Songe d'une nuit du Sabbat,' Allegro strepitoso. A few quotations will show the character of the themes employed :—

The 'idée fixe' (Example *a*) may be taken as a fair sample of Berlioz' melody—artificial rather than warm or spontaneous, and not susceptible of much variety of harmonic or contrapuntal treatment. The combination of tunes extending to some forty-eight bars (Example *b*) is an instance of that peculiar process of rabbeting which with Berlioz often takes the place of counterpoint, and may be compared with the subsequent treatment of the *Ronde du Sabbat* and *Dies irae*. The Valse tune approaches the commonplace:

The 'Scène aux champs,' the most consistent and most musical section of the symphony, shows the influence of Beethoven's Sinfonia pastorale, notably of the 'Scene am Bach.' Though there are no direct reminiscences of that movement, its mood is reproduced *tant bien que mal*; and an equivalent for the quaint imitation of bird notes at the end of it is sought in a theatrical effect of distant thunder, which is produced, very realistically, by four drummers on four drums struck with 'baguettes à tête d'éponge.' Berlioz ends his scene with a variant of the duo between oboe and corno inglese which forms the opening— a subtle and telling device that makes for symmetry :

The drummers are busy, with and without sourdines, ' et avec des baguettes de bois,' during the fortissimos in the *Marche au supplice*, as well as in the *Ronde du Sabbat*, and the travesty of the *Dies irae* which constitutes the Finale. In the latter movement they are assisted by two further drummers who beat a ' grosse caisse roulante,' and by a host of brass instruments, a pair of cymbals, and two bells behind the scenes.

Strings.

a.

Drums with
mutes.

dim.

Dies irae et Ronde du Sabbat ensemble.
Strings.

b.

Brass and Wood wind.

The limitations of Berlioz' mental horizon, his histrionic bias
and tendency to attitudinize, are nowhere so much in evidence
as in that collection of romantic platitudes, the monologues of
'l'acteur qui parle et agit seul sur l'avant-scène' in *Lélio,
ou le retour à la vie : monodrame lyrique*, which forms the
sequel to the *Symphonie fantastique*. It is a mere pasticcio
made up of heterogeneous fragments and pieces loosely strung
together by means of rhapsodical declamation.

Apart from his love for a loud noise, every page of his scores
manifests Berlioz' instinct for sonorousness and tone quality,
and the extraordinary care with which he worked out his
combinations of instrumental colour—indeed the lucidity and
beauty of his instrumentation throughout is remarkable.   A
number of his novel effects, however, be they beautiful, violent, or
grotesque, are produced by the mere sound of the instruments
rather than evolved from the musical conception; they seem
to have had some separate existence, perhaps in the composer's
notebook, before the notion of either programme or symphony
occurred to him. 'C'est fort beau, quoique ce ne soit pas
de la musique.'—From a technical point of view, Berlioz'
orchestration is chiefly remarkable for its distinctness.   It is,

as he calls it, *éclatant* in every sense of the word, varied, daring, original.   The stress is laid more often on the novelty than on the beauty, but things sound as they are intended.   The various procedures have nothing about them that might be called meretricious—no particular devices predominate.   His powers of invention, in this respect, are almost as great as Weber's and far greater than those of his disciples in orchestration such as Liszt, Félicien David, Saint-Saëns.

The second symphony, *Harold en Italie*, contains also a persistent melody, which, like that of the *Symphonie fantastique*, is somewhat jejune in character, and somewhat incapable of harmonic variety.

Originally designed as a concerto for Paganini, this work grew under Berlioz' hand into a ' Symphonie en quatre parties avec un alto principal '; and it is interesting to observe that two of its chief themes are taken almost exactly from the discarded overture to *Rob Roy*[1].   One, 'the persistent melody,' stands for ' une sorte de rêveur mélancolique dans le genre du Childe Harold de Byron[2].'   The other tune found a place in the first Allegro.   The entire symphony forms a record of the composer's musical recollections of Italy: I. 'Harold aux montagnes, scènes de mélancolie, de bonheur et de joie,' Adagio and Allegro. II. 'Marche de pèlerins chantant la prière du soir,' Allegretto. III. 'Sérénade d'un montagnard

[1] Written at Rome, 1832, and said to have been destroyed after a fiasco in 1833. The full score was, however, found and published in 1900.—When Lully, obeying his confessor, put the score of his *Armida* in the fire : ' Eh quoi, Baptiste, lui dit-on, tu as pu brûler une si belle chose ! — Paix, paix, j'en ai gardé copie.'

[2] *Recte*, Dans le genre du Réné, de Chateaubriand.

des Abruzzi à sa maîtresse,' a sort of Scherzetto.   IV. ' Orgie
de brigands, souvenirs des scènes précédentes,' Allegro frene-
tico.   The scheme is closely akin to that of the *Symphonie
fantastique*, embracing a similar order of movements, with the
histrionic Leitmotif in each, and Berlioz' favourite ' Orgie,'
by way of Finale.   The fragmentary restatement of themes,
described as ' Souvenirs des scènes précédentes ' is a device
derived from the Finale of Beethoven's Ninth Symphony (the
score of which appeared in 1826).   Advocates of Berlioz'
method can point to the ' Marche de pèlerins ' with its mysterious
charm, and the ' Sérénade,' as genre pictures of rare originality,
the undeniable success of which goes far towards justifying
realistic effects, such as the imitation of bells and the responses
of the Litany which occur at intervals in the march, or the
pseudo-contrapuntal ingenuity with which the Harold motive
is joined to the main theme :

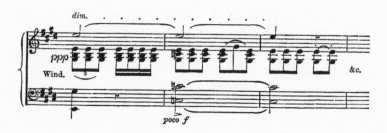

In the 'Sérénade' the interweaving of dissimilar melodies and rhythms is carried to an extreme with surprising cleverness and picturesque effect:

&c.

With ' *Roméo et Juliette* — symphonie dramatique, avec
chœurs, solos de chant et prologue en récitatif choral, composée
d'après la tragédie de Shakespeare' (1838)—Berlioz professed to
believe he had reached 'l'île merveilleuse où s'élève le temple
de l'art pur.' What he did in fact reach, or at least approach,
was a kingdom of Cockayne. And he seems to have been
dimly conscious of this fact when, in the preface ᵗⁿ the edition
of 1857, he tried to explain that his efforts were not meant to
be an ' opéra de concert' nor a cantata, but a 'symphonie avec
chœurs.'

In the first instance the work was undoubtedly intended to
be a symphony illustrating certain incidents of Shakespeare's
play. The conception comprised the following movements :—
Andante malinconico and Allegro (' Roméo seul,' ' Grande fête
chez Capulet'), Adagio (' Scène d'amour'), Scherzo ('La reine
Mab'), Finale, instrumental and choral (' Rixe des Capulets et
des Montaigus—Serment de réconciliation') ; evidently a scheme
resembling that of the *Symphonie fantastique* and *Harold*,
influenced by the vocal Finale of Beethoven's Ninth. If a
programme thus laid out had been furnished separately, or if
only the titles of the sections had been given, the composer
might have succeeded in justifying his scheme ; but he chose,
instead, to preface the principal instrumental movements by a
lengthy vocal introduction : which consists of a Prologue set as
a choral recitative, followed by two Couplets for contralto solo
containing sentimental reflections. Later on, the symphonic
movements are interrupted by a chorus of male voices singing

'Réminiscences de la musique du bal,' and again by a choral and instrumental piece, entitled : 'Convoi funèbre de Juliette.' This is followed by a melodramatic orchestral piece, 'Roméo au tombeau des Capulets'—and the close consists of a kind of operatic scena which includes a lengthy 'Récitatif et air du père Laurence' and a choral 'Serment de réconciliation.'

Thus the complete work has seven divisions : 1. Orchestral introduction, 'Combats, tumulte, intervention du Prince'; Prologue, 'Récitatif choral et Scherzetto, La Reine Mab,' tenor solo and chorus. 2. Roméo seul—'Tristesse,' orchestra alone; 'bruit lointain de bal et de concert; grande fête chez Capulet.' 3. Orchestra and chorus—'Nuit sereine; le jardin de Capulet silencieux et desert; les jeunes Capulets, sortant de la fête, passent en chantant; scène d'amour'—orchestra alone. 4. Scherzo—'La reine Mab, ou la fée des songes'—orchestra alone. 5. Orchestra and chorus—'Convoi funèbre de Juliette.' 6. Orchestra alone—'Roméo au tombeau des Capulets ; invocation, réveil de Juliette ; élan de joie délirante, brisé par les premières atteintes du poison ; dernières angoisses et mort des deux amants.' 7. Finale—Orchestra, solo voice, and double chorus—'La foule accourt au cimetière; rixe des Capulets et des Montaigus ; récitatif et air du père Laurence ; serment de réconciliation.'

Is it in any way surprising that such a conglomerate should prove a failure in spite of a host of novel and beautiful details ? Undoubtedly practical skill and insight is shown in the selection of incidents which lend themselves more especially to musical illustration, and produce once and again effects in a high degree striking and original. But the plan of the whole, if plan it can be called, is thoroughly unsatisfactory—the design of some of the separate movements equally poor. The constant reference to incidents in the play is the cause of much that seems musically inconsistent ; it accounts also for certain lapses into mediocrity and for an abundance of histrionic effects which tend to lower the general quality of the music. Effort after effort is made to

attain dramatic expression. The style recalls the rhetoric of
the grand opera. It is the music of attitudes. It constantly
seems to demand stage action, and to be striving to illustrate or
emphasize things more or less alien to musical art.

The vocal pieces, both choral and solo, are distinctly inferior
to the instrumental; the artificiality of Berlioz' melody reduces
their value. With the exception of the *Convoi funèbre*, the
touching effect of which is more truly orchestral than vocal,
they are not particularly interesting, either from the singer's
point of view or from that of the hearer. The opening of the
movement entitled ' Roméo seul—Tristesse ' is on a par with
the fine introduction to the *Symphonie fantastique.* Here is
genuine music; in both pieces the chromatic wail of strings
produces a striking effect of melancholy and longing. It is
interesting to compare such poignant chromatic passages in
Berlioz' symphonies with the richer and more musical employment of similar devices in the introduction to Wagner's *Tristan
und Isolde.* Compare also the melody and harmony of the
Andante malinconico with the chant of syrens in the first
scene of *Tannhäuser,* or the following bars from the finale (Père
Laurence) with the sixteenth to the twenty-fourth bar of the
overture to *Tannhäuser.*

In both cases Wagner's superiority is not less unmistakable than his indebtedness to Berlioz.

Then follows a Larghetto espressivo, and an Allegro; the themes of which are finally combined and produce an effect of extraordinary brillance. But in the next movement Berlioz has something better than brilliance to offer. The ' Scène d'amour' contains some 200 bars of the richest and most delicately passionate music in existence. There is nothing in the whole range of French music to approach it, and nothing but the ' O sink hernieder, Nacht der Liebe' in the second act of Wagner's *Tristan*, to surpass it. Unfortunately the instrumental recitatives, which are meant to represent Shakespeare's lines about the lark and the nightingale, produce an incongruous effect, and spoil the middle of the movement. The instrumentation is remarkable and beautiful from beginning to end:

Clarinets and Corno inglese.

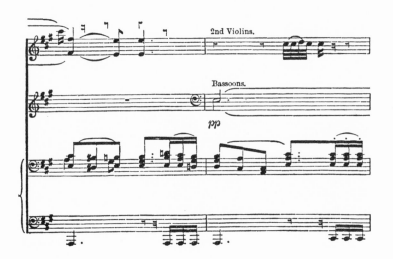

The Queen Mab Scherzo is an orchestral *tour de force*,
dealing largely in the sound of violin and harp harmonics. In
form it is akin to the Scherzos of Beethoven's Third and Seventh
Symphonies. The fantastic element predominates to such an
extent that the effect is more curious than beautiful, indeed,
borders upon the ludicrous—' un petit bruit semblable à celui des
seringues mal graissées.' The 'Convoi funèbre' which follows is
described in the score as a ' marche fuguée *instrumentale* d'abord,
avec la psalmodie sur une seule note dans la voix : *vocale* ensuite,
avec la psalmodie dans l'orchestre.' The following extract will
convey some idea of its effect:—

Of the reception of the sixth division, a melodramatic instrumental piece illustrating the scene in the tomb, Berlioz seems to
be in doubt, and the score contains a note advising its omission on
the ground that 'le public n'a point d'imagination; les morceaux
qui s'adressent seulement à l'imagination n'ont donc point de
public. La scène instrumentale suivant est dans ce cas, et je
pense qu'il faut la supprimer toutes les fois que cette symphonie
ne sera pas exécutée devant un auditoire d'élite auquel le
cinquième acte de la tragédie de Shakespeare avec le dénoûment

de Garrick est extrêmement familier, et dont le sentiment poétique est très élevé. C'est dire assez qu'elle doit être retranchée quatre-vingt-dix fois sur cent.' If imagination on the part of an intelligent audience can make up for incoherence on the part of the composer, this somewhat arrogant manifesto may perhaps be justified. Questions as to the appropriateness of his method seem never to have troubled Berlioz. But judged on its musical merits alone, the movement is a failure. There are genuine accents of passion here and there, and towards the middle the pathos of the ' Invocation' is well sustained for some four-and-twenty bars, then the strutting recitative of the operatic actor again makes its appearance, and the tragedy collapses. The incongruous and lengthy vocal scena, which forms the seventh and concluding division, shows traces of Meyerbeer's *Huguenots*. It needs no comment beyond the statement that it is as dull as it is elaborate. A few words of Wagner's[1] sum up the situation perfectly: ' Berlioz added to, altered, and spoilt his work. This so-called Symphonie dramatique, as it now stands, is neither fish nor flesh—strictly speaking it is no symphony at all. There is no unity of matter, no unity of style. The choral recitatives, the songs, and vocal pieces have little to do with the instrumental movements. The operatic Finale, Père Laurence especially, is a failure. Yet there are many beautiful passages in the work. The Convoi funèbre is a very touching and masterly piece. The opening theme of the Scène d'amour is heavenly ; the garden scene and fête at Capulet's wonderfully clever; indeed Berlioz was diabolically clever (*verflucht pfiffig*).'

Brief mention of the remaining orchestral pieces of Berlioz suitable for concert performance may conveniently be made here. They are : a *pièce d'occasion*, entitled: ' Symphonie funèbre et triomphale pour grande harmonie militaire, avec un orchestre d'instruments à cordes et un chœur ad libitum' (1834–40), and eight overtures, viz. *Waverley* (1827–8), *Les Francs-Juges*

---

[1] See Grove's *Dictionary of Music*, article Wagner.

(1827–8), *Roi Lear* (1831), *Rob Roy* (1832), *Benvenuto Cellini* (1837), *Le Carnaval romain* (1837–43), *Le Corsaire* (1831–44–55), *Béatrice et Bénédict* (1862). The Symphonie funèbre et triomphale, for military band—originally written for the ceremony of transferring to their monument in the Place de la Bastille the remains of the victims who fell in the revolution of July 1830—consists of a sombre and rather heavy march-like movement in F minor; and an ʻOraison funèbre' for trombone solo, followed by a cleverly contrived flourish of trumpets, cornets, trombones, and drums, leading to an ʻApothéose' for the combined orchestras, in which the chorus joins [1]. The overtures are satisfactory or the reverse according as the composer indulges or restrains his ʻpoetical intentions.' Thus *Waverley, Rob Roy, Les Francs-Juges*, are all open to objection on the ground of some deviation from musical common sense. *Le Roi Lear* and *Le Corsaire*, the latter remarkable for consistency of form on novel lines, i.e. lines analogous to those of the first movement of Beethoven's Sonata, Op. 109, in E major [2], though far behind Beethoven's ideal, follow in the track of *Egmont* and *Coriolan*; whilst *Benvenuto Cellini*, together with *Le Carnaval romain* and the overture to *Béatrice et Bénédict*, are frankly operatic and free from the burden of a programme. Technically there is little to choose between them.

Berlioz' eminent gift of calculation and combination, his peculiar method of interweaving heterogeneous phrases, arrests attention already in his early overture, *Les Francs-Juges* (F minor). This work, which belongs to the period of Berlioz' pupilage, shows as much reverence for orthodoxy of form as its mercurial composer ever allowed himself to exhibit. Yet even here the histrionic method appears. By way of working

---

[1] Here, again, it is instructive as well as curious to compare Wagner's two occasional pieces, the *Huldigungsmarsch*, originally for a military band, and the *Kaisermarsch*, with chorus. The spontaneity and technical superiority of Wagner's work are very striking.

[2] As has been pointed out by Mr. W. H. Hadow in his *Studies in Modern Music*, vol. i. p. 141.

out, an attempt is made to depict the gradual approach of a band of warriors. Scraps of melody, scraps of accompaniment are heard, the rhythmical beats as from afar, then the fragments coalesce, and the arriving hosts are greeted with a shout of welcome. Still more evident is the dramatic intention in the music of the overture *Le Roi Lear*. In this piece the form of expression, especially in the introductory part, is vivid enough for a tragic opera with Leitmotive which might be labelled Lear, Goneril, Regan, Cordelia; so vivid, indeed, that, given the general designation, even an unimaginative hearer is likely to take the composer's meaning, and to find the proper names for the themes.

We may agree with Felix Draeseke [1] in assigning to the overture *Benvenuto Cellini* (G major) the foremost place among Berlioz' shorter instrumental pieces. The companion piece, *Le Carnaval romain* (A major), invites comparison with the Saltarello of Mendelssohn's Italian Symphony, though not to its advantage in point of freshness or finish. It is made up of the principal tunes from the second finale of *Benvenuto Cellini*.

Berlioz, his partisans assert, was grand, sublime and powerful, terrible or comic as he chose; to which detractors not unfrequently retort that he was grotesque, inflated and pretentious. Perhaps there is a modicum of truth on both sides. He worshipped the grandiose. It is vain to look for traces of mental growth in his work; a comparison of dates reveals next to nothing in regard to the development of his genius, unless, indeed, the dates which belong to the last twenty years of his life be taken as marking retrogression.

One of his most ambitious efforts as an illustrator, the *Marche funèbre pour la dernière scène d'Hamlet* (1848), a piece little known and very rarely performed, deserves at least as much attention as any other bit of descriptive music by his Russian or German disciples. It is written for grand orchestra and

---

[1] *Die Musik*, p. 1257 (1902).

voices in chorus, plus '6 Tambours voilés ou sans timbre, Grosse caisse, Cymbales et Tambour.'

A curious fact in connexion with his programme music is the evolution of what is known as the Leitmotif from the 'Double idée fixe' of the *Symphonie fantastique* and the 'mélodie caractéristique' of *Harold en Italie*. The use of a musical phrase as a subordinate element of coherence, a ready-made appeal to the imagination and memory, was an innovation in Berlioz' time. It survives to this day as the technical process which has proved most serviceable among the many experiments that Berlioz made in search of novelty. Partially adopted by Meyerbeer in *Les Huguenots* and *Le Prophète*, and systematically developed by Wagner, it is now familiar to musicians as the method of employing representative themes, and serves as an efficient device in the technique of dramatic music or oratorio. At first it was an 'Erinnerungs-motif,' i.e. a motive appealing to the memory, which was gradually developed into the 'Leitmotif' as we now have it.

Among the few works directly inspired by the example of Berlioz, perhaps the most noticeable is the Ode-symphonie, *Le Désert*, by Félicien David. *Le Désert* was performed at the Conservatoire of Paris in 1844 and speedily made the round of Europe[1]. This work, inasmuch as it consists of orchestral movements, descriptive or melodramatic fragments, marches, dance tunes, vocal solos, and choral pieces for male voices, each preceded by some lines of explanatory verse or prose, resembles Berlioz' Mélologue *Lelio*, mentioned above. There is a cleverly contrived sequence of events—far less of a makeshift than the order of scenes in *Lelio*—showing the progress of a caravan through the Sahara and including a hymn to Allah, a struggle with the Simoon, and a rest at the well of an oasis. Effective use is made of typical Arabic phrases and tunes—as in the 'Prière à l'Allah,' the 'Chant du Muezzin,' and the 'Danse des

[1] Chiefly in consequence of a very appreciative article by Berlioz in the *Journal des Débats*, December 15, 1844.

Almées.'—There is nothing really symphonic about David's ode, but it pleased those who had a liking for descriptive experiments : and *Le Désert*, for a number of years, furnished hints to seekers after novel modes of picturesque expression [1]. The Muezzin's chant at sunrise, as David puts it, is well worth quoting :

[1] Compare Borodine's *Dans les steppes de l'Asie Centrale*, and the 'Au couvent' and 'Sérénade' in his *Petite Suite*; some of Rubinstein's *Persisch Lieder*; portions of Saint-Saëns' *Africa*, and his Fifth Concerto ; the 'Danse Indienne' in Rimsky-Korsakov's *Milada*; the *Rêverie orientale* and *Rhapsodie orientale* by Glazounov.

David's second Symphonie avec chœurs, *Christophe Colomb* (1847), failed to attract attention[1].

Liszt[2], with his largest productions—*Eine Symphonie zu Dantes Divina Commedia* (1847-55), and *Eine Faust-Symphonie* (1854-7)—shows less directly than David the trace of Berlioz' influence. Like Berlioz he aims at effects derived from a desire to illustrate, and he relies on points of support outside the pale of music proper. Saturated with contemporary literature, imbued with the Parisian romanticism and the spirit of the Catholic revival of 1830-40, and stimulated, musically, by the example of Berlioz, he set himself in his own way to work out, on poetic lines, the problem of musical illustration. Composed of imagination and impulse, his musical genius was one that could hardly express itself save through some other imaginative medium. He devoted his extraordinary mastery of instrumental technique to the purposes of illustrative expression; and he was now and then inclined to do so in a manner that tends to reduce his music to the level of decorative scene painting or *affresco* work. His orchestral compositions consist of the two symphonies already mentioned, two illustrations to Lenau's *Faust*, twelve lesser pieces with the happily chosen title ' Poèmes symphoniques,' and a few miscellaneous works of comparatively slight importance.

Of all the subjects Liszt chose for symphonic treatment the *Divina Commedia* was the best suited to his peculiar temperament, as it offered superb opportunities for the display of his powers as a master of instrumental effect. Already, in 1847, he had planned musical illustrations of certain scenes from Dante's poem with the aid of the newly-invented Diorama. The original

---

[1] Such was also the fate of his oratorio *Moïse au Sinaï*, the *Mystère Éden* (1848), the comic operas *La Perle de Brésil* (1851), *Lalla Rookh* (1862), *Le Saphir* (1865), and the grand opera *Herculaneum* (1859). David with advancing years gave way to an inartistic desire to illustrate all manner of non-musical ideas. He reached the height of absurdity in the score of *L'Avant-homme*, where by means of marginal notes he endeavoured to combine certain curious musical effects with a statement of the principles of antediluvian geology.

[2] Liszt was born at Raiding, Hungary, in 1811; he died at Bayreuth in 1886.

idea was never carried out, nor does there seem to be much connexion between certain sketches he made with a view to it and
the symphony as it now stands.   An eccentric ' Fantasia quasi
Sonata' for the pianoforte (*Années de pèlerinage* ii, 7),
suggested by a poem of Victor Hugo, 'Après une lecture de
Dante,' seems also to have been merely tentative.   A number of
lines from the *Inferno*, as at first selected for illustration, have,
however, been retained.   They now appear in the score of the
Dante Symphony, as inscriptions elucidating a number of
musical phrases which act as Leitmotive.   To give an idea of the
character of the whole composition would require more extensive quotation than is possible here, but the Leitmotive will at
least exhibit the general conception of the music.   The entire
work is laid out so as to form three divisions, entitled *Inferno*,
Purgatorio, and *Magnificat*—the last in place of Dante's
Paradiso.

The furious chromatics of the first Allegro, entitled *Inferno*
(D minor mainly), do full justice to the poet's words :

Diverse lingue, orribili favelle,
Parole di dolore, accenti d' ira,
Voci alte e fioche, e suon di man con
  elle
Facevan un tumulto, il qual s' aggira
Sempre in quell' aria senza tempo tinta,
Come la rena, quando al turbo spira.

Languages diverse, horrible dialects,
Accents of anger, words of agony,
And voices high and hoarse, with sound
  of hands,
Made up a tumult that goes whirling on
For ever in that air for ever black,
Even as the sand doth, when the whirl-
  wind breathes.

For musical reasons, much is made of the Paolo and Francesca
episode with its characteristic theme in $\frac{7}{4}$ time :—

The theme 'Lasciate ogni speranza' is repeated with tremendous vehemence at the end of the movement. The strains of the *Purgatorio*, after a tranquil introduction reflecting Dante's 'tremolar della marina,' are meant to suggest the soul's passage through expiatory pain and a state of contrition, towards a sense of beatitude:

The fugato, 62 bars in B minor (c), which forms the centre of the movement, its theme derived from a recitative for the bass Clarinet in the preceding movement, may be compared with the 'Convoi funèbre' of Berlioz' *Romeo* Symphony[1]. For the Magnificat, Liszt employs the intonation of the third tone, supporting it by long-drawn consonant harmonies consisting of major chords exclusively, which towards the end, where the bass descends by slow steps of whole tones (b), produces a novel effect of great beauty:

---

[1] Compare also with fugato in the third movement of Liszt's *Faust* Symphony.

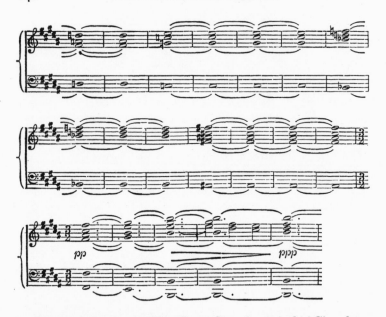

The ideal aimed at in 'Eine Faust-Symphonie in drei Charakter-bildern [1]' is akin to that of the Dante Symphony. The moods of Goethe's characters Faust, Gretchen, and Mephistopheles are depicted in three instrumental movements, and a chorus of male voices supplies a sort of comment by way of a close. The method of presentation is again by means of Leitmotive and by their reaction upon one another, as well as by allusions to those incidents of the play which are susceptible of musical illustration. The portraiture of Faust is the object of the first and weightiest movement : the Andantino which follows represents Gretchen : the spirit of Mephistopheles animates the Scherzo (Allegro ironico), in which the themes of the earlier movements are per-verted and caricatured, much as the 'Idée fixe' and the *Dies irae* are turned into burlesque in the Finale of Berlioz' *Symphonie fantastique*. A setting of Goethe's *chorus mysticus* 'Alles Vergängliche ist nur ein Gleichniss,' for tenor solo and male

---

[1] Ary Scheffer's Faust pictures had some influence on the conception of Liszt's *Faust* Symphony.

chorus, concludes the work.—The changing moods of doubt, despair, desire, enthusiasm, are shadowed forth in the Faust section. Like the Inferno of the Dante Symphony, this movement exhibits the outlines of symphonic structure ; exposition of themes, development, recapitulation ; but the details for the most part have reference to the exigencies of the 'poetical idea,' and such exigencies are permitted to overrule considerations of musical consistency and beauty.

The rather mechanical sequence of chords with the augmented fifth, which forms Liszt's principal theme :

may profitably be compared with the theme of Mozart's Fantasia in C minor (*a*), Rossini's *Guillaume Tell*, Act II (*b*), and finally, Wagner's *Die Walküre*, Act II (*c*).

The Andantino, a portion of which refers to the garden scene
in Goethe's poem, invites comparison with the 'Scène d'amour'
in Berlioz' *Roméo et Juliette*. Here, as there, and for similar
reasons, the thematic materials fail to produce their full effect.
The Gretchen themes are delicate and tender, the dainty illustration of 'Er liebt mich—liebt mich nicht,' is of charming
naïveté, and the modifications of the Faust subjects, quoted or
adopted from the first movement, are sufficiently eloquent.   Yet
the section, taken as a whole, produces an incongruous effect [1].
Liszt's endeavour to illustrate certain incidents directly leads to
combinations which are rather detrimental from the point of view
of consistent musical design.   On the other hand, it may be
asserted that the recurrence of Leitmotive furnishes a clue to the
spiritual connexion of one movement with another, a connexion
that certainly exists in this instance, and which probably could
not be so clearly expressed by other means.   In the Scherzo the
travesty of the Faust subjects (those referring to Gretchen are
barely touched upon) is piquant in the extreme.   Compared
with the violence of Berlioz' burlesque treatment of the themes
in the 'Songe d'une nuit de Sabbat,' Liszt's method is delicate
and light-handed, equally clever in instrumental device, and far
more successful in its appeal to the imagination [2].

The *chorus mysticus* ('Alles Vergängliche ist nur ein
Gleichniss') indicates one clear limitation of the descriptive
method : its inability to express those solemn emotions to which
devices and tricks of phrase are inappropriate.   It endeavours
to complete the story by combining themes assigned to the char-

---

[1] Just as in Berlioz' 'Scène d'amour,' where the composer tries and fails to
reproduce the sense of Shakespeare's words about the lark and the nightingale.

[2] Saint-Saëns in his *Danse macabre* follows Liszt in pursuit of the grotesque.

acters of Faust and Gretchen, but it is perforce confined within restrictions where pure music alone can move freely, and in its attempts to be reverent it approaches perilously near to dullness. Two other orchestral Faust illustrations, ' Zwei Episoden aus Lenau's Faust: (i) Der nächtliche Zug, (ii) Der Tanz in der Dorfschenke' (Mephisto-Walzer, No. I), are best mentioned here. They belong to the year 1859, and rank as rather eccentric ' paralipomena ' to the *Faust* Symphony.

Liszt's *Poèmes symphoniques* (1850–60), companion pieces to the *Faust* and Dante symphonies, may be described as the out-pourings of a musician's fancy as stimulated by certain pieces of poetry and painting. They are as follows :—

1. *Ce qu'on entend sur la montagne* (after a poem by Victor Hugo).

2. *Tasso: Lamento e Trionfo* (partly after Byron's · *The Lament of Tasso*).

3. *Les Préludes* (after one of Lamartine's *Méditations poétiques*).

4. *Orphée.*

5. *Prométhée* (an introduction to Herder's dramatic scenes, ' Der entfesselte Prometheus ').

6. *Mazeppa* (after Byron and Victor Hugo).

7. *Fest - Klänge* (Prelude to Schiller's ' Huldigung der Künste ').

8. *Héroïde funèbre* (Part I of a symphony composed in 1830).

9. *Hungaria.*

10. *Hamlet.*

11. *Hunnen-Schlacht* (after a painting by Kaulbach).

12. *Die Ideale* (after a poem by Schiller).

13. *Von der Wiege bis zum Grab* (after a sketch by Michael Zichy).

With the exception of the little masterpiece *Orphée*, which is pure self-contained music, all are impromptu illustrations, corresponding to some poem, or picture or group of concepts expressed in words. They are mere sketches arranged in accordance with some poetical plan, extraneous, and more or less alien, to music. The words 'Lamento e Trionfo,' which mark the two sections of *Tasso*, show the scheme of the majority; thus the essence of *Prométhée* is 'Malheur et gloire — Une désolation triomphante par la persévérance de la hautaine énergie'; Mazeppa's ride closes with a glorification, 'Il tombe... et se relève roi'; *Les Préludes* ends with an Allegro marziale; *Hungaria* with an Allegro trionfante; *Hunnen-Schlacht* with 'The triumph of Christianity'; *Die Ideale* with an 'Apotheosis' of certain symbolical themes. *Orphée*, as has already been said, is a gem in its way, and is exquisitely scored. *Les Préludes*, *Tasso*, and *Fest-Klänge* bid for popularity; they are melodious, effective, readily intelligible, but have a touch of the common-place. The two former are in reality Variations, arranged in accordance with the contrasted images contained in one of Lamartine's *Méditations poétiques* ('Notre vie est-elle autre chose qu'une série de préludes à ce chant inconnu dont la mort entonne la première et solennelle note?'), and with the composer's own meditations on the fate of *Tasso*. By means of rhythmical changes, contrasting subjects are evolved from the same order of notes—an ingenious device that seems to be Liszt's peculiarity, but which he derived from Berlioz, who again was by no means its originator [1].

Mazeppa and *Hungaria* are expansions of early pianoforte pieces : the first of an Étude, the germs of which are contained in Op. 1 (1826-7, aet. 16), the second of a 'Heroischer Marsch im ungarischen Styl' (1840-4). There is quite a family of Mazeppas, though only the two latest take the name: (1) A little 'Exercise in the manner of Czerny,' Op. 1, No. 4; (2) Grandes Études, No. 4 (1839); (3) Études d'exécution transcendante, No. 4, Mazeppa; (4) the Poème symphonique;

---

[1] The device in question is in fact at least as old as the Partite (variations) and Suites of Froberger and other seventeenth-century precursors of J. S. Bach, who frequently constructed successive movements upon subjects consisting of the same notes rhythmically changed. In Handel's Suites, too, movements occur which are variants of one another.

and finally (5) a transcription for two pianofortes of the latter piece.   The title *Mazeppa*, and the reference to Byron's 'Away, Away,' and Victor Hugo's 'Il tombe ... et se relève roi,' appear in the third version.   The early *Héroïde funèbre* (1830–56), *Hamlet* (1858–61), and a late piece *Von der Wiege bis zum Grab* (1881–3) exhibit his method in a less favourable light.

Ce qu'on entend sur la montagne (1848–56) and *Die Ideale* (1853–7) are the longest examples of thorough-going programme music among Liszt's works of that description.   On various pages of the score of *Die Ideale* he has inscribed extracts from Schiller's poem, much as mediaeval painters used to add legends to parts of their pictures.   Unity is sought by the use of representative themes, of which the principal one undergoes various rhythmical changes.   In its first and complete shape it recalls the effect of measured prose :

The sections are connected, and the main lines of symphony-form can be traced, though the contours are somewhat blurred and indefinite. Aufschwung, aspiration ... Allegro spiritoso; Enttäuschung, disillusion ... Andante maestoso; Beschäftigung, occupation ... Allegretto mosso; Apotheose ... maestoso, Allegretto fuocoso assai. The Leitmotive are summed up, as it were, in the final section. An episode in E major, symbolical of friendship it would seem, merits quotation for its tenderness and beauty. It is but a fragment, however, and remains undeveloped:

The singularities and oddities of Liszt's style roused the ire of contemporary critics and conservative musicians—such as Ferdinand David, Rietz, Hauptmann and other professors of the Leipzig Conservatorium. 'The bulk of Liszt's orchestral pieces,' it was said, 'is needlessly and gratuitously ugly—he delights in eccentric combinations solely because of their eccentricity.' Censure and hostility were directed, not so much against his 'poetic' tendencies and the nature of the subjects he chose for illustration (which latter to some extent appear to justify Liszt's system of procedure), as against ill-contrived outlines, forced connexion of chords, strained melody, and bluster. Uncouth, 'impure' harmony was the principal subject of complaint[1]. Liszt's friends and pupils, when they failed to discover satisfactory reasons for this or that ugly distortion, fell back on 'poetical intentions'—but an abundance of cases remained for which they found it hard to discover a plausible excuse. It is on record that certain extravagances in Liszt's early pianoforte pieces annoyed Chopin, and that sundry perversities in the Poèmes symphoniques puzzled Wagner.

What, then, can have induced a born *grand seigneur* in the realms of music, a man so highly gifted as Liszt, to put his trust in harmonic crudities and chromatic horrors, from which sensitive musicians shrink with an instinctive dislike ? One fact which throws a strange light upon the matter, is that Liszt in early days (about 1832) earnestly worked at a notion vaguely expressed

---

[1] This was Hauptmann's objection.

by Fétis, the lexicographer, as a possible *ordre omnitonique*: which *ordre*, according to Fétis, might be destined at some distant date to supersede our present tonality. But it is a fact stranger still that Liszt, all his life long, should have retained such a notion, and that he desired to make, and was ever ready to encourage, experiments in tonality which led to effects of interesting ugliness [1].

Another fact to be taken count of is the pianoforte virtuoso's prodigious mastery in chromatic ‘double stops,’ major and minor thirds, augmented fourths, diminished fifths and sevenths, and the like. This feature, conspicuous among the many specialities of Liszt's pianoforte technique, was the result of his strenuous practice of chromatic passages in every imaginable form. And it is indisputable that mechanical practice of chromatics, if carried to an excess, particularly on the pianoforte, will prove detrimental to the inner ear, and induce decadence of that native instinct for tonality and harmonic relation generally, without which a modern musician can hardly hope to keep steady and hold his own as a harmonist [2]. Thus it seems sufficiently clear that Liszt's habit and his taste were subject to many an out-of-the-way influence, and, without pressing the point further, it may be surmised that certain cases of harsh dissonance, juxtaposition of chords having little or no harmonic affinity, perverse and ugly modulation, may be the result of poetical or rhetorical guesswork, materialized through

---

[1] Witness certain curious productions of his old age, such as the close of the second Mephisto-Walzer—score published 1881—‘ La lugubre Gondola,’ and portions of the last number of *Années de pèlerinage*, iii, ‘Sursum corda,’ 1882. Not only in his original compositions but also in his numerous transcriptions and arrangements Liszt shows a predilection for harmonic piquancies and *hauts goûts*. ‘Gieb ihm Weissbrod, so streut er Paprika darauf,’ said Wagner in 1877:—‘ Give him white bread, he will sprinkle red pepper upon it.’

[2] Berlioz, when composing, professed to prefer the guitar to the pianoforte. Wagner always made use of the latter instrument for *testing* purposes; but his independence of any sort of digital mnemonics was remarkable. With him the inner ear was always paramount. For instance, the full orchestral score of *Tristan* was engraved long before the composer had heard a note of it, and not a note was ever altered.

the pianist's fingers. Other traits, such for instance as the tempestuous chromatic crescendos in *Les Préludes*, the harp glissandos representing gusts of wind in the Dante Symphony, and kindred effects of crude realism got by means of rapid chromatic scales or arpeggios arranged in chords of the diminished seventh—are but a reflex of certain technicalities of pianoforte playing and a reproduction of some of Liszt's peculiar ways at the pianoforte [1].

Though the widest difference of merit exists between the good and bad, it must be admitted that, from the point of view of musical design, a lax and loose conception of art prevails more or less through all the Poèmes symphoniques. In those pieces, in place of melody, Liszt offers mere fragments of melody —touching, it may be, and beautiful, passionate or tinged with triviality; in lieu of a rational distribution of centres of harmony in accordance with some definite plan, he presents clever combinations of chords, and ingenious modulations from point to point; in lieu of musical logic and consistency of design, he is content with rhapsodical improvisation. The power of persistence seems wanting, orchestral polyphony is not attempted. The musical growth is spoilt, the development of the themes is stopped or perverted by some reference to extraneous ideas. Everywhere the programme stands in the way and the materials refuse to coalesce.

No doubt, Liszt as sincerely believed in the symbolical efficiency of his representative themes as Berlioz believed in the dramatic significance of *L'Idée fixe* and *La Mélodie caractéristique*. Both the great illustrators were convinced that a close union of instrumental music and poesy is possible and desirable. Both masters may have erred in their method; and programme music, as they conceived it, may in the end prove to have been a dubious hybrid of insufficient vitality.

[1] Wagner to Liszt, 1856. *Letters*, vol. ii. pp. 129-30: 'So gelten mir deine Orchesterwerke jetzt gleichsam als eine Monumentalisirung deiner persönlichen Kunst, und unvergleichbar, dass die Kritik lange Zeit brauchen wird, um nur irgendwie zu wissen, wohin damit.'

CHAPTER VIII

ORATORIOS AND CANTATAS

THE steadily increasing tendency towards closeness of characterization, which forms the distinguishing feature of the romantic period, is apparent even in the work of Mendelssohn, who was by nature and training averse to innovation or experiment. Mendelssohn's attitude in regard to Protestant church music was peculiar. Looking at music mainly from the artistic point of view he thought it ill-placed in the Lutheran church service. He confessed his inability to see how artistic music could be made to form an integral part of such a service so that it would appear other than 'a mere concert with more or less of devotional effect'—as, for instance, is the case when J. S. Bach's Cantatas are performed in church[1]. Accordingly, he wrote his Psalms, the *Lobgesang*, and the oratorios, *St. Paul* and *Elijah*, for purposes not directly connected with worship, that is to say, for the use of choral societies and with a view to performance at festivals. Thus his choral work of this description must be considered as concert music of a serious kind—touched, it is true, with the spirit of devotion and with Christian symbolism, but by no means ecclesiastical.

Mendelssohn's strength in oratorio and cantata lies in the mastery of polyphonic choral technique which he had acquired by the study of Bach and Handel, in his facile gift of melody, and in his command of instrumentation. To this may be added a marked inclination towards the formal side of musical art; an instinctive love of form for its own sake; and also, perhaps, the influence of individual temperament, of hereditary

---

[1] Mendelssohn's *Briefe*, vol. ii. p. 75.

bias, and the love of religious emotion.   In the choice of the
scriptural account of St. Paul, and of Elijah as subjects for
oratorio, as well as in the arrangement of the ground-plan and
general disposition of the materials with a view to the best
musical effect, Mendelssohn relied upon his own judgement, and
friends merely supplied a choice of texts and occasionally the
wording of a recitative or an aria.

The book of *St. Paul*, which comprises a cento of texts
interspersed with Lutheran chorals, is mainly concerned with the
death of Stephen, the conversion of Saul, and the firmness of
the Apostle's faith.   In the first part of the book of *Elijah*, the
symbolical element which a Christian mind may find in the Old
Testament appears to be latent only; but it occupies a more
prominent position towards the close of the second part, where
allusion is made to the coming of Christ.   The Biblical account
of Elijah forms the groundwork, while a superstructure of texts
is arranged so as to serve musical purposes.   The framework
consists of a series of scenes and situations laid out dramatically, and held together by the figure of Elijah.   The narrative
in the form of recitative—which in *St. Paul* connects the vocal
numbers—is eliminated, so that in this oratorio the principal
character, the subordinate characters, and, in some instances,
even the chorus, are made to speak dramatically.   The book
embraces just enough action and contrast to sustain the
interest, and allows enough of expansion to give a chance to
the full musical expression of the inner aspect and the inner
ground upon which the events are set forth.

In *St. Paul* the narrative consists of recitative delivered by
soprano and tenor voices in turn, with simple accompaniments for strings.   The declamation, in German, is precise and
accurate, though without undue insistence.   When the narrative
demands the expression of emotion, the recitative rises to
cantilena—as at the death of Stephen—and such touches are
among the best and most sincerely felt details resulting from
the composer's mode of treatment.   Side by side with such

touches, rank the poignant accents of remorse and contrition in pieces such as the air, ' Lord, a broken heart, and a contrite heart'; the burst of rage and hate, ' Confound them all, Lord Sabaoth'; and the expression of strong indignation, as in the aria, ' Is not His word like a fire?'

From a musician's point of view, the weight and power of Mendelssohn's oratorio music is best seen in the choruses. They are masterly in the full sense of the word, characteristic and varied, and evince a command of contrapuntal resource beyond the reach of any of his contemporaries. The following are conspicuous examples from *St. Paul*:—the powerful opening chorus in A, ' Lord, Thou alone art God'; the chorus, ' Rise up, arise and shine '; the choruses of Hebrews, ' Now this man ceaseth not to utter blasphemous words,' and ' Stone him to death'; the chorus of Gentiles, ' O be gracious, ye immortals '; the earnest and serious chorus of Christians, in D minor, ' But our God abideth in heaven,' which contains the melody of a chorale, ' His will directeth all the world,' inserted after the manner of J. S. Bach. As in Bach's Passion-music, harmonized chorales are introduced at intervals between the airs and choruses to act like ideal comments upon events, and so as to enforce a mood or close a section.

The secret of the greater success—especially in England—of the later oratorio, *Elijah*, lies in its dramatic scheme, and in the enhanced opportunities for solo and concerted music which it afforded the composer. In *Elijah*, Mendelssohn exhibits his talent at its full maturity. Taken as a whole and compared with *St. Paul*, *Elijah* stands on a higher plane. It is stronger in spirit, freer, broader, more direct, and less tinged with Lutheran influences. Whether the composer was conscious of the fact or not, it is evident that every conspicuous feature in the method and technique makes for characterization. The dramatic force of the scenes, their conciseness and vivid colouring, the pointed rhythms of the choruses, the highly wrought orchestration, the energy expressed in the choruses of Baal's priests, the fierce savagery of 'Woe to him, he shall perish,' and certain almost histrionic effects in the rain scene, all point in the same direction.

The influence of the Lutheran service, which in *St. Paul* is apparent in the symbolism of the chorals and in the pietistic tone of certain airs and choruses, is less conspicuous in movements of the same order in *Elijah*. The dramatic sections of the latter oratorio are as free, as vivid, and as frankly pictorial, as anything in Handel. As an example, note the impressive 'prophecy of the drought' which, preceded by four solemn chords of brass and placed *before* the overture, produces a very remarkable effect. Further examples are contained in the scene of the widow, the priest's scene with the flesh, of fire from heaven, the scene of Elijah standing on the mount, and above all the great scene which describes the giving of the rain; all striking and expressive in idea, all remarkably original in form and workmanship. The choruses at the beginning of Part I describing the drought, and also the duet and chorus following —'Lord, bow Thine ear to our prayer,'—are both touching and impressive. In Part II the splendid chorus, 'Be not afraid,' and the chorus, 'He that shall endure to the end,' are typical examples of the master's sentiment in music and of his great knowledge of effect. The chorus last named—Andante sostenuto, F major—is especially attractive; it contains nothing that resembles or even aims at passion, nothing that is even telling, it is merely the record of a tranquil and peaceful mood, truly and beautifully expressed. Wonderfully characteristic in their way are the choruses of the priests of Baal. In the scene of Elijah standing on the mount, the repetitions of 'Behold, God the Lord passed by,' produce a kind of rhythmical effect, framing, as it were, the description of storm, earthquake and fire. An impression of resistance and striving against natural phenomena, and at the same time an irresistible onward impulse, is conveyed to the mind by the use of choral imitations leading to the crisis, 'And after the fire there came a still small voice: and in the still small voice onward came the Lord.' After the

Holy, Holy,' of the angels, and the arioso, ' For the mountains shall depart and the hills be removed,' Elijah is silent; his ascent to heaven is depicted in the chorus, ' Then did Elijah the prophet break forth like a fire.' The five numbers following, which point to the coming of Christ, form rather an anticlimax and are not particularly interesting as music.

Mendelssohn intended to compose another oratorio, *Christus*, as a sort of sequel to *Elijah*. He began to work at it in 1847, the year of his death.

Apart from the two oratorios Mendelssohn's other choral works demand little comment. Planned as a kind of choral symphony, the disposition of the *Lobgesang* (1840) is open to a charge of tautology, inasmuch as the choral movements following upon the instrumental, cover the same ground, and act as a restatement by the aid of words of that which has been already expressed by the orchestra without them. Connexion and unification is attained by the use of a leading phrase or motto, like Berlioz' ' Idée fixe,' which consists of the intonation of the eighth tone as sung to the Magnificat, and forms the subject of the first movement of the ' symphonia,' the first chorus, and the close of the cantata.

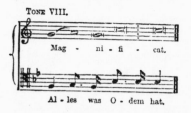

Like the overtures to Mendelssohn's oratorios, the three orchestral movements of this work are fluent and finished but not very fresh or spontaneous. The choral movements, six in number, have full measure of the technical merits that always characterize the master's choral pieces; yet they do not come near to the direct impulse and power, or to the warmth and tenderness of feeling he managed to express in certain choruses belonging to

Elijah and *St. Paul.* The entire work consists of serious music, individual and independent in style, but neither inspired nor inspiriting.

In the three motets, Op. 39, for female voices and organ (1830), and in the *Lauda Sion,* for chorus and orchestra (1846), Mendelssohn tried to compose in a style suitable for the Roman Catholic service. The Psalms for chorus and orchestra, ' As the hart pants,' ' Come, let us sing,' ' When Israel out of Egypt came,' ' Not unto us, O Lord,' though more or less important in the list of his works, belong to the Protestant concert-room.

The case is very different with Goethe's wild scene, ' Die erste Walpurgisnacht' (1831–32–43), which forms the subject of a cantata expressly intended by Goethe for music, and laid out with a view to that end:

> Möge dies den Sänger loben,
> Ihm zu Ehren war's gewoben.

This scene is one among three cantatas contained in Goethe's collection of ' Books of words for music '—a companion piece to the *Rinaldo,* so beautifully set by Brahms. The poem is triumphantly successful—a masterpiece in a field where masterpieces are extremely rare; so simple and consistent in motive that it seems like one spontaneous growth, so direct in its appeal to the imagination that there is no need of scenic accessories, yet so precise and vivid in its fantastical way, that it could be set, sung, and acted on the stage, without the change of a scene or a line. Whether it was expressly written for Mendelssohn does not appear, but it exactly met his views and afforded fine opportunities of which he thoroughly availed himself. On the approach of spring, in face of warning that heathen practices are punished with death, Druids assemble on the hill-tops at dusk to kindle flames in honour of All-father. Below, on the borders of the wild wood, they post sentinels who all night long, with diabolical din, feign a witches' orgy to scare the profane. Christian watchmen hold aloof for fear of devils, whilst the fires burn above, and the worship proceeds. As has already been pointed out, Mendelssohn in the ' Overture ' to this cantata is a musical illustrator with a definite idea before him.   In this Introduction—for such it is and not a true overture—he depicts in a realistic manner the rough winter weather and the gradual approach of spring ; then, by a series of vocal solos and choral songs, he leads up to one of the most vivid and striking of his pieces—the wild and fantastic chorus, ' Kommt mit Zacken und mit Gabeln,' Allegro molto, A minor, $\frac{6}{8}$, which recalls certain weird instrumental effects first heard in the incantation scene of Weber's *Freischütz*.   A kind of hymn for baritone solo and chorus—Andante Maestoso, C major, $\frac{4}{4}$, rounds off and closes the work.

Passing mention may here be made of the works which Mendelssohn wrote to order for the Court Theatre at Berlin : overture, solos, and choruses, to Racine's *Athalie* (1845), and the music to Donner's translation of Sophocles' *Antigone* (1841), and of *Oedipus in Colonos* (1845), for male voices and orchestra. The fragments of an opera, *Lorelei*, the text by Geibel, are essentially concert music, and one fails to see how it could gain by stage action.

Much more than in Mendelssohn's oratorios, the spirit of romanticism with its innocent striving after emotional expression pervades Schumann's *Das Paradies und die Peri*, *Der Rose Pilgerfahrt*, and other choral works for the concert-room. The presence of romantic emotion is felt throughout—even in bits of choral description, and in solo narrative, which in place of the ordinary recitative often rises into definite arioso.

After having produced a large amount of original and very interesting music for pianoforte solo, Schumann, about 1840, began in splendour the career as a composer of songs and choral pieces which he ended in darkness.   In the zenith of his brilliant genius he put forth a treasury of song ; from about 1850 onwards, in failing health, he flooded the market with vocal mediocrity.   His secular oratorio, *Das Paradies und die Peri* (1843-4), consists of the translation in rather perfunctory verse of Moore's story of 'Paradise and the Peri,' slightly expanded, and set as a series of three cantatas for solo voices, chorus and orchestra. It made a great impression and was immediately popular in Germany. Novel in style, romantic and sentimental in spirit, it won the sympathy of the upper bourgeoisie, and pleased the members of Singing Societies. To the luxurious oriental pictures of Moore's poem, the music adds a warmth of feeling peculiarly German and peculiarly Schumann's own. The airs contain an abundance of sweet, perhaps over-sweet, melody ; and several of the lesser choruses or choral songs are pleasant to sing, as, for instance, the delicate 'Sleep on, in visions of odour rest,' which closes the second cantata, the canon for female voices called the 'Song of the Houris,' and the choruses of the Genii of the Nile—the two latter forming part of the few slight additions to Moore's poem. The larger choruses, however, fall short of the mark. Schumann's choral technique is almost always defective. It will not bear comparison with that of Handel, Bach, Haydn, or Mendelssohn. It is often inept, inefficient, and trying to the voices. The lack of practical experience is seen to be a real drawback. Despite strenuous efforts and a not inconsiderable display of contrapuntal skill in choruses—such as 'Denn heilig ist das Blut,' and 'O heil'ge Thränen inn'ger Reue '—the result is disappointing. Yet such occasional shortcoming in choral and orchestral effect does not detract much from the originality of the work taken as a whole. The true source of its weakness lies rather in the disposition of the poem and the decrease in interest as it proceeds. Moore's story of the three gifts that should open the gate of Eden to the disconsolate Peri exhibits a sequence of events diminishing in excitement and picturesqueness. From 'Mahmudh of Gagna's wrath ' and 'The warfield's bloody haze,' to 'Blest tears of soul-felt penitence,' there is a diminuendo very detrimental to the total effect of the music.

The historical interest which belongs to *Paradise and the Peri* will probably be found to exceed the intrinsic value of the

work. It is the first instance of a long poem not especially
written for music, being set from beginning to end without
interference with the verse or the disposition, and with minute
attention to the poet's meaning. Schumann's music covers
Moore's poem like a close-fitting garment. Formerly, poems
intended for music were expressly contrived to meet the real or
supposed exigencies of the art ; or else composers appropriated
some poet's work, and cut, compressed, or by means of repetition, expanded it to suit their particular purposes—as, for
instance, Handel expanded the ' Alexander's Feast ' of Dryden.
It was not until after Beethoven's time that musical resources
were sufficiently developed to allow of a composer attempting
so difficult a task as the complete absorption and adequate
reproduction of a poem of some length. Nowadays, and since
Schumann set the example, any poem that is musical in its
nature may be aptly treated, and presented in conformity with
the poet's intention. It has been proved that the sequence of
moods which makes a good design in poetry will also make
a good design in music [1].

With the exception of *Paradise and the Peri*, a portion of the
music to the second part of Goethe's *Faust*, i.e. the ' Transfiguration,' the ' Requiem für Mignon' (1849)—one of the poems
contained in Goethe's *Wilhelm Meister*, Op. 98 *b*—and the short
Nachtlied, Op. 108 (poem by Hebbel), which also belongs to 1849
and is both poetically and musically suggestive and original, none
of Schumann's choral works have stood the test of time. *Der
Rose Pilgerfahrt*, a companion piece to *Paradise and the Peri*,
was a production for the market. The music to the *Adventlied*
—a kind of choral ode (poem by Rückert), 1848—is reminiscent

---

[1] Beethoven's cantata *Meeresstille* and Mendelssohn's *Walpurgisnacht*, together
with Schumann's successful initiative in *Paradise and the Peri*, and in part of his
music to Goethe's *Faust*, may be regarded as the starting-points of that extensive
development of the Ode and Cantata which starts from Bach, and which Brahms
furthered in his setting of Hölderlin's *Schicksalslied* and Goethe's *Rinaldo*. The
development culminates in some recent versions of great English poems by English
composers.

of Mendelssohn's Psalms, but does not reach their level of
excellence. The Balladen for solo voices, chorus and orchestra
(1851), *Der Königssohn, Des Sängers Fluch, Das Glück von
Edenhall* (after poems by Uhland), the four Balladen by Geibel
(1852–3), entitled 'Vom Pagen und der Königstochter,' are
failures one and all. The motet, 'Verzweifle nicht im Schmer-
zensthal,' for a double choir of male voices, with organ *ad
libitum*, 1849 (poem by Rückert), has several fine moments,
but it is monotonous, long, and heavy; and, owing to certain
chromatic progressions, rather difficult to sing. There is hardly
any relief to the forte of the chorus and organ, and the effect of
the intricate harmonies at the words 'Harre aus im Leid' is
distressing. For the sake of completeness certain lame and
tame attempts at church music—a Mass and a Requiem, both
composed in 1852 and published after the composer's death—
may be mentioned here. The Requiem has a few points of
interest. The Mass was stillborn. In the Requiem the
opening and closing movements, 'Requiem aeternam dona
eis Domine,' which are written in a tender and delicate strain—
the fugal 'Pleni sunt coeli,' which has a certain degree of life
and power—portions of the closing section of the Benedictus—
and also the Sanctus and Agnus Dei, are still worth the
attention of the student.

The ecstatic verses of the closing scene of Goethe's *Faust*,
Part II, the Transfiguration, exercised a peculiar fascination
over Schumann's mind; he set them line by line, for solo
voices, chorus and orchestra. The music pertaining to this
section belongs to his best period, about 1848; it is complete
in itself and important.—In later years (1853–6) he tried his
hand at certain other scenes from both the first and second
part of *Faust*. Ultimately the detached pieces were gathered
together and prefaced by an overture, so as to form a kind of
concert oratorio. Thus the huge posthumous publication
entitled 'Scenen aus Goethe's Faust' is in fact a mere conglo-
meration, having no more real coherence than can be claimed

for its rival, Berlioz' *Damnation de Faust*. The first division consists of portions of Goethe's garden scene, Gretchen before the shrine of the Mater dolorosa, and the scene in the cathedral. The second contains the scene of the dawn and Ariel's hail to sunrise, the scene of the 'four grey sisters'—Want, Guilt, Misery, and Care—striking Faust with blindness, and the scene of Faust's death. The third, as has been stated, is concerned with the mystical Transfiguration, the translation of Faust's soul to heaven.

The spirit of Goethe's great scene in heaven exactly suited Schumann's temperament and stimulated his genius to its best. He seems to have had no difficulty in dealing with the verse. Except in the chorus ' Gerettet ist ' and the *chorus mysticus* at the end, hardly a line is repeated. There is little flagging or shortcoming ; things seem to take form and fall into their place quite naturally. The rhythmical variety of the verse is reflected in the movement and speed of the music ; and the gradual increase of animation and ecstasy expressed in the words of the Hermit-fathers and the Doctor Marianus, in the chorus of blessed youths and the younger and elder angels, the chorus of female penitents, and the voice of ' una poenitentium—sonst Gretchen genannt ' is rendered to perfection.

The delicate swing and balance of rhythm in the choral song, ' Dir, der Unberührbaren,' is a good specimen of the ease and spontaneity that distinguishes Schumann's declamation. The Doctor Marianus and chorus address the Mater Gloriosa thus :—

nom - men, Dass die leicht Ver - führ - ba - ren Trau - lich zu dir

CHORUS.

kom-men, Dir, der Un - be - rühr - ba - ren, Ist es nicht be -

nom-men, Dass die leicht Ver - führ - ba - ren Trau-lich zu dir kom-men.

&c.

From the beginning to the end of the Transfiguration, Goethe's verse is reproduced in melody of equal beauty and subtlety. Of the opening and concluding choruses two versions have been published. The principal choral numbers are difficult to sing; but the effect of a correct rendering is distinctly fine almost throughout. The music emphasizes the points of the poem, and explains its meaning more effectually than any commentary. This is particularly the case with the words of the Doctor Marianus, and the final *chorus mysticus* :—

Alles Vergängliche	All things transitory
Ist nur ein Gleichniss;	But as symbols are sent;
Das Unzulängliche,	Earth's insufficiency
Hier wird's Ereigniss.	Here grows to event;
Das Unbeschreibliche,	The Indescribable,
Hier ist es gethan;	Here it is done;
Das Ewigweibliche	The Woman-Soul leadeth us
Zieht uns hinan.	Upward and on.

If Schumann's *Faust* music is but a conglomerate of scenes from Goethe's poem arranged in a sequence for concert purposes, the so-called *Légende dramatique, La Damnation de Faust*, by Berlioz (1846), may be described as an accumulation of stray pieces—some taken from the composer's first publication, ' Huit scènes de Faust, œuvre Ier,' which was cancelled, some totally alien, like the arrangement of the Rakoczy March, and some few specially written to fill up gaps in the curious scheme of a grand opéra or rather of an opéra de concert, in accordance with which the materials were finally put together. The designation ' Légende dramatique' (Légende fantastique would have been more appropriate) merely serves to conceal the absence of any definite plan. In his preface, Berlioz is quite frank on this subject. ' Pourquoi l'auteur a-t-il fait aller son personnage en Hongrie ? — Parce qu'il av: it envie de faire entendre un morceau de musique instrumentale dont le thème est hongrois. Il l'avoue sincèrement. Il l'eût mené partout ailleurs, s'il eût trouvé la moindre raison musicale de le faire.' As to the violence done to Goethe's poem, the author of *La Damnation* asserts that ' Le titre seul de cet ouvrage indique qu'il n'est pas basé sur l'idée principale du *Faust* de Goethe, puisque dans l'illustre poème Faust *est sauvé*.' Portions of the libretto are taken from Gérard de Nerval's translation of *Faust*; the first, fourth, sixth, and seventh scenes were written for Berlioz by an acquaintance, the remainder by Berlioz himself.

The separate airs, choral songs, and orchestral pieces, which go to make up the four main divisions are picturesque in effect, highly coloured, and superbly scored. As regards intrinsic musical value they differ greatly. Occasionally, in scenes such as Faust in the fields, or Marguerite in her room alone, when the situation appeals to the sober and more serious side of his mind, the composer rises to heights of noble and original music. In the Chansons called ' Histoire d'un Rat,' ' Histoire d'une Puce,' and in the ' Sérénade du Diable,' the comical and ironical sense of the words is well brought out. In this last piece (which in the suppressed Opus I appears as a song for a tenor voice with guitar accompaniment), in Marguerite's beautiful romance just mentioned, 'D'amour l'ardente flamme,' in her Chanson gothique, 'Le Roi de Thulé,' in the graceful and delicate 'Danse des Sylphes,' the 'Menuet des Follets,' and the famous 'Marche Hongroise,' the cleverness of the instrumentation is remarkable even for Berlioz, with whom the treatment of the orchestral instruments is always a strong point. The choral numbers are comparatively weak. The Easter hymn, 'Christ vient de ressusciter,' is not particularly impressive. The burlesque fugato on the subject of the song of the Rat, 'Requiescat in pace, Amen,' is in fact rather a display of Berlioz' shortcomings as a contrapuntist, than a telling skit on fugal composition as he meant it to be. Compare the queerly contrapuntal double chorus for male voices (soldiers and students) in *La Damnation de Faust*.

The 'Course à l'abîme' (Faust's and Mephistopheles' ride to hell), and the scene in 'Pandaemonium,' with its 'Chœur de démons et damnés' screaming in Swedenborgian 'langue infernale,' attempt to inspire terror, but achieve no more than distaste, whilst the 'Épilogue sur la terre,' and the chorus of blessed spirits singing the 'Apothéose de Marguerite dans le ciel,' are trite and rather insignificant. They would appear wholly commonplace were it not for a new and beautiful effect at the end which is obtained by an ingenious combination of harps and boys' voices.

All the numbers—airs, vocal ensembles, and orchestral pieces —are more or less redolent of the opera. There is a sense of theatrical rhetoric, of musical pose and tirade, quite correct in its way and perhaps effective in an opéra de concert, but not always good music. At times the instrumental noise—as in the 'Marche Hongroise' and the scene in 'Pandaemonium'—is almost deafening. By devices of orchestration the colourist tries to reach that which the melodist fails to attain for want of warmth, the harmonist for want of power, and the designer for want of skill. Everywhere the composer is prone to speak in tones acceptable to that kind of public taste which is caught by peculiar tricks of sound or glaring colours. For the most part the music is histrionic in style, it stimulates the nerves and is frequently constrained to attract attention by strange or barbaric sounds, or to excite interest by appeals to ideas and associations outside the pale of musical art. Purely musical expression, as we find it in Bach, or Beethoven, or Brahms, may not have been intended; but even where it does in fact exist, it is not well sustained, and its quality is hardly pure enough to tell as absolute music. From a rhetorical point of view, Berlioz in this his 'œuvre le plus accompli' is successful enough; not so, tested by the standard of the greatest masters.

Berlioz' Salon Oratorio, the *Trilogie sacrée, L'Enfance du Christ* (1854)—a series of three cantatas—consists of nine short scenes of studied conciseness, irregularly grouped in three divisions: 1. Le Songe d'Hérode; 2. La Fuite en Égypte; 3. L'Arrivée à Saïs. The music is daintily written for a small chorus, small orchestra, solo voices and solo instruments. By the side of much that is essentially dull—like the 'Marche nocturne,' the overture to 'La Fuite en Égypte,' and 'L'Arrivée à Saïs'—or both dull and grotesque, like the conjuration of the soothsayers (said to be based on Hebrew tunes)—this triptych of cantatas contains several movements distinctly interesting and charming from a musical point of view—as, for example, the choral song, 'Il s'en va loin de la terre,' the Chœur mystique, 'Ô mon âme' (which Berlioz palmed off on a select Parisian audience as the work of a forgotten mediaeval composer), the duo 'L'Étable de Bethléem,' and the interlude 'Le Repos de la Sainte Famille.' The latter movement is most delicately scored for wood wind and strings, to which at the end are added a tenor voice and eight female solo voices representing angels at a distance. The following extract will give an example of its melody:—

Two pieces by Liszt may fitly be mentioned here. One is a Chorus of Reapers, A major, $\frac{3}{4}$—No. IV of an ambitious set of choruses for Herder's 'Entfesseltem Prometheus' (1856), to which the Poème symphonique 'Prometheus' forms the over-ture. An oasis in a desert, this 'Chor der Schnitter' is a good specimen of a Pastorale, closely akin to certain pieces belonging to the cancelled Album Suisse and now contained in *Les Années de pèlerinage*, i, such as 'Églogue' and 'Au bord d'une source.' The other is a setting of the opening scene of Longfellow's *Golden Legend* (1875), 'Die Glocken des Strassburger Münsters,' for baritone solo, chorus, full orchestra, and organ. This approaches the category of Schumann's Balladen, being rendered in the manner of a dramatic dialogue between baritone and chorus. The liturgical motif of the Preludio recurs in the Vorspiel to Wagner's *Parsifal*, and elsewhere in that work.

CHAPTER IX

RELIGIOUS MUSIC

THE Romantic movement in France was a revolution which invaded not only the theatre and the concert-room but the Church also. Not that it set up any worship of the ' Goddess of Reason '—from this, indeed, it was in many ways removed— but it made a definite and conscious effort to break through all ecclesiastical restrictions, and to treat religion as one department of human feeling, different in object but not different in kind from the sentiments evoked by natural beauty or by the tragedy of history and romance. Liszt, in a letter to the *Gazette Musicale* (1834), described his own and Berlioz' ideal of romantic religious music thus : ' For want of a better term we may well call the new music Humanitarian. It must be devotional, strong, and drastic, uniting—on a colossal scale—the theatre and the Church, dramatic and sacred, superb and simple, fiery and free, stormy and calm, translucent and emotional.' And Berlioz furnished a practical example of what such music would be like, when in 1836-7 he composed the Requiem Mass which was performed in the church of the Invalides at a memorial service for General Damrémont and the French soldiers who fell at the taking of Constantine.

The words ' on a colossal scale, theatre and Church, dramatic and sacred ' suffice to indicate Berlioz' views when he wrote

this wilfully eccentric score. He particularly emulated, and
hoped to eclipse, the fame which Cherubini, the then Director
of the Paris Conservatoire, had gained with a grand Requiem
mass in C minor [1]. When, in the most striking movement of
Cherubini's Requiem, to the trumpets and trombones of the
'Dies irae,' a gong is struck, fortissimo, we may readily understand that the impressiveness of the subject has passed beyond
the ordinary resources of the composer. But what is the beating
of a gong or a sudden clash of cymbals to Berlioz' *Tuba mirum*,
with its 'Quatre orchestres d'instruments de cuivre placés aux
quatre angles de la grande masse chorale et instrumentale,'
together with sixteen kettledrums and a grosse caisse roulante,
a gong, three pairs of cymbals, and another grosse caisse 'avec
deux tampons'? No such volumes of sound had been heard in
Paris since the taking of the Bastille. No such orchestra had
ever been collected—Gossec's *Te Deum* is pale and ineffectual in
comparison.

There is not space to quote the host of instruments in detail,

Laissez le mouvement s'animer très peu.

but some of the drums, the cymbals, and the gong, figure in the score as follows :—

After this the 'cellos and basses resume the tune of the 'Dies irae,' *piano*, accompanied by little phrases played upon the corno inglese and bassoons, while the tenor voices, also *piano* and 'avec un sentiment d'humilité et de crainte,' sing 'Quid sum miser tunc dicturus.' This short movement makes a subtle appeal to the imagination. It acts, of course, as a contrast and relief, and is, in its way, both novel and beautiful, though the musical substance does not rise much above mediocrity. A similar effect of contrast is expressed in the next movement between the *fortissimo*, 'Rex tremendae maiestatis,' and the supplication, *piano*, 'Salve me.'

The monotonous psalmody of the Offertoire produces a calculated effect on the nerves[1]. As in the Convoi funèbre from the symphony *Roméo et Juliette*, the device here consists of a long-drawn instrumental fugato, 154 bars (A), interrupted at intervals by a plaintive wail of voices on two notes only which are repeated again and again (B).

---

[1] Wagner admired the skilful contrivance of this Offertoire, and repeatedly spoke of the singular effect it produces : 'If a man cares to be hypnotised musically, here is his chance.'

The 'Hostias' which follows depends for its effect upon a surprising trick of instrumentation, i. e. chords played *piano*, *crescendo*, and again *piano* by three flutes and eight trombones:—

This contrivance, though but little suited to the dignity of the occasion, is a capital example of Berlioz' ingenuity and

keenness of perception in matters of instrumental effect, and
of the marked attention he paid to those remoter capabilities
of the orchestral instruments with which the majority of
professional musicians in his day were not familiar.   The score
contains a note drawing attention to a particularly clever contrivance in the employment of certain bass notes of the tenor
trombone at the end of the movement [1].

The most musicianly number is the opening ' Requiem
aeternam,' which is repeated in a shortened form at the close
of the work.   It is original, sincere and consistent ; marked
by a touch of austerity which is rare in Berlioz, and approaching more nearly than was his wont to a contrapuntal style.   Its
various themes are effectively contrasted :—the sombre melody
with which it begins, the whispered monotone of its ' Kyrie
eleison,' the transition to the major mode at the words 'Te
decet hymnus.'

[1] ' Ces notes graves de trombone ténor sont peu connues même des exécutants ;
elles existent cependant et sortent même assez aisément lorsqu'elles sont ainsi
amenées.'

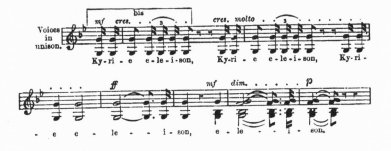

And as this is the most ecclesiastical number so the 'Lacrymosa' is the most operatic. Written with every consideration for the voices, and admirably scored, it is wholly theatrical in character; it is no more suited to the Church than Rossini's *Stabat Mater*, and in the midst of all its artificial passion and histrionic effect it even stops to borrow a moment's inspiration from Bellini:

In other movements, however,—notably in the unaccompanied 'Quaerens me'—this charming trait appears as a mere trick that comes in conveniently when contrapuntal invention fails. Sometimes, too, as in the 'Dies irae,' the choral writing has an instrumental air. The words are put under the notes, in accordance with the popular French formula of progress, 'Marche, ou je t'assomme[1].'

---

[1] Cited by George Sand in *Lettres d'un voyageur*.

Curiously enough, the instrumental phrases thus sung by the tenors recur in the Offertoire (bars 96–105), where, more appropriately, they are allotted to the strings.

Taken as a whole, the *Requiem* shows little of religious resignation, quiescence, or repose of the soul. Grandiloquent effects predominate. It is musical scene-painting; illustration on a large canvas and with glaring colours.

The *Te Deum* (1849–54) was performed once only during Berlioz' lifetime, and under his personal direction, in the church of St. Eustache, Paris, April 30, 1855—to celebrate the opening of the Palais de l'Industrie on the day following. For its due performance the composer demands an orchestra of 134 executants, a double choir of 200 voices each, and a choir of 600 children's voices [1]. In a note prefixed to the score, he directs that the orchestra and two principal choirs, with the third choir on a separate platform and at some distance from them, are to be placed at one end of the church opposite to the organ.

It is difficult to speak plainly and without exaggeration of this very ambitious but very disappointing work. The rather limited range of Berlioz' melody has already been criticised, and there is little evidence of increase or development in the measure of his genius. Indeed, the later date of the *Te Deum* (1854) as compared with that of the *Requiem* Mass (1837), and of the operas *Les Troyens* and *Béatrice et Bénédict* as compared with *Benvenuto Cellini*, would seem to indicate a decadence of inventive power. Musicians are agreed that strange instances of inept harmony or melody occur in the early works, and it cannot be said that they are less frequent in the later; indeed, ineptitude gradually becomes more obvious. In a general sense the *Te Deum* is distinctly inferior to the *Requiem*. The composer alters the arrangement of the ritual text, and repeats or omits words for the sake of dramatic effect. Side by side with passages undeniably clever though rarely beautiful, it contains much that is inchoate, dull or perverse, and much that is marred by abstruse and laboured details, instances of vain effort and errors of tact and taste which 'a man of forty ought not to have committed [2].'

---

[1] The use of such choral Masses was not an entire novelty in the churches of Paris at that time. Méhul, in the *Chant du 11 juillet* 1800, had already employed three independent choirs and full orchestra.

[2] Schumann: private letter to Ambros. Franchomme, the violoncellist, Chopin's friend, asserted that as early as 1833 Chopin declared that he had expected better things from Berlioz, and that Berlioz' music was of 'such a quality as to justify any man who chose to break with him'—a singular expression of opinion on the part of one so reticent as Chopin, if it is strictly true as reported.

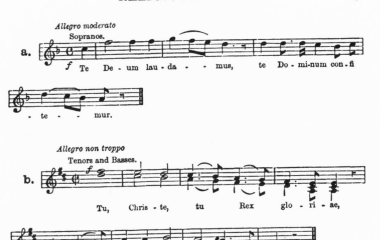

These quotations, which show the theme of the first number, the 'Te Deum laudamus' and the scale-like theme of the 'Tu Christe,' cannot be said to possess much distinctive character. Neither of them is particularly suitable for contrapuntal treatment, and the manner in which they are developed is never really effective. Although the orchestral and choral means employed are abundant and the cumulative mass of sound is great, both movements are tedious.

The sixteen bars of an Andantino which form the opening and the end of the second number—Hymne, 'Tibi omnes angeli incessabili voce proclamant'—are perhaps the most fluent in the entire work.

The close of the third number—'Prière: Dignare Domine '—
on the whole a weak number, approaches the same level:

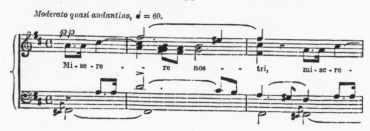

But the one movement that really shows the composer's power
and originality is the ' Iudex crederis,' No. 6. This is a piece
of large dimensions, grandiose in style, and in spirit akin to the
' Rex tremendae' and the ' Lacrymosa' of the *Requiem*. It
resembles the latter in the cast of the themes and mode of
treatment. A very powerful and original effect is attained by
the restatement a semitone higher, step by step, of its striking
and vigorous melody :—

Allegretto un poco maestoso.

♩. = 69.

Iu - dex cre - de - ris es - se ven - tu . . rus.   In

te, Do - mi - ne, spe - ra - vi, non con - fun - dar . . in ae -

- ter - num, non con - fun - dar in ae - ter - num.

The final movement, a 'Marche pour la présentation des
drapeaux,' in B flat, Allegro non troppo, leaves the impression
of empty rhythmical noise rather pretentiously put forth.

It has been pointed out that Liszt's orchestral Programme-
music derives in a large measure from Berlioz' *Symphonie
fantastique, Harold en Italie,* and *Roméo et Juliette.* In like
manner it may be asserted that much of Liszt's miscellaneous
church music and a large portion of the oratorios *St. Elisabeth*
and *Christus* emanate from Berlioz' *Requiem* and *L'Enfance
du Christ.* Wagner's method of employing representative
themes is adopted by Liszt in the *Graner Festmesse* (written for
the consecration of the Basilica at Gran, 1855–6), as well as in
Die Legende von der heiligen Elisabeth (1861–5) and *Christus*
(1866–72).

In *St. Elisabeth,* which is published as a concert-oratorio,
Liszt virtually produced something like an opera sacra—in which
guise the work has been performed at Munich, Weimar, Hanover,
Leipzig, &c.   According to .the authorized biography[1] the
success of *St. Elisabeth,* when performed with scenic accessories,
came as a surprise to the composer.   But, however that may be,
the nature and structure of the work seem to call for theatrical
pomp and circumstance.   The conception of *St. Elisabeth* is
rooted in the enthusiastic admiration felt by both Wagner and

[1] Lina Ramann, *Franz Liszt als Künstler und Mensch,* iii. p. 444.

Liszt for certain of Calderon's *Autos sacramentales* [1]. A libretto
was wanted which should give a composer of sacred music an
opportunity to illustrate the legend of a saint, as Wagner had
illustrated the stories of *Tannhäuser, Lohengrin,* and *Siegfried.*
Taking his cue from the order of Moritz v. Schwind's frescoes,
which illustrate the history of St. Elisabeth of Hungary in the
restored hall of the Wartburg at Eisenach, Liszt planned six
scenes for which Otto Roquette [2] furnished the verses. The
scenes are: 1. The arrival of the child from Hungary—a bright
sunny picture; 2. The rose miracle—a forest and garden scene;
3. The crusaders—a picture of mediaeval pageantry; 4.
Elisabeth's expulsion from the Wartburg—a stormy nocturne;
5. Elisabeth's death; 6. Solemn burial and canonization.
Five sections belong to the dramatic presentation of the story.
The sixth and last, the burial and canonization, is an instrumental
and vocal epilogue balancing the long instrumental movement
which acts as a prologue. The 'Leitmotive,' five in number,
consist of tunes of a popular type:

1. 'In festo Sanctae Elisabeth [3]':

2. A Hungarian folk-tune:

3. A Pilgrims' Song:

---

[1] See the Wagner-Liszt correspondence, anno 1858.
[2] Author of the well-known poem *Waldmeisters Brautfahrt.*
[3] Compare Brahms' *Geistliches Wiegenlied,* Op. 91, No. 2

4. A hymn-tune assigned in the oratorio to Saint Elisabeth:

5. The intonation of the Magnificat—frequently employed by Liszt as symbolical of the Cross [1]:

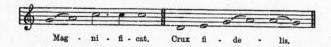

Mag - ni - fi - cat.   Crux fi - de - lis.

Of these tunes the first proved the most pliable and the most fruitful of results. Its gentle contours supply the main lines and suggest the development of the two best sections of the oratorio—the instrumental Introduction and the scene of the Rose-miracle. The latter is a little masterpiece: the most touching and most artistic scene in the whole work, and altogether one of the best things Liszt ever produced. The story is one of charming *naïveté*, and seems to call for music: Landgrave Ludwig, Elisabeth's husband, is surprised to meet her in the wild wood alone, carrying a covered basket. In reply to his questions, she timidly pretends to have wandered while gathering roses. Questioned further, she confesses to be on her way to the sick poor with bread and wine. At the Landgrave's command, she uncovers the basket, and it is found to be full of roses. 'A wonder, a marvellous wonder hath the Lord done unto us.'

---

[1] For example, in the Dante Symphony, *Granermesse : nächtlicher Zug*—No. 1 of the illustrations to Lenau's *Faust*, and in the Poème symphonique *Die Hunnenschlacht*.

Landgrave.

un poco rall.

Ge - lieb - te, kannst du mir ver - zeih - n?

Elisabeth. *un poco rall.*

Er - schüt - tert steh' ich und er - ho -

- - ben.

p

espress.

poco rall.

p

The chorus enters and continues in the same strain with subtle changes leading to a climax of praise; then the two solo voices, alternating with the chorus, resume their song, and the scene ends as quietly as it began.

Everything following this scene is comparatively weak. The chorus and march of the Crusaders are poor and trivial; the scene of the expulsion culminates in a theatrical thunderstorm: that of Elisabeth's death recalls the last act of *Tannhäuser*; indeed, a steady diminution of power and effect is manifest from the close of the miracle scene to the close of the work. There is as complete a miscalculation in this case of *St. Elisabeth* as in that of Schumann's *Paradise and the Peri*—the subject of which offered material enough to make one fine cantata, whereas Schumann wrote three weak ones—and Liszt chose to write a series of six.

Next to *St. Elisabeth*, the setting of the thirteenth Psalm—for tenor solo, chorus and orchestra (1855–65)—occupies a prominent place among Liszt's contributions to sacred music. In Luther's version of the Psalmist's words the force of the personal pronoun comes out strongly: 'Wie lange soll ich sorgen? *Ich* aber hoffe—*Ich* will dem Herrn singen.' This is Liszt's cue. He exhibits the Psalmist's passionate appeals, his trust and hope, and his final conviction that he has been heard and will find help. In his own words, 'the tenor part (that of the Psalmist) is very important.'—'I have permitted myself to sing *personally*, and I have tried to convert the ways of my own flesh and blood to the ways of King David[1].'

The following recitative-like setting of the words 'How long wilt Thou forget me, O Lord? for ever? how long wilt Thou hide Thy face from me?'—shows the character of the main themes:—

[1] Liszt, Letter to Brendel.

The chorus repeats these supplications and the orchestra strengthens and enforces them. The first appeal is followed by a fugato[1]: 'How long shall I take council in my soul, having sorrow in my heart daily? how long shall mine enemy be exalted over me?'

Then comes another supplicating strain: 'Consider and hear me, O Lord my God; lighten mine eyes, lest I sleep the sleep of death'; after which the supplications are again resumed, and again the pain seems assuaged: 'But I have trusted in Thy mercy; my heart shall rejoice in Thy salvation.'

---

[1] Compare the contrapuntal fragments quoted above, pp. 120 and 133, from Berlioz' *Symphonie fantastique* and from *Roméo et Juliette*. Liszt's essays in counterpoint are, perhaps, more successful than those of Berlioz, though his fugue subjects are equally artificial and he fails to make the most of them. Both masters seem to have concocted rather than composed their fugues.

Espressivo

Ich a‑ber hof‑fe dar‑auf, dass du so gnä‑dig, so gnä‑dig bist

The close consists of an Allegro impetuoso, ' I will sing unto the Lord [1].'

Allegro impetuoso

ff

ten.   Ich will dem

Herrn sin ‑ ‑ ‑ gen, will dem

Among Liszt's many contributions to the répertoire of Catholic church music [2] the *Missa solemnis,* known as the ' Graner Festmesse,' is the most conspicuous. Written to order in 1855, performed at the Consecration of the Basilica at Gran, in Hungary, in 1856, it was Liszt's first serious effort in the way of church music proper, and shows him at his best in so far as personal energy and high aim are concerned. ' More prayed than composed,' he said, in 1856, when he wanted to smooth the way for it in Wagner's estimation—' more criticised

[1] In connexion with the setting of the thirteenth Psalm it is curious to note the contrast between Liszt's ultra‑romantic pose of passion, and Brahms' studied reticence and purity of diction when dealing with the same words. Liszt's setting was published in 1865 ; Brahms' Op. 27, ' Der 13. Psalm für dreistimmigen Frauen‑Chor mit Begleitung der Orgel,' appeared at about the same time. Party strife was then at its height ; and the two versions may be taken to represent as nearly as possible the conflicting ideals of style, under the influence of which German musicians ranged themselves in hostile camps —' Zukunftsmusik ' on the one side, uncompromising classicism on the other.

[2] I. Missa quatuor vocum ad aequales (two tenors and two basses), concinente organo. II. 'Graner Festmesse.' III. Missa choralis quatuor vocum, concinente organo. IV. 'Ungarische Krönungsmesse.' V. Requiem, for male voices and organ. Psalms 13, 137, 23, 18, 116, 129. VI. Twelve Kirchenchorgesänge.

than heard,' when it failed to please at the Church of St. Eustache, in Paris, in 1866. It certainly is an interesting and, in many ways, a remarkable work.

Liszt's instincts led him to perceive that the Catholic service, which makes a strong appeal to the senses, as well as to the emotions, was eminently suited to musical illustration. He thought his chance lay in the fact that the function assigned to music in the ceremonial is mainly decorative, and that it would be possible to develop still further its emotional side. The Church employs music to enforce and embellish the Word. But the expansion of music is always controlled and in some sense limited by the Word—for the prescribed words are not subject to change. Liszt, however, came to interpret the Catholic ritual in a histrionic spirit, and tried to make his music reproduce the words not only as *ancilla theologica et ecclesiastica*, but also as *ancilla dramaturgica*. The influence of Wagner's operatic method, as it appears in *Tannhäuser, Lohengrin*, and *Das Rheingold*[1], is abundantly evident; but the result of this influence is more curious than convincing. By the application of Wagner's system of Leitmotive to the text of the Mass, Liszt succeeded in establishing some similarity between different movements, and so approached uniformity of diction. It will be seen, for example, that his way of identifying the motive of the Gloria with that of the Resurrexit and that of the Hosanna, or the motive of the Sanctus and the Christie eleison with that of the Benedictus, and also his way of repeating the principal preceding motives in the ' Dona nobis pacem,' especially the restatement, at its close, of the powerful motive of the Credo, has given to the work a musical unity which is not always in very clear accordance with the text.

Liszt's illustrative, decorative, and dramatically expressive style is seen in the Kyrie and Christe, as well as in the Gloria, of which movements the following quotations will give some notion :—

---

[1] The score of *Das Rheingold* was finished in 1854.

A.

- - nae   vo - lun - - ta - - tis

The sentences of the Credo, so difficult to weld into a consistent musical whole, are treated separately, and a semblance of unity is attained by means of repetition and expansion of the principal subject.

Altogether it may be said that Liszt's treatment of the text of the Mass—his treatment of the Gloria, for instance, as a chorus of angels with the accompaniment of whirring violins—is here and there strikingly picturesque and effective. Compare the example C, above. But it must be added that with the exception of the Kyrie and its little offshoot, the Benedictus, no complete movement is sufficiently well knit together to bear severe scrutiny; that the music is made up of scraps of melody, of fragmentary counterpoint, and sudden changes of key; and that the prevailing restlessness and the theatrical character of some of its instrumental effects are not in just accord with the spirit of a religious ceremonial.

In the Hungarian Coronation Mass ('Ungarische Krönungsmesse,' 1866-7) Liszt aimed at characteristic national colour, and tried to attain it by persistently putting forward some of the melodic formulae common to music of the Hungarian type, such as:

A.

B.

which occurs in the national 'Rakoczy March' and in numberless popular tunes—or an emphatic melisma, such as:

known to everybody through the famous *Rhapsodies*. From beginning to end the popular Hungarian element is represented by devices of this kind in a manner which is always ingenious and well suited to the requirements of a national audience. The following bars from the Benedictus and the Offertorium will serve for examples :—

B.

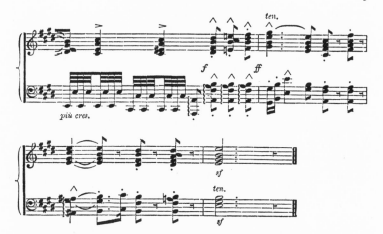

But the style of the entire Mass is as incongruous as a gipsy musician in a church vestment—doubly strange to students of the present day, who in Liszt's *Rhapsodies* and Brahms' *Ungarische Tänze* have become familiar with the rhythmical and melodic phrases of the Hungarian gipsy idiom, and who all along have known them in their most mundane aspect. Apart, however, from its incongruities of style, the Offertorium is a shapely composition with a distinct stamp of its own [1].

Liszt's manner of writing for solo and choral voices is generally practical and effective. The voice-parts are carefully written so as to lessen the difficulties of intonation which the many far-fetched modulations involve, and are skilfully disposed in point of sonority. The orchestration, always efficient, is frequently rich and beautiful.

The oratorio, *Christus* (1863-73), the largest and most sustained of Liszt's efforts, and the *magnum opus* of his later years, is remarkable for the fact that its conception is essentially Roman Catholic, devotional, and contemplative in a Roman Catholic

[1] Allowing for 'ce double caractère national et religieux,' Liszt asserts that 'dans ces étroites limites, *La Messe du Couronnement* est plus concentrique qu'écourtée, et que les deux tons principaux du sentiment national hongrois et de la foi catholique s'y maintiennent et s'harmonient d'un bout à l'autre.'—*Letters to Madame de Wittgenstein*, iii. 181.

sense both in style and intended effect. It contains nothing
that is not in some way connected with the Catholic ritual or
the Catholic spirit; and, more than any other work of its
composer, recognizes and obeys the restrictions imposed by the
surroundings of the Church service. The Latin book of words
(Liszt's own selection) consists of Biblical and liturgical texts,
with the Beatitudes (Matt. v. 3–10) for the centre. The person
of Christ is treated with great reticence, though His words are
used in the Beatitudes, in the illustration of the storm, ' Quid
timidi estis, modicae fidei ? ' and in the scene of the Passion,
' Tristis est anima mea usque ad mortem.' There are three
main sections: 1. Christmas oratorio; 2. After Epiphany;
3. Passion and Resurrection. These sections or parts are
subdivided thus : Part I. Christmas Oratorio—1. Instrumental
introduction with the prophet Isaiah's words for a motto:
' Rorate coeli desuper et nubes pluant iustum, aperiatur terra
et germinet Salvatorem.' 2. Instrumental Pastorale, and the
Annunciation : ' Angelus Domini ad pastores ait [1].' 3. ' Stabat
Mater speciosa.' 4. Instrumental Pastorale, the music of the
shepherds. 5. Instrumental March, the Three Kings, ' Et ecce
stella quam viderant in Oriente antecedebat eos.' Part II. After
Epiphany : 1. The Beatitudes. 2. ' Pater noster.' 3. The
foundation of the Church : ' Tu es Petrus et super hanc petram
aedificabo Ecclesiam meam.' 4. The storm-miracle. 5. The
entry into Jerusalem : ' Hosanna, Benedictus qui venit in no-
mine Domini, Rex Israel.' Part III. Passion and Resurrection :
1. ' Tristis est anima mea.' 2. ' Stabat mater dolorosa.' 3.
Easter hymn, ' O filii et filiae.' 4. Resurrexit.

A mere *cento*, it may be said. But it would be difficult to
make a better selection for the special purposes which Liszt
had in view.

Of the Leitmotive, several of which consist of liturgical

From ' Angelus Domini ' to the words ' Coelestes exercitus ' Liszt quotes the
Gregorian chant note for note (soprano solo) ; even the chorus ' Laudantium Deum
et dicentium,' which follows, is almost entirely taken from the same source.

phrases and are therefore meant to be taken for symbolical as
well as representative themes, two may be quoted[1]: 1. The
intonation of the ' Rorate coeli ' (Introitus ; Advent IV)—

which Liszt has as follows :

2. The intonation of the ' Pater noster ' :

which Liszt has thus :

The themes of the introductory fugue, the first Pastorale
(*a*, below), and the March of the Three Kings (*b*, below), are
evolved from No. 1, above :

The phrase from the first bar of No. 1 appears in the introduction
to the Beatitudes, Part II, in the Easter hymn, Part III, and

---

[1] Compare Bäumker, ' Das katholische deutsche Kirchenlied in seinen Sing-
weisen,' where ' Gesangbücher' of Mayence, 1661 and 1665, are quoted, i. p. 476.

elsewhere. Both the Pastorale movements and the March, though they are somewhat long-drawn-out, considering the quality of the musical texture, are full of simple, popular melody and effective instrumentation. Instances may be found in the *pifferare* tunes of the second Pastorale, the tender melody in F major from the same number, the picturesque effect of the high notes of the violins and flutes in the trio of the March, meant to depict the star of Bethlehem, or the rich sound of the following passage, also from the March, illustrating the adoration of the Magi, 'Apertis thesauris suis, obtulerunt Magi Domino aurum, thus et myrrham':

The 'March of the Three Kings,' it is said, was inspired by
a picture in Cologne Cathedral. 'Stabat mater speciosa,' No.
3, Part I, in spite of its cloying sweetness proves singularly
impressive in performance. On the whole, the entire Christmas
section—the first part of the oratorio—is distinctly good, and
in its naïve way deserves to rank with the charming Children's
chorus of welcome and the fine scene of the Rose-miracle in
St. Elisabeth. With one exception, namely, the beautiful
illustrations to the Sermon on the Mount (the Beatitudes), it
cannot be said that the second and third parts take rank with
the first. There is an increasing preponderance of effort and
dubious experiment as the work proceeds.

The exception, however, is very noticeable. The Beatitudes
contain more refined music, convincing in itself by reason of its
beauty, than all the later movements put together. The
antiphonal disposition of this piece is simple and very effective.
The protagonist, baritone solo, begins: 'Beati pauperes
spiritu' (E major), and the chorus repeats and responds:

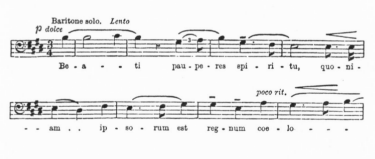

Advantage is taken of the opportunity for expressive modulation offered by the third, fourth, and fifth versicles:

and of the chance to introduce an effect of energy at the eighth
response : ' Beati, qui persecutionem patiuntur propter iustitiam.'

'Beati, Beati, Amen' forms the close, *pianissimo*. Then comes the 'Pater noster,' a choral movement in a similar mood, equally well written for the voices, though far less original. The section entitled 'The foundation of the Church' ('Tu es Petrus)' consists mainly of a choral song, 'Simon Ioannes, diliges me?' written in 1863, under the title of 'L'Hymne du Pape,' and published with French and Italian words, in 1865, at a time when there was talk of Liszt being appointed Maestro della Cappella Pontifica. The storm-miracle in *Christus*, like the wild storm-scene in *St. Elisabeth*, is a piece of decorative *affresco* work—partly instrumental with descriptive indications such as 'Ipse vero dormiebat,' printed in the score, partly choral with short exclamations chanted by a chorus of male voices : 'Domine, salva nos, perimus' ; it culminates in a phrase sung by a baritone voice which represents the voice of Christ : 'Quid timidi estis, modicae fidei?' This curious specimen of hybrid composition comes as near to failure as any similar deviation in Berlioz' work.

In the scene of the entry into Jerusalem the music, admirably adapted to the pageant, culminates in an animated fugato, 'Hosanna Filio David,' with a coda, in graver mood, to the words 'Benedictum quod venit regnum patris nostri David : hosanna in altissimis.'

The 'Tristis est anima mea usque ad mortem' of Part III illustrates the sufferings of Christ as realistically as it is possible to present them in terms of music. The persistent chromatics affect the ear as an excess of sombre chromes and browns may affect the eye in a picture. In the somewhat prolix 'Stabat mater dolorosa,' the process of emphasizing the expression of suffering is continued with similar insistence, by an ingenious and at times really fine accumulation of tones. The poignant expression is carried to an extreme of pathos, strikingly dramatic in nature and effect : such, for instance, as the following passage from the 'Inflammatus' :—

But the main impression left by this part of the oratorio, i. e. the Tristis and the Stabat, is as wearisome and oppressive as that of a collection of realistic pictures of martyrdom [1].

[1] We have got accustomed to all manner of chromatics and the most poignant dissonances in *Tristan*, *Götterdämmerung*, and *Parsifal*; but we have also learnt to appreciate the closeness of Wagner's musical diction, which responds at once and precisely to the stimulus of emotion. Moreover, the extremes of emotion, as

A naïve little hymn, a favourite old tune tastefully set for female voices with harmonium (or flutes, oboes, clarinets and corno inglese), is introduced by way of relief and contrast after the Stabat. It is intended to be sung and played by invisible choristers and instrumentalists :

The oratorio closes with an ecstatic, and indeed somewhat militant, 'Resurrexit,' in which the voices are almost overpowered by the tumult of brass instruments. The following excerpt may serve to illustrate the manner in which it is conceived :

Wagner sometimes deals with them, are explained by the dramatic action. Thus the utmost violence in musical combinations may be intelligible and justifiable from the dramatist's point of view, even when, taken as mere music, combinations of the kind seem to pass the limits of intelligibility, and appear simply ugly and repelling. Compare Wagner's own view as expressed in *Ueber die Anwendung der Musik auf das Drama*, Schriften x. 231-50.

Was Liszt's bias essentially histrionic, as the use of representative themes and operatic effects of illustration in his Programme-music seems to suggest; or was it ecclesiastical, as the use of Intonations serving as symbolical Leitmotive in his Masses, Psalms, oratorios, and even in a number of instrumental pieces, would imply? Perhaps both. All his life long Liszt was a faithful, if somewhat wayward, son of the Catholic Church; and from the first, some of his music echoes the tone of the cloister, and bears traces of the *faicts et gestes* of the priesthood. It is difficult to deal justly with a certain class of Liszt's productions—pieces imbued with religious sentiment and produced at all stages of his career—from the morbid 'Pensée des morts' of 1834, the rather austere 'Pater Noster' (in C) or the devout 'Ave Maria' (in B♭) of 1847 [1], and the painfully chromatic 'Stabat mater dolorosa' (F minor) of 1886 (*Christus*), to the various azure and ultramarine Pieties, such as the 'Ave Maria' (in E) of 1863, the 'Pater Noster' (in A♭) of 1866 (*Christus*), or the Angelus 'Prière aux anges gardiens' (in E) of 1883 [2]. Several of these effusions are very ambitious: the scene of the canonization of St. Elisabeth, for instance, or the distressing 'Stabat mater dolorosa' just mentioned, or the beautiful Beatitudes; others are so slight as to be hardly appreciable, like the 'Stabat mater speciosa,' and the naïve Easter hymn, 'O filii et filiae' (*Christus*), the Sposalizio of the *Années de pèlerinage*, or the delicate little

---

[1] *Harmonies poétiques et religieuses*, Nos. 2, 4, 5.
[2] *Années de pèlerinage*, iii. No. 1.

pianoforte pieces called ' Consolations.' Among such widely
divergent compositions, religious in tone and character, those of
later days than the simple ' Pater Noster' of 1847 are by no means
extravagant or problematic, or in any sense outside the pale of
music proper ; yet the majority of them can hardly be accounted
good music in the full sense of the word. Taken simply as
music, and without regard to any symbolism or casual associa-
tion with the ritual, they convey an undefinable sense of effort
and weakness. Nevertheless, some of these very pieces, notably
the ' Stabat mater speciosa' and the Beatitudes, have been known
to make a deep impression on persons not particularly susceptible to influences of an ecclesiastical description or subject to
sudden devotional impulses.

Looked at from a musician's point of view—apart from the
glamour of an ancient ceremonial, apart also from the fascination
of Liszt's unique personality—a large proportion of these
compositions appear wanting in that specific musical character
and in those distinctive features which make for consistency
and coherence of musical interest. Pieces, to a certain degree
well put together, are found to contain bare and arid stretches,
full of intention perhaps, and full of feeling, but full, also, of
wearisome and pointless particulars. The means of effect
employed by Liszt are neither commonplace, nor especially
eccentric, extravagant, or in any technical sense deficient.
The devotional feeling that prompts their use is evidently
sincere, amounting now and again to true fervour and passion ;
yet, in the end, the entire endeavour fails to convince the mind's
ear, and leads to little that is complete or even likely to prove
of enduring value as artistic work. If a man chooses to
employ the pianoforte or the chorus and orchestra for devotional
purposes he is bound to be watchful of his mode of musical
expression; mere emotional improvisation will not suffice ;
for his experienced hearers are always inclined to resent any
shortcomings in the musical substance or workmanship, and
to assert, with increasing emphasis, that the cause of piety

is but ill served by deficiency in the essential elements of composition [1].

The *pièces sacrées* of Rossini and Verdi may fitly be mentioned here. Rossini's consist of the well-known *Stabat mater*, begun in 1831, finished and performed 1841–2; three choruses for female voices: La Foi, L'Espérance, and La Charité (1844), of which the first two belong to a forgotten opera, *Oedipus*; a 'Tantum ergo' for two tenors and bass with orchestra, a 'Quoniam' for bass solo and orchestra, and 'O Salutaris' for four solo voices; and the so-called 'Petite Messe Solennelle' (1864), the scoring of which was completed in 1867, shortly before his death. Writing about the first Parisian performance of Rossini's *Stabat Mater*, in 1842, Heine [2] slyly stated that the impression he had received reminded him of a curious representation of the Passion by little children, which he professed to have witnessed at Cette. 'The ineffable martyrdom was presented and reproduced, but in the most naïvely juvenile way—the terrible plaint of the Mater dolorosa was intoned by little maiden voices,' &c.—It is sufficient to state broadly that Rossini's *Stabat* is fine music from the professional singer's point of view, and not always devoid of devotional sentiment. The Introduction and first Chorus, the duet, 'Quis est homo,' the 'Inflammatus,' and the unaccompanied quartet, 'Quando corpus morietur,' rank with the most effective of Rossini's work.

Verdi's contributions to sacred music are a *Requiem Mass* for solo voices, chorus, and orchestra, in memory of Alessandro Manzoni; a *Pater Noster* for two soprani, contralto, tenor, and bass; an *Ave Maria* for soprano and strings, and 'Quattro pezzi sacri.' In 1875, his sixty-second year, Verdi, amid rare enthusiasm, made the tour of the principal European concert-rooms with the *Requiem*. It is in the nature of things that the religious music of a man who from youth to old age devoted

---

[1] Witness in recent years the failure of Gounod's oratorios *The Redemption* and *Mors et Vita*, Tinel's *Franciscus*, Perosi's *Transfiguration*, &c.

[2] *Werke*, x. 331.

himself exclusively to the composition of operas should have
something dramatic about it. The marvel, under the circumstances, is rather that this religious music of his (it is not
precisely church music) should have so little of the histrionic
or the theatrical about it. The expression of sorrow, terror,
despair, supplication, and hopeful expectancy in the *Requiem*
is perhaps too personal and passionate, but it is sincere. There
is no trace of frivolity, and, what to a musician is more
important, it will bear inspection from a strictly musical point
of view. Much of it is admirable in its way, and convincing ;
some portions, where the contrapuntal treatment of choral
parts comes in sporadically, are now and then weak, though
by no means inept. The best numbers owe their success to
the composer's native gift for vocal melody, to his able treatment of the voice-parts in *ensemble* pieces, also in some
measure to certain realistic effects produced by choral noise
and orchestral blare, as in the 'Tuba mirum,' which shows that
Verdi had studied Berlioz' *Requiem* to some purpose. The
elegiac reposeful numbers have the charm of sincerity and
tender feeling ; such is particularly the case with the ' Requiem
aeternam,' in which a subdued expression of sorrow alternates
with a tender ray of hope, and the Kyrie and Christe. The mezzo
soprano solo, ' Liber scriptus,' and the bass solo, ' Confutatis,'
which form part of the ' Dies irae,' are remarkably effective.
The extremely simple 'Agnus Dei' is as original as it is masterly,
a melody of thirteen bars six times repeated with ingenious
changes in the voicing, and a few bars of coda. The closing
'Requiem aeternam' is as touching as the opening of which it
is an expansion. Of the two fugues, 'Sanctus' and ' Libera me,'
the second is the best as regards the invention of the subject
and also in point of workmanship ; its climax acts as a telling
foil to the *pianissimo* of the final ' Libera me.'

In the course of 1898, his eighty-fifth year, Verdi published
the latest of his religious pieces : *Quattro pezzi sacri, Ave Maria*
(scala enigmatica armonizzata a quattro voci), *Stabat mater*

(per coro a quattro parti ed orchestra), *Laudi alla Vergine Maria* (per quattro voci bianche), and *Te Deum* (per doppio coro a quattro parti ed orchestra). The first of these, the *Ave Maria*, a harmonic puzzle, looks as if it were a *jeu d'esprit*, meant to be a skit upon certain curious experiments of Liszt's in chromatics. It is based upon an ' enigmatic ' scale—ascending C, D♭, E, F♯, G ♯, A♯, B, C; descending C, B, A♯, G♯, F♮, E, D♭, C. This ' scala ' in minims is employed as a cantus firmus, first in the bass, then successively in the tenor and alto, finally in the soprano. The queer counterpoint which Verdi applies to it is far-fetched and difficult of intonation; the total effect is almost, if not quite, as musical as it is curious. From a vocalist's point of view, the ' Laudi per *voci bianche*,' female voices, is an exquisite piece—sweet and tender, showing Verdi as a singer of genius. It produces a wonderful effect of purity and happiness. The words are from the last canto of Dante's *Paradiso* :

Vergine Madre, figlia del tuo Figlio,	Thou Virgin Mother, daughter of thy Son,
Umile e alta più che creatura,	Humble and high beyond all other creature,
Termine fisso d'eterno consiglio,	The limit fixed of the eternal counsel,
Tu se' colei che l'umana natura	Thou art the one who such nobility
Nobilitasti sì, che il suo Fattore	To human nature gave, that its Creator
Non disdegnò di farsi sua fattura.	Did not disdain to make Himself its creature.
Nel ventre tuo si raccese l' amore,	Within thy womb rekindled was the love,
Per lo cui caldo nell' eterna pace	By heat of which in the eternal peace
Così è germinato questo fiore.	After such wise this flower was germinated.

The *Stabat* and *Te Deum*, in the violent contrasts of colour employed, the noisy instrumentation, and the crude use of chromatics, show traces of the operatic stage of Berlioz' *Requiem*, and even of Liszt's *Christus*; but they also exhibit high imagination and some genuine musical quality.

Wagner's *Das Liebesmahl der Apostel : eine biblische Scene*, for male voices and orchestra, belongs to this part of the subject, though it can hardly be ranked under the head either

of orthodox or of secular church music. It is religious in spirit
and tinged with the partly religious, partly humanitarian and
political, enthusiasm of the years which preceded the revolution
of 1848. It was composed as a *pièce d'occasion,* for a festive
gathering of men's choral societies in Dresden. Like some
scene from an opera seria of Spontini, it is planned to form
one continuous movement. Remarkable rather for the spirit
in which it is conceived than for its actual musical value,
Das Liebesmahl recalls the style of Wagner's first successful
opera, *Rienzi* (1840–2). As in *Rienzi,* the melodic and
harmonic effects are simple, direct, and telling, though occasionally somewhat blatant and commonplace. Certain passages—
'Sende uns deinen heiligen Geist,' 'Machet euch auf, redet
freudig das Wort'—show traces of that mystical fervour which
many years afterwards found fuller expression in the choruses
of the Knights of the Grail in the first act of *Parsifal.* Three
separate choirs *a cappella* (each consisting of tenors and basses
divided), who represent the Disciples, are supplemented by
twelve solo bass voices, who represent the Apostles, and by a
choir of 'voices from on high,' who represent the Trinity;
ultimately the mass of voices is joined by a very full orchestra,
which, as in *Rienzi,* includes certain extra wind and percussion
instruments such as additional bassoons, a 'Serpent,' valve
horns, valve trumpets, a bass-tuba and two kettledrums, besides
the usual trumpets, horns, trombones, and timpani. The
sound of 'voices from on high' as in *Parsifal*—'Seid getrost,
Ich bin euch nah, und mein Geist ist mit euch'—was heard
in its fullest beauty when the words were sung from the
cupola of the Frauenkirche, at Dresden, on the sixth of July,
1843; and the fine effect thus produced was made to serve again,
thirty-nine years later, in the first and third acts of *Parsifal*
(1882)—'Der Glaube lebt, die Taube schwebt.'

CHAPTER X

CONCERTOS AND CHAMBER MUSIC

CONCERTOS and shorter pieces chiefly for pianoforte or violin with orchestra are conspicuous among the instrumental music of this period. They may be ranged under two heads: pieces remarkable for originality of conception and a high quality of material and workmanship—such as Weber's Concertstück for pianoforte, Spohr's eighth Concerto, 'In modo d'una scena cantante' (1816), Mendelssohn's Concerto for violin, and Schumann's for pianoforte (both 1845); secondly, pieces wherein stress is laid on a display of the solo player's attainments as a virtuoso —such as Paganini's violin Concerto in D (1820), Ernst's in F ♯ minor (1836), Vieuxtemps' in E (1835) and D minor (1853), Moscheles' third pianoforte Concerto in G minor [1] (1822), Henselt's in F minor, Liszt's in E♭ and in A, his concert variations on the *Dies irae* known as 'Todtentanz' (*Danse macabre*), 1850, and furthermore, three characteristically National concertos, distinctly belonging to the period of romanticism, though comparatively recent in date, viz. Joachim's Hungarian Concerto in D minor for violin, Grieg's Norwegian Concerto in A minor for pianoforte, and Tchaikovsky's Russian Concerto, also for pianoforte, in B♭ minor.

Weber's Concertstück (1821), ' Larghetto affettuoso, Allegro passionato, Marcia e Rondo giojoso,' was first designed on the scheme of a romantic story, which Weber finally did not publish, since he deemed the sequence of movements sufficiently intel-

---

[1] The first movement of which contains music of a high order, undeservedly neglected, and represents the technique of Hummel, grafted on that of Clementi and Beethoven.

ligible without verbal explanation. His own views on the
subject of this piece and its relation to 'programme music' are
expressed with great frankness: 'I am planning,' he wrote to
Rochlitz, the critic, 'a pianoforte concerto in F minor. The
choice of key seems curious—seeing that concertos in a minor
key so rarely please unless there be some rousing idea connected
with them. A sort of story has somehow taken hold of me;
it will serve to link the movements together and determine their
character in detail, as it were, dramatically. I intend to entitle
them: Allegro, "Separation"; Adagio, "Lamento"; Finale,
"Deepest grief, comfort, return and jubilation." I find it very
difficult to accustom myself to this conception, as I particularly
dislike all musical pictures with specific titles—yet it irresistibly
forces itself upon me and promises to prove efficacious. In
any case i do not care to put it forward for the first time at
any place where I am not already well known, for fear of being
misunderstood and counted as a charlatan.'

As the Concertstück now stands, the sequence of movements
reflects the changes of mood in some operatic scena, thus:
A lady sitting in her bower and thinking of her knight, who
has gone to the Crusade (*Larghetto affettuoso*). She fancies
him in battle (*Allegro passionato*) and longing for one more
sight of her before death. She is near to fainting away, when
suddenly from the woods without comes the sound of men
approaching (*Tempo di marcia*). She looks out anxiously.
There is her lover—and with a wild cry she rushes into his
arms (*Presto giojoso*)[1]. Technically, the Concertstück marks
a new departure in the treatment of the pianoforte as a concert
instrument, and is full of ingenious devices both in the solo
part and the orchestration.

---

[1] An ingenious commentator, C. F. Weitzmann (the first good historian of
clavier music), inspired by Liszt's grand rendering, regarded the piece from
a political point of view, as an echo of the glorious uprising of Germany towards
the close of the Napoleonic wars, and not without some reason, in so far as the
spirit of the music is concerned.

The novel effect of a sustained melody with arpeggiando and quasi-pizzicato accompaniments, senza pedale (Introduction), has been reproduced by Mendelssohn in his Capriccio brillante, mentioned above; and the staccato octaves, rippling semi-quavers, and certain details of instrumentation (Finale) reappear in Mendelssohn's Concerto in G minor. The plaintive wail produced by the high notes of the bassoon against the throbbing chords of the strings—an operatic effect—just before the Tempo di Marcia, is singularly telling in its place :

After this the hearers are astonished by rapid octave glissandos over the white keys of the pianoforte, a virtuoso effect comparatively easy on the old Viennese instruments, but next to impossible on modern grands [1].

There is yet another even more surprising effect, and more distinctly Weber's own, but too long for quotation—the sustained crescendo from pianissimo to fortissimo for sixteen bars before the first Allegro on the same harmony, where the sound of the instrument is allowed to accumulate with the dampers raised [2].

Before the Concertstück Weber wrote two concertos, one in C and another in E♭. The second of these appeared in 1812, a year after Beethoven's great Concerto in E♭. Thus Weber's surprising choice of the key of B major for the Adagio [3] is accounted for; it appears as a reflex of Beethoven; there are also other points of resemblance—slight but unmistakable.

Though not strong enough for performance in public at the present day, Weber's Concerto for bassoon in F, his concertino in E♭, Op. 26, and the Concertos in F minor and E♭ for clarinet, and especially the interesting Concertino in E minor for horn (1806–18)—occasional pieces rapidly written for virtuoso friends —deserve notice as containing the best solo music extant for

[1] It is apparently due to Beethoven, who made use of it in his Trio in C minor, Op. 1, in the first Concerto in C, and in the Finale of the Waldstein Sonata.

[2] This is the celebrated crescendo that Goethe asked for when Weber visited him in 1812. Here again Beethoven was the initiator, and Weber, with his theatrical 'flair,' the first to make the most effective use of it.

[3] Virtually C♭ major—the key-note E♭ becomes D♯ and forms the third of the new key.

the particular instruments. The latter piece, for the first time in recorded music, exhibits a curious trick of obtaining the effect of three- or even four-part harmony from a solo horn. (The player 'blows' a note and at the same time sings or rather 'hums' another—if this is done perfectly in tune the acoustical result is of a chord in three or four parts.) Taken together Weber's show-pieces for wind instruments form a compendium of the good effects the instruments can produce individually, and here again, as with some of the solo pianoforte pieces to be mentioned later on, the details appear like studies for something to come. Compared with Spohr's early violin concertos, the freshness of Weber's pieces is remarkable, in spite of their rather flimsy texture. The best piece in which the clarinet takes part is the duo concertante Op. 48, in E♭, a spirited and showy sonata for that instrument and pianoforte.

Musicians and virtuosi of the present day are agreed that after Beethoven's concertos in C minor, G major, and E♭, and before Brahms' in B♭ major and Tchaikovsky's in B♭ minor, Schumann's is the great pianoforte concerto; and similarly, that after Spohr's 'Scena cantante,' and Beethoven's concerto in D, but before Joachim's 'Hungarian' in D minor and Brahms' in D major, Mendelssohn's is the great concerto for the violin. So grateful to the violinist and so much in vogue with the public is the latter, that it bids fair to outlast the interest in the rest of Mendelssohn's solo and ensemble pieces.

The device of joining the movements of a concerto so as to form a continuous whole has frequently been ascribed to Spohr, who, in his 'Scena cantante' (*Gesangsscene*) just mentioned, imitates an operatic scena of tragic import. Moscheles in his 'Concerto fantastique' worked on similar lines. Mendelssohn made use of it with very good effect in both of his pianoforte concertos and in the concerto for violin. But the credit of having originated the happy innovation belongs to Beethoven, whom Weber followed in the Concertstück (compare the beautiful transition from the Adagio to the Finale in Beethoven's E♭

concerto with Weber's bassoon passage quoted above). Mendelssohn's method of combining the movements derives directly from Weber's Concertstück, as Spohr's design derives from Mozart's fantasias in D minor and C minor. Mendelssohn's concertos for pianoforte, the Capriccio brillante, the Serenade and Allegro giojoso, and the Rondo brillante, are not included in the first rank of concert pieces for the reason that even the best of them, the G minor concerto and the Capriccio, bear palpable traces of borrowing from Weber, and the remainder, though clever in detail and eminently practical, exhibit conspicuous mannerisms.

Schumann's pianoforte concerto stands with Weber's Concertstück as a typical representation of the Romantic period. The opening Allegro was written first as a lyric fantasia; the Intermezzo and final Allegro were added after an interval of some years. Traces of Schumann's aphoristic manner are present throughout, particularly in the first movement, but the design is firmly and consistently maintained. Among his larger instrumental pieces there is none that offers a more complete and well-balanced expression of his individuality, and in none of his works (the *Manfred* overture and the Adagio of the C major Symphony excepted) has he so perfectly succeeded in setting forth the delicately passionate sentiment and the fiery exaltation that represents the normal state of his musical mind. The technique of the solo part is original and sufficiently effective, though there is not a bar of display for mere display's sake. The instrumentation, without being striking or clever, yet leaves nothing to be desired. Less satisfactory is the Introduction and Allegro appassionato, Op. 92, an ambitious work, but rather monotonous and ineffective, and still less the Concert Allegro with Introduction, dedicated to Brahms, Op. 134.

Chopin's two concertos were early works (1833–6). In the general outlines they recall the style of Hummel, as is shown in the arrangement of tuttis and solos, the distribution of cantilena and passage work, and in certain technicalities belonging to the treatment of the solo instrument. The cantilena

in the E minor concerto is Italian in spirit, and, like much of
Chopin's melody, shows traces of the influence of Bellini [1].

Against both concertos and indeed against all Chopin's pieces
with orchestra—the Krakoviak, which ranks with the Rondos
of the concertos, the Andante spianato and Polonaise in E♭, Op.
22, the Fantasia on Polish airs, Op. 13, the variations on 'La
ci darem,' all of them fascinating from a virtuoso's point of
view and very clever as compositions—there is serious objection :
they appear to better advantage without orchestra, and with the
accompaniment played on a second pianoforte. Chopin did not
know enough about orchestral instruments, either singly or in
combination, to employ them with proper effect. His tuttis
lack sonority, and when the pianoforte enters, the would-be
accompaniment fails to blend with the solo instrument. One
or two fine and original effects, however, must not be overlooked,
viz. the alternation of strings, pianissimo and unisono, with
soft chords of wood winds, in the beginning of the Larghetto in
the F minor concerto ; and the long tremolo of strings interspersed with the solemn pizzicato of the double basses which
supports the recitative of the pianoforte in the same movement [2].

Regarded from the pianoforte player's point of view, Henselt's [3]
concerto in F minor (1838), the most ambitious among that
pianist's pieces, has very considerable merits. As a record of
Henselt's personal achievements at the keyboard, the work is
remarkable for the rich effects of sound attained by the use of
widespread chords in the most complex form of arpeggio, the
intricate filigree work of passages, the rapid *fioriture*, the broken

---

[1] The Italian eighteenth-century vocal cantilena as transferred to the violin by
Legrenzi, Tartini, Viotti, and afterwards from the violin to the pianoforte,
constitutes the cantilena of Mozart's and Hummel's concertos, and from Mozart
and Hummel, Field and Chopin in the main derive theirs.

[2] Attempts at re-instrumentation, such as those of the F minor concerto by
Klindworth and of the E minor concerto by Tausig, or of instrumentation direct
such as that of the Allegro de Concert in A by Nicodè, have not justified their
existence. Almost throughout, the solo part, as Chopin has it, is complete in itself.
The accompaniments, whether the composer's own or added by commentators, act
as drags and obscure rather than enhance the effect.

[3] 1814–89.

octaves, and the other devices which afford such ample opportunity to the skill and endurance of the virtuoso. But in spite of the brilliancy of the protagonist's part, and the fairly good orchestration, there is a noticeable lack of convincing effect. One misses the chief of Henselt's peculiarities—that smooth, sentimental 'Lieder ohne Worte' tunefulness, which distinguishes many of his Études and Impromptus—and this perhaps more than anything else has stood in the way of a complete success. Though the concerto is well planned and carefully written, it breathes an air of pedantry, chiefly owing to the rather trite character of the themes—which have all the médiocrité distinguée of Henselt's master, Hummel. Certain details in the two principal movements, Allegro patetico and Allegro agitato, are obviously appropriated from Chopin's F minor concerto, and thus derive from Hummel at second hand. The middle movement—Larghetto in D♭ major and C♯ minor, ⁶⁄₈, a piece more distinctly Henselt's own in point of melodic invention and sentiment, starts and terminates as a kind of Nocturne after the manner of Field or Chopin. The centre portion, C♯ minor, very remarkable from a pianist's point of view, contains a bold effect of sonority [1] : a broad cantilena for both hands in double octaves sustained by the pedal,—in imitation of heavy bass and tenor instruments,—at first *piano*, later on *forte*, and then *fff* played simultaneously with the accompanying chords, which, also laid out for both hands, follow each main note of the melody in semiquavers higher up on the key-board.

Schumann expressed a wish to write a piece which should consist of an extended movement, the opening section to stand for the first Allegro, a cantabile section for the Adagio, and a bright close for the customary Rondo. Liszt tried to carry out some such idea. Taking a hint from Berlioz' *L'Idée fixe* and Wagner's system of Leitmotive, as employed in *Tannhäuser* ·and *Lohengrin*, Liszt strove for unity by making a single

[1] Recently copied—key, effect, notation on four staves—by S. Rachmaninoff, in the celebrated C♯ minor Prélude.

subject serve both in quick and slow time, by making a continuous movement of the entire piece, and by stringing together the
main subject with its variants and all accessory melodies in the
final peroration. This novelty in form, designed as self-dependent music without regard to a programme, proved to be a success.
Indeed Liszt's two concertos in E ♭ and A major, to which may
be added the so-called Concerto for two pianos without orchestra
in E minor, and the ' Todtentanz ' (*Danse macabre*), would rank
among the best of concert pieces, were it not for the lack of
weight and beauty in their main themes. As virtuoso pianoforte
music these efforts are magnificent, the orchestration superb—
particularly in the Concerto in A and the wildly fantastic ' Dance
of Death [1].' The *Danse macabre*, sketched in 1839 (written
and rewritten in 1849 and 1859)—a piece that belongs to the
category of Berlioz' *Nuit d'un sabbat*, the *Orgie des brigands*,
and Liszt's own Scherzo ironico, *Mephistopheles*, has for an
avowed programme Orcagna's frescoes representing the Dance
of Death, at Pisa, together with a reminiscence of Holbein's
Dance of. Death, at Basle. The piece consists of a series of
grotesque variations on the old intonation of the ' Dies irae ' used
by Berlioz in the *Nuit d'un sabbat*. Remarkably clever as an
example of the extremes of pianoforte technique, and equally
clever as an example of grotesque instrumentation, it is very
effective when properly played to an audience in the mood for
such things.

Bare enumeration must suffice for John Field's pianoforte
Concerto in A ♭ (the 7th), Ferdinand Ries' in C ♯ minor (the
3rd), Sterndale-Bennett's in F minor (the 4th), Ferdinand Hiller's
in F ♯ minor (1863), Rubinstein's in G major and in D minor,
Joachim Raff's in C minor (1870), as well as for Schumann's
Concerto for violoncello, and his Concerto for four horns. All
these works stand, more or less, apart from the main line of

---

[1] The Concerto in E ♭ and a good number of Liszt's earlier works owe much
of their telling effect to Joachim Raff, who for several years acted as Liszt's
secretary.

gradual change which marks the Romantic period, and none of them have left an appreciable impression upon professional executants, to whom they were, in the first instance, addressed and whom they mainly concern.

Both Mendelssohn and Schumann made strenuous efforts in concerted chamber music for pianoforte and strings. Mendelssohn's two trios, D minor and C minor, and his two sonatas for 'cello and pianoforte, fine and finished as they are, particularly in the first movements and the Scherzos, have, for the present at any rate, lost their vogue. His three early pianoforte quartets are of small moment.

Written in 1842, Schumann's famous Quintet in E♭ soon became, and (apart from Brahms's in F minor) still ᵣemains, the favourite of concert audiences, despite the lugubrious *In modo d'una marcia*, which has been maliciously described as an 'Elegy on the death of a Philistine.' Next to this ranks the pianoforte quartet also in E♭. Schumann in his later years wrote three trios—in D minor, F major, and G minor—of which the first is the strongest and the last a failure. With the exception of the first Allegro of the Trio in D minor and perhaps the Adagio of this and the Larghetto of the Trio in F, none of Schumann's trio movements reach the level of Mendelssohn's. Two sonatas for violin and pianoforte, in A minor, Op. 105, and D minor, Op. 121, not so well considered, in point of form, as Mendelssohn's 'cello sonatas, belong to the period of Schumann's decline, when he wrote in feverish haste. The themes of the first movements of both sonatas are passionate, but the treatment produces an effect of effort and forced agitation. The slow movements, in F and G respectively, especially the first one, are in their way good, the finales mediocre. It is enough to mention the three Phantasiestücke, Op. 73, for clarinet (or violin) and piano, and the three Romanzen, Op. 94, for oboe (or violin) and piano, as pieces perhaps better suited for the violin than either the oboe or clarinet. *Märchenbilder*, for pianoforte and viola, Op. 113, *Märchenerzählungen*, for pianoforte, clarinet,

and violin, and *Stücke im Volkston*, for violoncello and pianoforte, Op. 102, are in the main dull, though not without an
occasional glimpse of beauty.

In his three string quartets, Op. 41, Schumann tried to make
each movement exhibit some definite mood, in a manner which
should depend for its effect upon a concise and direct expression
of the idea rather than upon a complex scheme of contrasting
subjects and balanced developments. And he thus managed to
say things aphoristically which had never been so expressed
before. He was well aware that in the most intellectual department of instrumental music, the string quartet, any effect
produced by mere mass or colour, anything which gave the
impression of trickery, would instantly be revealed as an error
in style, and in this respect his three quartets are more
satisfactory than Mendelssohn's seven. Not that Mendelssohn's music for stringed instruments can be called other than
masterly; but the fact remains that his Quartets and Quintets
contain, here and there, certain effects which suggest the
orchestra or the pianoforte—such, for instance, as the use of
the tremolo in the first Allegro of the D major Quartet, Op.
44, No. 1, and the Quintet in F minor, Op. 80, or the use
of syncopated accompaniments in the first Allegro of the
Quartet in E minor, and other devices of the kind. Mendelssohn's fine Octet for strings, published as Op. 20, with its very
clever and poetically suggestive Scherzo, is too well known to
need any detailed description. It was a truly astonishing feat
for a boy half-way through his seventeenth year [1]. Unification
is attempted by a repetition in the Finale of the principal
subject of the Scherzo—with the same end in view, subjects
from the first movement of the Quartet, Op. 12, in E♭, are also
reproduced in the Finale.

Verdi's one contribution to chamber music, a string quartet
in E minor, is interesting and original throughout. It consists
of the usual four movements: (1) a rather lengthy, yet effective,

---

[1] Compare Sir George Grove in the article on Mendelssohn, *Dict.* ii. p. 258.

Allegro, $\frac{4}{4}$, consistent in form, masterly in treatment, and full of novel effects; (2) an Andantino, $\frac{3}{4}$, in C, of piquant invention both as regards melody and modulation; (3) a short Scherzo Prestissimo; and (4) a Scherzo Fuga, $\frac{4}{4}$, allegro assai mosso, very cleverly elaborated and brought to a bright close in E major. The work, like Borodine's second quartet, is worthy of more serious attention than it has received.

CHAPTER XI

PIANOFORTE MUSIC

AN anthology of Weber's compositions for the pianoforte would exclude all the variations on popular tunes and include the Concertstück, the sonatas in A♭ major and D minor, the so-called Perpetuum mobile (Finale, Sonata in C), the Momento capriccioso, the Rondeau brillant in E♭, the Polacca in E, the *Aufforderung zum Tanz* (*L'Invitation à la valse*) and a few of the four-hand trifles, Op. 60. It is a small list, but a weighty one, for it consists of the most original and technically the most advanced pieces after Beethoven and Schubert and before Schumann and Chopin. In most of these pieces Weber has broken new ground and has proved to be the pioneer of later developments : in almost all of them he added a good deal to the keyboard technique of Dussek, Clementi, and even of Beethoven. Thus, for instance, taking a hint from Beethoven, he produced special and very distinct effects of sonority without the aid of the pedals, or by some particular use of them ; he developed Dussek's showy passage work of scales and broken chords—as we know it in that master's sonatas in F minor, Op. 77, called *L'Invocation,* and Op. 70 in A♭, called *Le Retour à Paris*—still further in the direction of pliant grace and glitter. Unfortunately Dussek's rather lax and patchy construction also reappears in the Allegros of Weber's sonatas, which, like those of Dussek, are concert pieces intended for the use of professional players. The predominance of sentiment over closeness and concentration of design is fully apparent —as for instance in the fine first movement of the Sonata in A♭. A number of Weber's early pianoforte works look

like stepping-stones to his operas; even the Polacca in E, the
Invitation, and the Concertstück seem to belong to the same
group and to point in the same direction. It is worthy of note
that up to the present day Weber's influence is felt in the
ball-room. The chevaleresque spirit and subtle grace of his
Aufforderung zum Tanz (*L'Invitation à la valse*)[1] has changed
the character of the German Walzer, which it made the richer
by a note of brilliant gaiety, of dignified ease, and gentle manners,
unknown before. Up to Weber's time the Walzer resembled
a rustic dance known as the Ländler (compare the Waltz in
Der Freischütz, or the middle part of the Presto alla tedesca
of Beethoven's Sonatina, Op. 79), or else it was like a fluent
Minuetto with a touch of sentimentality like Schubert's so-
called *Sehnsuchtswalzer* in A ♭, Op. 9, No. 2.

Then came Weber with his dashing *Allegro con fuoco*, and
his frank enjoyment of life and movement. Thus, together
with Schubert, he appears as the originator of the modern Valse
and the father of the music of the Strausses and other masters
of the dance. His influence is perceptible even in Chopin,
whose lighter valses owe as much of their freshness and charm
to the Invitation as some of his Polonaises owe their fire to
the Polacca in E[2].

Before passing on to the works of Mendelssohn, Schumann,
and Chopin, John Field must be mentioned[3]. To find anything so dainty in sentiment, so novel and perfect in diction,
as Field's Nocturnes, No. 4 in A, $\frac{4}{4}$ and No. 7 also in A, $\frac{6}{8}$, one
would have to go back to Mozart's Rondo in A minor, or
forward to certain Nocturnes of Chopin. The designation
'Nocturne' is Field's own, and only nine or ten of the pieces

---

[1] The graceful pantomimic music of the Introduction and the Epilogue accounts
for that title.

[2] Viennese dance music from 1820 to 1850, with Labitzky, Strauss the elder,
and Lanner, reflects the spirit of the South German *bourgeoisie* of that time.
With the younger Strauss and Gungl the valse becomes Pan-Germanic and
cosmopolitan. With Chopin and Brahms it leaves the confines of the public
ball-room and returns to the domain of graceful fancy.

[3] Field, a pupil of Clementi, was born in Dublin 1782, he died in 1837.

so called are genuine[1]. Field's frail little pieces are remarkable for originality of spirit ánd novel technique. Each bar
shimmers with the gleam of romance. To realize their merit
it suffices to remember their date, and to compare them with
some of their offspring, such as Nos. 1, 18, 19, 37, of Mendelssohn's *Lieder ohne Worte*, or the first set of Chopin's
Nocturnes, Op. 9. High and varied as is the artistic quality
of these particular pieces of Mendelssohn's and Chopin's, the
mysterious voice of poesy does not so unmistakably resound
in them as in Field's. Besides the two Nocturnes just mentioned, those in B♭, A♭, and E♭ merit attention[2]. It is
evident that Chopin in his elegiac mood is much indebted to
Field. The kind of emotion expressed in Chopin's Nocturnes, the type of melody with its graceful embellishments,
the waving accompaniments in widespread chords with their
vaguely prolonged sound supported and coloured by the pedals,
all this and more Chopin derived from Field. Even from the
executant's point of view, there is as much trace of the study
of Field's pieces in Chopin's case, as there is of Clementi's or
Berger's[3] in Mendelssohn's, or of Cramer and Hummel in
Schumann's.

Mendelssohn intended his *Lieder ohne Worte*, eight books
in all, to be straightforward, simple, and naïve, that is to say,
Mozartian in the expression of emotion. In their effects the
majority of the Lieder are graceful and pleasing. There is
refined musical sentiment, perfect savoir-faire, balance, complete finish, but *not* music in the fullest and warmest sense,
as we get it so often in Schumann and Brahms. In spite of
occasional titles—Gondellied, Volkslied, Jagdlied, Frühlingslied, Spinnerlied (the three latter, though generally adopted,
are not furnished by the composer), each Lied rests solely upon
its musical merits. Among the finest of them we may point

---

[1] Publishers, by including arrangements, have increased the number to 18.
[2] The latter is the prototype of Chopin's Op. 9, No. 2, also in E♭.
[3] Berger was Clementi's pupil and Mendelssohn's teacher.

to the Gondellied in A minor, the Volkslied in the same key,
the so-called Spring Song in A major, the first Lied, in E major,
of Book I [1], and the first, E ♭ major, of Book II [2].

Besides the Songs without words, Mendelssohn's most important contributions to the solo literature of the pianoforte
consist of six Preludes and Fugues, a Scherzo a capriccio in
F♯ minor, Op. 35, and the Variations sérieuses, Op. 54. The
first of the six fugues, in E minor, is a masterpiece on the lines
of J. S. Bach, whose manner it often recalls both in texture
and in movement [3]; but with the remaining numbers the
interest lies more in the Prelude, e.g. the one in A♭, F minor,
and B♭. The 'Serious' Variations on a beautiful theme in
D minor, Andante $\frac{2}{4}$, are remarkable for ingenuity of treatment
and grouping, and for skilful handling of the instrument. The
scheme is akin to that of Bach's Chaconne for violin and
Beethoven's Variations in C minor with the very effective turn
to the major key towards the end common to both, and a
showy close in the minor. These Variations in the matter of
invention break no new ground—as, on the contrary, is the
case in all of Beethoven's, the majority of Brahms', and in some
of Schumann's Variations—but the unity of style, the balance
of effects, and the mature craftsmanship shown throughout are
qualities beyond praise.

Other sets of variations, the posthumous Op. 82 in E♭ and
those in B♭, look like preparatory studies for the Variations
sérieuses. The two sets last mentioned can hardly count as
representative pieces, though they are quite up to the average
level of the master's work.

When Schumann took to composing, at first he devoted

---

[1] Chopin's favourite.

[2] It may be added that several of the Lieder make good studies for specialities
of touch—like Nos. 10, 11, 15, 18, 24, 30 and 32. Fanciful sub-titles, such as
have been furnished for all the Lieder by Stephen Heller, or poems cited by way
of illustration, are entirely superfluous and often misleading.

[3] Compare the wonderful fugues in Beethoven's Op. 101, 106, and 110, which
are also written on the lines of Bach, but in every bar bear the stamp of
Beethoven's impetuous individuality.

himself exclusively to the pianoforte—he relied more upon his temperament and his gift of improvisation, than upon any system or tradition of style ; and from the earliest sketches for pianoforte to the apotheosis of Faust, he was influenced by the romantic spirit of the time as it reached him through literature. With regard to the pianoforte pieces, it is wonderful that so early in his career he should have been able to condense and express so many heterogeneous suggestions emanating from non-musical sources. When he began to publish, his actual professional attainment was insufficient, distinctly less than that of Mendelssohn, Chopin, or Berlioz. His early manner, from Opus 1 to about Opus 9, was modelled on the style of his favourite author Jean Paul. ' I have learnt,' he said, ' more counterpoint from Jean Paul Richter than from any music-master.' The counterpoint is not particularly in evidence; but Heine's humorous account of Jean Paul's manner will throw some light on the matter. ' Jean Paul's periods,' wrote Heine, ' are constructed like a series of diminutive chambers, which are often so narrow that if one idea happens to meet another there is sure to be a collision ; the ceiling above is provided with hooks to hold up all manner of ideas, and the walls are furnished with secret drawers to conceal emotion [1].' And Schumann's style, like Jean Paul's, was the result of impulsive improvisation and a constant desire to symbolize, with apparently no knowledge of the art of selection. He seems to be trying to reproduce Jean Paul's figurative and metaphorical mode of expression in terms of music, and appears to be playing with poetical metaphors, unable to find full expression for his meaning. In the early sets of solo pieces with suggestive titles, Schumann deals in terse epigrammatic phrases, which he joins one with another, but with little or no attempt at evolving anything further. So long as such phrases are sufficiently novel and the pieces concise, the result is both striking and fascinating, as is the case in the *Intermezzi*, Op. 4,

[1] *Heine-Schriften*, vii. p. 268.

the *Davidsbündlertänze*, Op. 6, the Scènes mignonnes entitled
Carneval, Op. 9, *Kreisleriana*, Op. 16 (1837) (the title is
meant to recall the fantastic figure of E. T. A. Hoffmann's
Capellmeister Kreissler), particularly the highly original numbers 1, 2, 4, and 6.   The fantastic miniatures [1] that go to make
up the majority of Schumann's publications from Op. 9 to 23,
some numbers of the Phantasie in C and *Kreisleriana*, the
Allegro Op. 8 and the Sonatas excepted, are each the brief
expression of a single mood, each remarkable for concentration
and power of suggestion.   But this method of stringing together
a number of independent paragraphs, as in the lengthy *Humoreske*, Op. 20, or in the last of the *Novelletten*, F♯ minor,
Op. 21, does not commend itself.   The result is ill-balanced,
incongruous, and, at times, even wearisome.   In several sets
of pieces earlier than the *Carneval*, such as *Papillons*, Op. 2,
Intermezzi, Op. 4, *Impromptus*, Op. 5, *Davidsbündlertänze*,
Op. 6, there is much that is inchoate, though not exactly
indefinite.   Even in later and more mature pieces surprises
and contradictions abound, as for instance in No. 7, *Traumes-
wirren*, where a series of abstruse chords interrupts a lively
piece of salon music.   Sometimes Schumann obtrudes his
particular whims and even his personality, for instance when
he introduces mysterious quotations from his own *Papillons*
in the *Carneval* or from the 'Abegg' variations in the last
number of the *Intermezzi*, Op. 4.

Schumann in his early days reproduced what he had been
taught or what he had studied.   It is not surprising, therefore,
that his early pieces contain traces of Hummel and of
Schubert.   His indebtedness to Schubert has been frequently
pointed out, but that to Hummel and even to Moscheles has
been overlooked.   The Allegro in B minor, for instance, might
well be called 'Réminiscences d'Hummel'; compare also the
Finale of the Sonata in F♯ minor, Op. 11, and the Toccata,
Op. 7, with Hummel's Sonata in F♯ minor, Fantasia in E♭, and

---

[1] Hauptmann called them *Sächelchen*, Tit-bits.

the Scherzo of the Sonata, Op. 106, in D. The fantastic titles, some of them interchangeable *ad libitum*—such as Arabesque, Blumenstück, Novelletten, Humoreske, Nachtstücke, Kreisleriana—derive directly from Jean Paul and E. T. A. Hoffmann. It has already been pointed out with regard to Schumann's orchestral works that he stopped short of actual programme music, although here and there he makes use of an inscription or a motto in verse or a musical quotation from some work of his own or of his bride, Clara Wieck. The same practice appears in his pianoforte music. For example, the great Phantasie in C major, Op. 17, exhibits the following lines of F. Schlegel's by way of a clue:—

Durch alle Töne tönet .	Midst all tones that vibrate
Im bunten Erdentraum	Through earth's mingled dreams
Ein leiser Ton gezogen	One whispered note resounds
Für den der heimlich lauscht.	For ears attent to hear.

The 'ear attent to hear' will readily perceive the uniting tones that run through all the pictures which the imagination of the composer unrolls.

Again, the Intermezzo No. 2, Op. 4, is inscribed ' Meine Ruh
ist hin,' i. e. Gretchen's song from Goethe's *Faust* ; *Novelletten*
No. 3, as at first published, had a motto taken from *Macbeth*,
and ' Verrufene Stelle ' in *Waldscenen* has a motto from Hebbel.
Such things are meant to be merely accessories, indications of
the mood in which the piece is to be heard or interpreted.   Out
of a total of seventy-four instrumental pieces thirty-four have
characteristic titles and musical quotations.   In the majority
of instances the titles and inscriptions help to explain the mood
of the music.   It may be that the hearer misses his way if
he goes from the piece to the inscription or the qubtation,
but from the inscription to the piece the path is straight and

a knowledge of what is intended adds to the pleasure of
listening. The delicate touch of romanticism shows to perfection in pieces like *Des Abends*. This little masterpiece
conveys just that which music can convey, and words or
colours cannot. There is something new here, both in spirit
and in technique. In the latter respect the novelty lies in the
continuous contradiction of the prevailing $\frac{2}{8}$ time of the harmonic
accompaniment and the quaver triplets of the melody, to which
the constant use of the pedal adds a vague atmospheric effect;
a mere trifle, it may be, but complete and perfect in itself.
The companion piece entitled *Warum?* is equally good. Here
the charm lies in the syncopation of the accompaniment against
two responding parts which overlap, one phrase beginning
before the other has come to an end. There is no need to
dwell upon other such buds and flowers of poesy; but attention
must be called to Nos. 4 and 6 from *Kreisleriana*, 'Arlequin'
and 'Eusebius' from *Carneval*, 'In der Nacht' from *Phantasiestücke*, Op. 12, the Aria from the Sonata in F♯ minor,
the last of the Études symphoniques in G♯ minor, and, above
all, to those inimitable examples of musical miniature, the
Kinderscenen, Op. 15.

Apart from his Concerto in A minor, none of Schumann's
larger pianoforte works, i.e. the three Sonatas, the Études
symphoniques, the Phantasie in C, Op. 17, the *Faschingsschwank*, the *Humoreske*, Op. 20, the *Novelletten*, are entirely
without flaw or shortcoming. The power of invention and the
emotion displayed are astonishing; so is the wealth of detail
in rhythm, harmony, melody, and the persistency in the attempts
to produce new effects of sonority. But the formative power
is defective or imperfectly developed; the materials are not
completely welded together, the profusion of detail tends to
obscure or upset the balance, the structure shows a lack of
unity, the music is not so much an organic whole as it is a
fusion of parts, and, at times, the treatment of the instrument
leaves much to be desired. Indeed the key-board technique is

here and there so clumsy that the novel effects fail to be effective.

To make Schumann's pianoforte music sound right a far greater and more persistent use of the pedal is required than in the music of any earlier composer. He is generally content with the indication ' con pedale,' and leaves the application in detail to the executant. If the use of the pedal, no matter how frequent, were restricted to the sustaining of particular notes or harmonies there could be no objection; but if a composer chooses to sustain certain important notes or chords in defiance of the context and without regard to the ' muddy' confusion and contradiction of harmony which results, he wilfully does an injury to his cause. Compare for instance, Schumann's *Faschingsschwank*, the Intermezzo in E ♭ minor, bars fourteen and fifteen and bars twenty-nine and thirty, or Études symphoniques, No. VIII, the last four bars—where the blur of conflicting harmonies is the unavoidable result of the prescribed ' pedal obbligato,' and these bars cannot be played without the pedal. As instances of impracticable technical experiments see the Intermezzo entitled ' Paganini' (No. 16 of the *Carneval*), and note the chords *ff* and *pp* before the return ; other examples occur in the last twenty bars of *Kreisleriana*, No. 3, in the *Humoreske* (middle of the Intermezzo), and in the third section of the *Blumenstück*, where during some sixteen bars the thumb of the right hand is expected to hold down certain keys whilst the left hand is to touch the same keys *staccato*.

Of the three Sonatas (in F♯ minor, Op. 11; F minor, Op. 14; and G minor, Op. 22), the first two are the strongest and warmest ; the third is formally finished, but not very significant. The Adagio Introduction to the Sonata in F♯ minor, ' the most romantic of sonatas,' as Liszt was wont to call it, is full of passionate melody ; the Allegro which follows is forcible and vigorous, though, by a curious error of judgement, it reaches its emotional climax before the close required by the sonata form, and thus the interest declines at the very point where, with Beethoven, it would have been chiefly concentrated. This means that the design of the entire movement is feeble with regard to the distribution of key centres. The boisterous Scherzo has an intermezzo 'Alla Burla' and a burlesque instrumental recitative to lead back to the theme. The Finale contains fine points, notably the first subject and a coda of entrancing warmth; but it is long and patchy, there is evidence of its having been still longer in the first instance, and the shears seem to have been ruthlessly applied, so that the relative positions of key centres is even more anomalous than it is in the first Allegro. Compare the section in E♭ and in C with the context. For the absurd title of the Sonata in F minor, Op. 14, 'Concert sans orchestre,' Schumann disclaimed responsibility. The second edition presents a revised and partially rewritten text. In turn fiery, passionate, tender, humorous, the work covers a wide range of feeling, though it suffers from uniformity of key, all the movements being in F minor. As is the case with the first of the solo sonatas, the materials are not completely unified, and there is now and again a sense of incoherence.

The phrase that acts as a musical motto is part of the subject for the Variations that form the third movement. Under various disguises it appears throughout the work. Among these disguises the last of the variations is particularly interesting as a very characteristic and personal effusion—striking in its emotional sincerity.

The final Presto, a sort of Toccata akin to the Finales of
Beethoven's Op. 27 and 54, with its incessant, almost delirious
whirl of rapid semiquavers and the persistent rhythmical
anticipation with every change of chord, produces a disquieting
effect on the hearer[1]. The Andantino belonging to the Sonata
Op. 22, $\frac{6}{8}$, a moonlight scene 'mit allem romantischen Zubehör[2],'
is the best of the four movements, the final Rondo the weakest.
The *Novelletten*, a total of eight numbers, are pieces of an
illustrative kind—in some sense programme music. To the

[1] This movement is an extreme instance of the mechanically contrived effects of
anticipation and syncopation, of which Schumann was so fond. Compare the
long series of hardly interrupted syncopations in the middle of the first movement
of *Faschingsschwank*, Op. 26.

[2] Schumann's letter to Miss Laidlaw anent the *Phantasiestücke*, Op. 12.

exquisite little miniatures called *Kinderscenen* already mentioned may be added the second of the *Romanzen* (F ♯ major), the charming trifles contained in the *Album für die Jugend*, the *Albumblätter*, Op. 124, and the four-hand pieces, Op. 85.

The *Carneval*, so called by Schumann himself, consists for the most part of very clever variations on a rather unmusical theme of four notes—A, E ♭ (German Es), C, and B ♮ (German H); thus A-S-C-H, which notes, besides being the musical letters in Schumann's own name, also happen to spell the name of the birthplace of his friend Ernestine von Fricken [1]. These notes will be found embedded in most of the little pieces. The arrangement with a view to contrast, and the notion of a musical carnival, were an afterthought. The enigmatic presentation of the four notes as 'Sphinxes' is evidently intended as a joke in the manner of Jean Paul—a riddle without an answer [2]. J. S. Bach in his younger days set the example of using the letters of his name in this way, and Schumann took the hint in his six Fugues on the name of B-A-C-H, as did Liszt afterwards. The theme of Schumann's 'Abegg' variations, Op. 1, is a sort of musical acrostic belonging to the same style of experimental composition; so is the little *pièce d'occasion*, 'Greeting to Gade,' G-A-D-E, in the *Album für die Jugend*, and several others. The signatures Florestan and Eusebius (in imitation of Jean Paul's Walt und Wult) which Schumann appended to his critical articles, and which appear as *noms de guerre* in the *Davidsbündlertänze*, and the F ♯ minor Sonata, are meant to represent Schumann himself in his humorous and sentimental moods. The series of sketches entitled *Waldscenen*, already mentioned, contains one number, 'Einsame Blumen,' that in its delicate loveliness ranks high among the lesser pieces [3]. 'Canonische

---

[1] The 'Estrella' of the *Carneval*.

[2] Of course the breves are not meant to be played, though Anton Rubinstein used to bang them, slowly, fortissimo,—and look solemn.

[3] 'Gesänge der Frühe,' the latest publications for the pianoforte, belong to the last sad years that were darkened by Schumann's *genius ater*.

Studien' and 'Skizzen' for Pedalflügel, Op. 56 and 58, together with the six 'Bach' Fugues, Op. 60, for the organ, seven 'Characterstücke in Fughetten form' for pianoforte, Op. 126, are fruits of the special studies in Counterpoint that Schumann began to make about the middle of his career. They are all interesting; some, like the first of the Canonische Studien (a minor $\frac{12}{8}$) and Nos. 1 and 2 of the 'Bach' Fugues, are ingenious and beautiful.

As a composer of pianoforte music Schumann had but one superior among his contemporaries—Chopin, pre-eminently the poet of the piano, the genius of the instrument, who by divine instinct realized the impossible and hardly seemed conscious of the fact. There is in his best work a breath and glow as of the south wind. His fervour of spirit, the fire and force of his fancy, his pathos, and, in his lighter moods, his ease, grace, and consummate taste, are unique. Some part of his work, not a large part, appears over-refined, hectic, and morbid; a small part belongs to the Parisian salon; most is poetical work of a high order, perfect, not only in fragments and sporadically, but in entire pieces and entire groups of pieces. The music rings true. Chopin does not pose for pathos and emphasis. The sensitive delicacy of his nature kept him within the limits of courtesy and prompted him to shun the more violent accents of passion; his canon of taste was the result of his temperament. He shrank from the robust, open-air power of Beethoven and was now and then inclined to emphasize those elements that make for sensuousness. The most artistic of romanticists, he never forgot or over-stepped the limits of the art. He avoided everything that might seem pedantic, dogmatic, or theoretical. He had nothing to preach or teach, unless it be his own incommunicable gift of beauty. The fire of his genius increased in intensity as time went on. His skill 'in the use of the sieve for noble words' enriched his work and saved it from extravagance.

To a student, the perfect finish of Chopin's pieces affords

evidence of the care and labour that he expended upon them.
A comparison of the rather flimsy early pieces which were
published as *œuvres posthumes* with those that he published
himself, say from Op. 9 to Op. 65, inclusive, will suffice to
show that he rejected music enough to fill scores of pages. As
he was fond of types such as the Mazurka, the Polonaise,
the Nocturne, in which some sort of rhythmic and melodic
scheme is prescribed at the outset, he virtually set himself the
task of saying the same thing over and over again. Yet he
appears truly inexhaustible; each Impromptu, Prelude, Étude,
Nocturne, Scherzo, Ballade, Polonaise, Mazurka presents an
aspect of the subject not pointed out before; each has a
birthright of its own. Chopin indeed is one of the rarest
inventors, not only as regards the technicalities of pianoforte
playing, but as regards composition. Besides being a master
of his particular instrument, he is a singer in that high sense
in which Keats, and Coleridge, and Tennyson are singers. He
tells of new things well worth hearing, and finds new ways of
saying them. He is a master of style—a master of flexible
and delicate rhythm, a fascinating melodist, a subtle harmonist.
The emotions that he expresses are not of the highest: his
bias is always romantic and sentimental. In his earliest
productions his matter and manner are alike frequently weak;
in his latest now and then turgid. But in the bulk of his work,
be the sentiment what it may, he makes amends for any
apparent want of weight by the utmost refinement of diction.
With him the manner of doing a thing is the essence of the
thing done. He is ever careful to avoid melodic, rhythmic, or
harmonic commonplace; and he strove so hard to attain
refinement of harmony that in a few of his latest pieces, such,
for instance, as the Polonaise-Fantaisie, the Violoncello Sonata,
and the last set of Mazurkas, he appears to have spun his
progressions into useless niceties. The impressions Chopin
received in Poland during boyhood and youth remained the
principal sources of his inspiration. Personal impulses, later

on, added radiance and intensity to his expression of passion, but the influence of the Parisian environment is felt only in such pieces as the Valses, the Bolero, the Tarantella, and a few of the Nocturnes.

Seen on paper, much of Chopin's work appears to be unduly ornate. Frequently, indeed generally—except in the cantabile of the Nocturnes, Scherzos, and Sonatas—the thought is stated in terms of ornament. In consequence there is a softening and clouding of outlines and things look very complex on paper, but in performance the main lines stand forth clearly enough.

A considerable variety and novelty of form may be found in the collection of pieces such as Preludes, Études, Impromptus, Mazurkas, and Ballades; and, with the exception of the first movements of the Concertos and of the three Sonatas, Op. 35, 58, and 65 (the last of which is the Sonata with violoncello mentioned above), there is no shortcoming. A very delicate feeling for balance and proportion is generally present; no matter how novel the scheme or how complex the details, the outlines are simple, telling, and self-contained, requiring no title or explanation. Certain exceptional works, such as the Preludes in E minor and D minor, the Prelude, Op. 45, in C♯ minor, the Études in A minor and C minor, Op. 25, the Berceuse, the Barcarolle, the Nocturne in G major, Op. 37, No. 2, the Finale of the Sonata in B♭ minor, Op. 35, seem to mark a new departure, as of poems upon new lines. The art is here so complete that it disappears.

Beethoven excepted, Chopin invented more that is valuable in the way of pianoforte effect and the technical treatment of the instrument, than any of his predecessors or contemporaries. His pupils and other witnesses agree in using the same words to convey a notion of his mode of playing his own pieces: 'veiled, graduated, accentuated, evanescent,' 'the harmonic notes vaguely blending, yet the transitions from chord to chord and phrase to phrase clearly indicated,' 'ever-changing and undulating rhythms,' 'indescribable effects of chiaroscuro,' i.e.

effects of sustained tone produced with the aid of the pedals. Heine, who was intimate by instinct with the nuances of Chopin's musical expression and style of playing, speaks of him with becoming warmth: 'Not only does he shine as a virtuoso with a perfect technique, but he accomplishes things of the highest value as a composer. He belongs to the sphere of Mozart or of Raphael. His true home is the dreamland of poesy. When I hear him, I entirely forget the mastery of his pianoforte playing and sink into the sweet abysses of his music.' (*Heine-Schriften*, x. pp. 287 and 342.)

Of his solo sonatas two alone count: Op. 35 in B♭ minor and Op. 58 in B minor; the third in C minor (Op. 4) is an early and immature work which was published posthumously.

Op. 35, the sonata that contains the funeral march (published 1840), is a great composition, Chopin's own from the first note to the last. There is no hint as to the composer's meaning in the title of any of the movements; all that we know is that the extremely emotional music was called forth by the struggle for independence in Poland, and that the spiritual connexion of one movement with another is to be sought in this direction. The first movement conveys a sense of strife, of a resolve to conquer or to die. It is a true sonata movement, with the usual two contrasting subjects, a working-out section and a recapitulation. Then follows a fervent Scherzo, having something of the same fierce impulse in its leading part, with a *più lento* exquisitely tender and graceful; then the Marcia funebre, with the cantilena which we all know by heart; finally there is a wail, like the night wind's cry over the graves of vanquished men [1]. If this Finale is played exactly as Chopin directs—pianissimo and with hardly any gradation of tone—the effect produced is weird in the extreme. This is the movement of which Mendelssohn is reported to have said: 'Oh, I abhor it. There is no music—no art,' and of which Schumann asserted that it contained 'more mockery than music.' But

[1] Compare the Prelude in E♭ minor, Op. 28, No. 14.

supposing it to be on the verge of, or even outside the pale of
music proper, what is it to be called? It is a piece unique in
its way, and of a genius not less than that of the three movements
preceding it. Both Mendelssohn and Schumann seem to have
overlooked the fact that the little toccata is perfectly orthodox
in form [1]. The Sonata in B minor, Op. 58, published some
five years later (1845), is less concise and less well planned; this
is particularly the case in the first movement, of which the working-out section is as lax in design as overwrought in style, and
consequently somewhat chaotic in effect no matter how well
played. But the long-drawn-out melodies of the Allegro
maestoso and the Largo are remarkable even for Chopin, the
supreme master of elegiac cantilena. In such melodies of
Chopin there are frequent touches of Bellini—no note-for-note
resemblance, but obvious spiritual connexion. Such, for example, are the second subject of the first Allegro in Chopin's
E minor concerto; the corresponding passage in his B minor
Sonata, Op. 58; the long melody in D♭ of the Scherzo, Op. 31;
the melody that forms the trio of the *Marche funèbre*; the
principal melodies in the Nocturnes in F♯ and A♭ and C♯
minor; the second part of the Nocturne in B, Op. 9, No. 3;
the posthumous Impromptu in C♯ minor; the Prelude in D♭,
and many others.

The majority of Chopin's Études, unlike those of Clementi,
Cramer, and Moscheles, have no didactic purpose; the best are
characteristic pieces, studies for masters, not for pupils. The
'Etüden,' Op. 2 and 5 of Henselt, the 'Études d'exécution
transcendante' and 'Études de concert' of Liszt, may be said
to vie with them. But if we look for originality, beauty, and
variety of effect, Henselt's Studies are left far behind, and
Liszt's, though remarkable from a virtuoso's point of view, lack

---

[1] After four introductory bars it starts in the key of B♭ minor; with the
24th bar it moves on to something like a second subject in the relative major, D♭;
with the 39th bar the four introductory bars recur, and the return from the 43rd
bar to the end, in B♭ minor, forms a complete recapitulation of the first section.
The movement is in fact unified on the lines of certain Preludes of J. S. Bach.

the musical inspiration of Chopin's [1]. In a number of cases Chopin contrives to exhibit the theme of an Étude in different aspects and under different lights. The Étude in A♭, for instance (Op. 10, No. 10), weaves into a single texture the diverse aspects of the leading figure. Other such Études are Op. 25, Nos. 3 and 5. But, technicalities apart, the most glorious of the Études are the two in C minor, Op. 10, No. 12, and Op. 25, No. 12, and No. 11 in A minor, Op. 25—passionate lyrics in the form of studies. Some of the Preludes, Op. 28, many of them little tone-poems that convey something of a passing perfume, correspond in style with particular Études contained in Op. 10 and Op. 25, though with the exception of Nos. 8, 16, 19, and 24 (F♯ minor, E♭, B♭ minor, and D minor), which are Études in the full sense, they are but sketches [2].

The Impromptus, so called by Chopin, have some affinity to the Impromptus and Moments musicaux of Schubert; the exquisite melody and style are of course Chopin's own [3]. Two or three of the early Nocturnes, Op. 9, No. 2, parts of Op. 32, Nos. 1 and 2, show traces of Field [4], but in all the rest Chopin speaks in his own magical way. The Nocturne in G major, Op. 37, No. 2, is one of the most original and subtly beautiful pianoforte pieces extant. Other fine pieces are the Nocturnes in C♯ minor and D♭, Op. 27, the tragic Nocturne in C minor, Op. 48, No. 1, the dreamy and perhaps a little over-elaborated Nocturne in E major, Op. 62, No. 1, and the Duet-Nocturne in E♭, Op. 55, No. 2, to which professed students of Chopin

[1] In two instances, at any rate, Liszt's Études are Chopin at second hand. Compare Liszt's very clever ' Étude de concert ' in F minor (No. 2) and the ' Étude d'exécution transcendante ' (No. 10) with Chopin's two Études in the same key. Henselt too imitates and dilutes Chopin—witness Études, Op. 5, Nos. 2, 9, and 10.

[2] Taken as sketches they may be compared with the second and third set of Beethoven's ' Bagatelles '—merely experiments, it may be, but of high value.

[3] Compare Schubert's Moment musical, No. 4 in C♯ minor, with Chopin's fourth Impromptu, the posthumous one, also in C♯ minor.

[4] As Leopardi's darker mood reflects the pessimism of Byron, so Chopin's elegiac melancholy is closely in touch with that of Field and Bellini.

have not yet given the attention that it deserves. 'I do not care for the Ladies'-Chopin,' Wagner remarked in 1877, 'there is too much of the Parisian salon in that'; but, whether one cares for the salon or not, the wit and finesse of French society seem to be more accurately caught and reflected in some of Chopin's lighter pieces than anywhere else in art. Undoubtedly, within these confines of elegance and pleasant trifling, Chopin is unrivalled. But let no one suppose that the true weight and significance of his music is to be found there.

It is difficult to say anything adequate of that glorification of Polish national music which Chopin has accomplished in his Polonaises and Mazurkas. The latter range from mere *jeux d'esprit* to highly elaborated pieces. Some of the Polonaises, such as those in A, C minor, A♭ and F minor, are grandiose pictures of pomp and pageantry. In both Mazurkas and Polonaises melodic and rhythmical idioms belonging to Eastern Europe abound. To a western ear some of the exotic melodies based on unfamiliar scales and the resulting harmonies sound strangely impressive. The impulsive rhythm, the delirious swirl, or the languor of certain Mazurkas (Nos. 39, 3, 10–13, 40, 22, 23, 29–32), the dithyrambic enthusiasm, the barbaric din and clang, of certain Polonaises (A♭, F♯ minor, Op. 53 and 44), convey impressions as of oriental exaltation, languid sensuousness, militant enthusiasm, or dithyrambic excess. Compared with the fresh open-air spirit of Beethoven's Scherzos, the burly humour of Schumann's, the bustle of Mendelssohn's, Chopin seems to have struck a new vein; he invented the sardonic Scherzo. In the four pieces which he calls by this title, the music has an air of impatience and questioning irony that alternates with moments of dreamy pathos. A fifth Scherzo, the best of all, that in E♭ minor, contained in the Sonata, Op. 35, already mentioned, belongs to this group. It is remarkable for conciseness, for concentrated energy, and for the strange grace of the trio —four-bar and five-bar rhythms overlapping. In the Barcarolle, the Berceuse, and the Ballades—pieces of an illustrative cast, experiments with an unwritten but implied programme—Chopin discovered a form of expression peculiar to himself; the music, especially in the Ballades, appeals to the imagination, like a narrative poem. The third Ballade, in A♭, is the most perfect as a well-balanced and carefully-designed piece; the second, in F, is the most fascinating and fantastic—one longs for a clue to the mysterious tale which the music unfolds; the first is perhaps the most impassioned; the fourth is the most elaborate, as it is the richest. Certain harmonies that look unfamiliar in Chopin's text because of the complex notation with all manner of accidentals, sound like pure chords[1]. The practice of employing transient chromatic harmonies in the same manner as transient chromatic single notes or groups of notes began with Chopin, as, for instance, in the trio of the Polonaise, Op. 40. It has been much extended by later composers, notably by Wagner in *Tristan und Isolde* and in *Parsifal*.

Chopin always kept a metronome on his teaching piano. His *tempo rubato* was not an eccentric swaying to and fro in point of speed. 'The singing hand,' he taught, 'may deviate—the accompanying hand must keep time.' 'Fancy a tree with all its branches swayed by the wind—the stem is the steady time, the moving leaves are the melodic inflexions[2].' It follows that certain readings of Chopin, which are dear to the heart of many a virtuoso, must be discarded as caricatures. He disliked exaggerated accentuation: 'It produces an effect of didactic pedantry.' 'You must *sing* if you wish to play—hear good singers and learn to sing yourself.'

Since the expiration of the copyrights, Chopin's text has suffered much at the hands of editors. It is true that Chopin's method of notation does not always express the full musical sense, inasmuch as the effects of sustained sound, which are

[1] Compare the Barcarolle, the Sonata in B minor, first movement, the Polonaise-Fantaisie.

[2] This saying is vouched for by Liszt.

best gained by the use of the pedal, are written out only in so far as the player's finger can hold down the key. In like manner his notation of fioriture, consisting of an irregular number of delicate grace-notes, expresses exactly what the fingers are to do, but no more. Nor is anything more desirable. Attempts to write out note-values in full, or to group the little ornamental notes so as to fit them into the time of the bar, are thoroughly misleading, for they tend to destroy the graceful ease of the music and to foster pedantry on the part of the executants. Tellefsen's presentation of the text, based upon Parisian proof-copies (the only proofs read by Chopin himself), is perfunctory and insufficiently revised for the press. Klindworth's valuable edition, a marvel of careful musical philology, contains too much of the editor's own views as to details of notation, fingering, &c.; it is Chopin seen through the temperament of a very masterful editor. The only recent edition free from undue interference with the notation, valuable also as a partial [1] record of Chopin's peculiarities in the matter of fingering, pedalling, and the like, is that of Mikuli, the last of the master's professional pupils.

Chopin and Liszt, as pianists and composers for the pianoforte, have often been compared. Facing the audience Liszt was triumphant. But when it is asserted that Liszt has outstripped Chopin as a composer for the instrument we must protest—the fact being that Liszt, in many instances, is but the imitator or the exaggerator of Chopin. Liszt's publications for the pianoforte solo may be ranged thus: I. *Fantaisies dramatiques*. II. *Années de pèlerinage*. III. *Harmonies poétiques et religieuses*. IV. Sonata, Concertos, Études, and miscellaneous works. V. *Rhapsodies hongroises*. VI. Partitions de piano of Berlioz and Beethoven's Symphonies, Beethoven's and Weber's Overtures, &c.; Transcriptions of Paganini's Caprices, Rossini's Soirées musicales, Schubert's Soirées de

---

[1] Frequently when Mikuli has no authentic materials as to fingering, he falls back upon Klindworth; hence certain inconsistencies.

Vienne (Valses), Songs by Schubert, Schumann, Robert Franz, arrangements for two pianos of Beethoven's ninth symphony, Beethoven's Concertos in C minor, G, and E♭ ; and also the majority of Liszt's own orchestral pieces [1].

Liszt was always ready to make speculative experiments in form. The earliest of these were the 'Fantaisies dramatiques,' which belong to the period of his early manhood, 1830-49-50, when he led the life of a travelling virtuoso. These pieces derive from the 'Variations brillantes' and 'Variations de concert,' mainly on operatic tunes, which were equally beloved by the virtuosi and the public of those days. Starting from such facile types Liszt added an Intrada, certain connecting links to make the design continuous, and a Finale. The idea was to combine the tunes and variations in such wise that the entire piece, from the introduction to the final climax, should consist of a crescendo of effects reproducing the mood of some dramatic situation or condensing an entire act. By means of dazzling execution and the personal magic of Liszt himself, some of these fantasias, such as *Norma*, *Sonnambula*, *Robert le Diable*, and *Don Juan*, took the musical world by storm. As the vogue of the theme wanes the chances of arresting the attention of an average audience diminish. Still the beauty of certain melodies such as Mozart's 'La ci darem la mano' and the Finale of Bellini's *Norma* will support Liszt's pianoforte effects for a long while to come. From the virtuoso's point of view, the technical difficulties contained in the fantasias remain as a supreme test of the executant's efficiency. Liszt exhibits true fancy in the general arrangement, and remarkable cleverness in the treatment of finger and wrist. The most celebrated of the fantasias, *Don Juan*, apart from its merits as a piece of display, is really interesting as a composition. Liszt takes Mozart's entire duet

---

[1] At Rome in 1839 Liszt, finding no proper partner for ensemble music, gave the first of those pianoforte recitals of which we have since felt the benefit and the boredom. In his case the 'ennuyeux *soliloques* musicaux,' as he frankly called them, were entirely a one-man show, executant and composer combined.

'La ci darem la mano' for the subject of his variations, and frames them by means of an Intrada, derived from the overture to *Don Giovanni* and a final presto based on the Brindisi from the third act. The whole piece is well designed and leaves nothing to be desired in consistency and unity of effect. The fantasias, *Robert le Diable, Norma, La Sonnambula,* and others, contain clever combinations of two or three different tunes played simultaneously—a virtuoso trick contrived in imitation of Berlioz' practice of dovetailing diverse melodies and rhythms [1].

Taking into account the restricted possibilities of the keyboard and the difficulties which arise from it, the following bars from *La Sonnambula* show the highest degree of manipulative ingenuity. They contain a combination of two tunes and a staccato bass, with a persistent trill at the top.

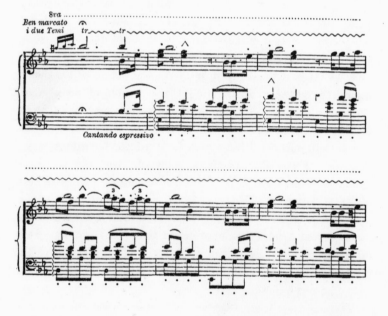

---

[1] For examples of Berlioz' methods see pp. 120, 125.

A curiosity called *Hexameron*, 1837, which bears Liszt's
name and is included in the thematic catalogue of his works,
claims a few words. It consists of a series of variations on
a melody known as 'La Marche des Puritains' from Bellini's
I Puritani; the variations were composed and played upon six
pianofortes by six pianists of repute : five played on full grands,
Chopin sat at a two-stringed semi-grand. Liszt contributed the
Intrada, the connecting links, and the Finale ; the others one
variation each. Chopin's variation, a little Larghetto in E major,
17 bars of square time, shines like a gem set in pinchbeck.

Les Années de pèlerinage, published in three divisions, bear
dates ranging from 1835 to 1883. For the most part the pieces
are but slight sketches—several among them, belonging to the
first division, are strikingly true to nature and suggestive.
They appear to be records of impressions directly derived from
natural sights and sounds—the beginnings of what may be called
l'impressionisme musical. The charm of such trifles as 'Au
lac de Wallenstadt,' 'Pastorale,' 'Au bord d'une source' is
indefinable. For adroitness and elegance in the treatment of
the pianoforte it would be difficult to match the latter piece.
Personal effusions, like 'Tre Sonetti di Petrarca,' which belong
to the second division and are transcriptions for the pianoforte
of certain melodies set to Petrarca's sonnets, have the peculiarly
Italian note of ecstasy that distinguishes the melodies of Bellini.
Other pieces, like 'Sposalizio,' after Raphael's picture in the
Brera Gallery at Milan, 'Il Penseroso,' after Michael Angelo,

' D'après une lecture de Dante,' after a poem by Victor Hugo so entitled, show the first attempts at illustration made by the great musical illustrator. The third division of *Les Années* is a collection of lesser value belonging to Liszt's old age. *Harmonies poétiques et religieuses*, of which No. 1, ' Bénédiction de Dieu dans la solitude,' and No. 10, 'Cantique d'amour,' are the best, is made up partly of transcriptions of vocal pieces and partly of attempts at the illustration of poetry. All have descriptive titles or mottoes in verse. A set of six little pieces called ' Consolations,' belonging to Liszt's prime, about 1850, may be taken as corollaries to the Harmonies. Distinguished by a dreamy personal note, the meditative and pious ' Consolations ' take as high a rank among Liszt's pieces as the naïve *Kinderscenen* among Schumann's. Nothing better than these little sets of miniatures could be found to exhibit the two composers' widely divergent temper and mode of work.

The Études, which head the thematic catalogue of Liszt's works, show, better than anything else, the transformation his style has undergone; and for this reason it may be well to trace the growth of some of them [1]. ' Études en douze exercices, par François Liszt, Op. 1,' were published at Marseilles in 1827. They were written during the previous year, Liszt being then under sixteen. The second set of Études, 'dédiées à Monsieur Charles Czerny,' appeared in 1839, but were cancelled ; and the 'Études d'exécution transcendante,' again dedicated to Czerny, ' en témoignage de reconnaissance et de respectueuse amitié de son élève,' appeared in 1852. The now cancelled copy of the Études which Schumann had before him in 1839, when he wrote his brilliant article [2], shows these studies to be more extravagant and, in some instances, technically more difficult than even the final version. The germs of both the new versions are to be seen in the Op. 1 of 1827. Schumann transcribed a couple of

---

[1] With the permission of Messrs. Augener & Co. the above paragraph regarding the ' Études d'exécution transcendante ' is quoted from the preface to the complete edition of Liszt's Études which the present writer prepared for them in 1899.

[2] *Gesammelte Schriften*, iii, pp. 166–8.

bars from the beginning of Nos. 1, 5, 9, and 11, from both the
new and the old copies, and offered a few of his swift and apt
comments. The various changes in these Études may be taken
to represent the history of the pianoforte during the last half of
the nineteenth century, from the 'Viennese Square' to the
concert grand, from Czerny's *Schule der Geläufigkeit* to
Liszt's *Danse macabre.* Czerny might have written the
original exercise No. 1, but it would not have been so shapely
a thing as Liszt's final version. The difference between the two
versions of No. 1 is, however, considerably less than that which
separates Nos. 2, 3, and 4 from their predecessors. If the
earlier and the later versions of No. 3 in F and No. 4 in
D minor were signed by different composers, the resemblance
between them would hardly attract notice. Of No. 2 little
remains as it stood at first. Instead of a reduction there is an
increase (38 to 102) in the number of bars. Some harmonic
commonplaces which disfigure the original, as, for instance, the
detour to C (bars 9-16), have been removed. The remainder is
enlarged, so as to allow of more extensive modulation, and thus
to avoid redundancy. A short introduction and a coda are
added, and the diction throughout is thrown into high relief.
'Paysage,' No. 3 in F, has been subjected to further alteration
since Schumann wrote about it. In his article he commends
the second version as being more interesting than the first, and
points to a change of movement from square to triple time, and
to the melody which is superadded, as improvements. On the
other hand he calls an episode in A major 'comparatively trivial,'
and this, it may be noticed, is omitted in the final version. As
it now stands, the piece is a test study for pianists who aim at
refinement of style, tone, and touch. The Étude entitled
'Mazeppa' is particularly characteristic of Liszt's power of
endurance at the instrument, and it exhibits the gradual growth
of his manner, from pianoforte exercises to symphonic poems
in the manner of Berlioz. It was this Étude, together perhaps
with Nos. 7 ('Vision'), 8 ('Wilde Jagd'), and 12 ('Chasse-neige'),

that induced Schumann to speak of the entire set as 'Wahre
Sturm- und Graus-Etüden' (Studies of storm and dread), studies
for, at the most, ten or twelve players in the world[1]. The
original of No. 5, in B♭, is a mere trifle, in the manner of J. B.
Cramer—the final version entitled 'Feux follets' is one of the
most remarkable transformations extant, and perhaps the best
study of the entire series, consistent in point of musical design
and full of delicate technical contrivances. 'Ricordanza,' No. 9,
and 'Harmonies du soir,' No. 11, may be grouped together as
showing how a musical 'Stimmungsbild' (a picture of a mood
or an expression of sentiment) can be evoked from rather trite
beginnings. Schumann speaks of the melody in E major, which
occurs in the middle of the latter piece, as 'the most sincerely
felt'; and in the last version it is much improved. Both pieces,
'Ricordanza' and 'Harmonies du soir,' show to perfection the
sonority of the instrument in its various aspects. The latter
piece, 'Harmonies du soir' in the first, as well as in the final
version, appears as a kind of Nocturne. No. 10, again, begins as
though it were Czerny's (*a*), and in the cancelled edition is
developed into an Étude of almost insuperable difficulty (*b*).
As finally rewritten, this study is possible to play and well worth
playing (*c*).

---

[1] This is no longer the case; we might multiply the twelve by ten and still be
below the number, so much has the mastery over the mechanical difficulties of
pianoforte-playing increased of late.

No. 12 also has been recast and much manipulated, but there is no mending of weak timber. We must also mention 'Ab Irato,' an Étude in E minor cancelled and entirely rewritten; three Études de concert (the second of which has already been mentioned as Chopinesque); and two fine Études, much later in date and of moderate difficulty, 'Waldesrauschen' and 'Gnomentanz.' The Paganini Studies, i. e. transcriptions in rivalry with Schumann of certain Caprices for the violin by Paganini, and far superior to Schumann's, do not call for detailed comment. They were several times rewritten (final edition, 1852) as Liszt, the virtuoso, came to distinguish between proper pianoforte effects and mere haphazard bravura,

and also, as the pianoforte makers afforded him better opportunities in point of touch and carrying power.

About Liszt's technique as pianist and composer of pianoforte music, it may be said that it rests on the teaching of
Czerny, who brought up his pupil on Mozart, a little Bach, more
of Hummel and still more of Czerny himself. Hummel, the solid
respectable classic, on the one hand, and Carl Czerny—a trifle
flippant perhaps, and inclined to appeal to the gallery—on the
other: these are the musical ancestors of the young Liszt.
Then appears the Parisian *incroyable* and grand seigneur; then
the imitator of Paganini and Chopin; and last the passionate
and devoted student of Beethoven, Weber, Schubert, and
Berlioz. Thus gradually there develops the mature master who,
both as player and composer, bore to the end of his days the
double marks of his origin [1].

Taken together with the Concertos, Liszt's ambitious Sonata
in one movement, B minor ('Sonate in einem Satz, an Robert
Schumann'), completely represents him in his more serious and
manly mood. Études and *Rhapsodies hongroises* apart, it
shows the ripest phase of his technique both as pianist and
composer. The scheme consists of a novel and rather speculative device, akin to that of the Concertos; that is to say, the
composer strives for unity by employing single phrases in quick
as well as in slow time, and by arranging the materials so as to
make a continuous movement of the entire piece. And in the

---

[1] From about 1863 onwards the writer has at times had the good fortune to
hear Liszt play, in private, pieces of such various descriptions as the following:
a number of Bach's Preludes and Fugues and single movements from the five later
and several of the earlier sonatas of Beethoven, bits of Chopin, some of his own
Rhapsodies, transcriptions from Schubert's '*Divertissement à la Hongroise*,' sundry
valses by Schubert, fragments from his own operatic fantasias, &c. There was
an air of improvisation about his playing—the expression of a fine and grand
personality—perfect self-possession, grace, dignity, and never-failing fire. His
tone was large and penetrating, but not hard; and every effect was produced naturally
and easily. Performances, it may be of the same pieces, by younger men, such as
Rubinstein or Tausig, left an impression as of Liszt at second hand, or of Liszt
past his prime. None of Liszt's contemporaries or pupils were so spontaneous,
individual and convincing in their playing; and none, except Tausig, so infallible
with their fingers and wrists.

case of this sonata as in the Concertos already discussed he does so on consistent musical lines without reference to a programme. The work is a curious compound of true genius and empty rhetoric, which contains enough of genuine impulse and originality in the themes of the opening section, and of suave charm in the melody of the section that stands for the slow movement, to secure the hearer's attention. Signs of weakness occur only in the centre, where, according to his wont, Liszt seems unable to resist the temptation to tear passion to tatters and strain oratory to bombast. None the less the Sonata is an interesting study, eminently successful in parts, and well worthy the attention of pianists.

Two Ballades, a Berceuse, a Valse-impromptu, a Mazurka, and two Polonaises sink irretrievably if compared with Chopin's pieces similarly entitled. The 'Scherzo und Marsch,' in D minor, an inordinately difficult and somewhat dry piece, falls short of its aim. Two legends, ' St. Francis of Assisi preaching to the birds,' a clever and delicate piece, and ' St. Francis of Paula stepping on the waves,' a kind of Étude, are examples of picturesque and decorous programme-music.

At the present day Liszt's reputation as a composer of pianoforte music rests largely upon the success of his *Rhapsodies hongroises*. These transcriptions of Hungarian songs and dances, ostentatiously rhythmical, and by no means discreet in character, are the most dazzling of show pieces in the hands of virtuosi. The arrangement of some of them for full orchestra has doubled their brilliancy and increased their intoxicating effect.

Liszt adopts the incisive Hungarian tunes as the itinerant gipsy bands are wont to play them; he finds many ingenious modes of imitating the orgiastic sounds of the cymbalon and ably develops the luxurious semi-oriental ornamentation and the crude harmony[1]. The Rhapsodies, starting from short transcriptions of Hungarian tunes, were elaborated at intervals,

---

[1] It seems worth while to add here that Brahms, in his Ungarische Tänze and all other movements that show the Hungarian influence, was careful to preserve

published, cancelled, rewritten, and republished in some cases
three times over. Schubert's *Divertissement à la Hongroise*
was the prototype of Liszt's *Ungarische Melodien*, which
began to appear in 1838; *Mélodies hongroises* followed in
1846; the final version, entitled *Rhapsodies hongroises*, in
1854; this consists of a total of fifteen pieces, ending with the
' Rakoczy March [1],' and was accompanied by a curious attempt
to prove the existence of a Gipsy epic.

In the so-called ' Partitions de piano,' transcriptions reproducing orchestral effects as closely as the pianoforte permits and
without regard to difficulties of execution, Liszt has accomplished
some of his best work. The task he set himself was akin to
that of an engraver, who must have knowledge of the painter's
and designer's art ere he can hope to apply his own technique
to advantage. It is astonishing to find how well Liszt succeeded
in the apparently impossible cases of Berlioz' *Symphonie
fantastique* and *Harold en Italie*. The transcriptions of
Beethoven's first eight symphonies, for pianoforte solo, and
especially that of the ninth (choral), as well as those of the three
Pianoforte Concertos in C minor, G, and E♭, for two pianofortes,
are marvels of skill. So are the transcriptions of Beethoven's and
Weber's overtures, the overtures to Berlioz' *Francs Juges* and to
Wagner's *Tannhäuser*, and of sundry other pieces culled from
Lohengrin, Tannhäuser, Der fliegende Holländer, Tristan, and *Die
Meistersinger*. Together with the ' Partitions de piano ' certain
arrangements for orchestra deserve to be mentioned, such as
the arrangement of Schubert's Fantasia in C, set out so as to
serve as a pianoforte concerto ; Weber's Polacca in E, to serve
as a concert-piece with orchestra, the instrumentation of Schubert's ' Marches à quatre mains,' and the accompaniments to
some of Schubert's songs.

the principal rhythmical and melodic characteristics of Hungarian music; that he
generally reproduced them in his own firm idiom, and very rarely touched upon the
Gipsy vernacular.

[1] Later additions to the number, all feeble, are of no account, be they authentic
or not.

Liszt was also a master in the notation of pianoforte music —a very difficult matter indeed, and one in which even Chopin frequently erred[1]. His method of notation coincides in the main with that of Beethoven, Berlioz, Wagner, and Brahms. Let the player accurately play what is set down and the result will be satisfactory. The perspicuity of certain pages of Liszt's mature pianoforte pieces, such as the first two sets of *Années de pèlerinage*, Consolations, Sonata in B minor, the Concertos, the *Danse macabre*, and the *Rhapsodies hongroises*, cannot be surpassed. His notation often represents a condensed score, and every rest not absolutely necessary is avoided ; again, no attempt is made to get a semblance of an agreement between the rhythmic division of the bar and the freedom of certain rapid ornamental passages, but, on the other hand, everything essential to the rendering of accent or melody, to the position of the hands on the key-board, to the details of special fingering and special pedalling, is faithfully recorded. Thus the most complex difficulties, as in the Fantaisies dramatiques, and even apparently uncontrollable effects of *tempo rubato*, as in the first fifteen Rhapsodies or the Étude 'Ricordanza,' or the 'Tre Sonetti di Petrarca,' are so closely indicated that the particular effect intended cannot be mistaken. One simple example of the notation of *tempo rubato* will suffice to show the method. In the vocal version of the first Sonnet (recently republished with the composer's latest emendation) the effects are obtained by the contrasting rhythms of the voice-part and the accompaniment (*a*), and a corresponding effect in the pianoforte transcription by means of slightly delaying the main notes of the melody (*b*).

---

[1] As he did in the second part of the Nocturne in F♯, Op. 15, No. 2 ; and in which Schumann frequently showed himself regardless of practical expediency— as, for instance, in the first Intermezzo belonging to *Kreisleriana*, No. II, where what is intended for both hands is crowded into the lower stave, whilst the upper stave is left empty, or in *Novelletten*, V. (Vol. iv. p. 55 of Madame Schumann's edition), where, besides the perversely crabbed diction, a most awkward task is assigned to th left hand.

CHAPTER XII

THE romantic problem, the many-sided question of an equipoise between poesy and music, has presented itself under various aspects again and again since Beethoven's time. One important side of it, the relation of verse to music and of music to verse, is best studied in connexion with the German Lied, in which direct appeal to the heart of man is made by the fusion of the two. In countless instances attempts at such an alliance or interchange of forces have failed, chiefly for the reason that lyric verse possesses greater rapidity of movement than music. Even with the Germans, whose lyric poetry is closely akin to the folksong and therefore best fitted to associate with music, instances of complete success, such as Schubert's *Gretchen am Spinnrade*, Schumann's *Frühlingsnacht*, Mendelssohn's *Frühlingslied, Durch den Wald,* Robert Franz' *Zu Strassburg auf der Schanz* and *Stille Sicherheit,* Wagner's *Träume,* Brahms' *Wann der silberne Mond, Feldeinsamkeit,* and *Wie rafft' ich mich auf in der Nacht,* are by no means common. Another reason is that poets often aim at effects resembling actual vocalization—as Tennyson does in that despair of composers, the ' Bugle Song '—or cast their stanzas in epigrammatic form with the point at the end, in which case the composer is at a loss, and must pass on to something else ere he can bring his melody to a satisfactory conclusion. On the musician's side it may be contended that the musical exposition, inasmuch as it is more protracted, makes a stronger appeal to the senses and therefore acts more powerfully on the emotions than verse alone.

Thus, for instance, the music in Brahms' song *Wie rafft' ich mich auf in der Nacht*, just mentioned, enforces the passion and melody of Platen's verse in a truly wonderful manner. But in every case the balance between the poetical and the musical factors is a matter of considerable difficulty, and a completely successful fusion is a rare achievement.

Apart from Brahms, who belongs to a later period, Schumann taken at his best is the greatest composer of songs after Schubert. When composing a song he was always instinctively guided by the idea rather than by any traditional conventions. Whether he utters a poet's passion or his own personal cry, Schumann is true and strong. In a supreme degree his best Lieder, such as *Widmung, Über'm Garten durch die Lüfte, Mondnacht, Die Lotosblume, Schöne Fremde, Er der herrlichste von allen, Waldesgespräch*, possess the rare quality which Wordsworth failed to discover in certain metrical works of Goethe's old age—absolute spontaneity. 'The verses are not inevitable enough' was Wordsworth's way of putting it. But the lyrical pathos of Schumann's songs is indeed inevitable, original, spontaneous. Schumann produced the bulk of his Lieder in 1840, the year of his marriage. Saturated as he was with German romantic literature—Jean Paul Richter, E. T. A. Hoffmann, translations of Byron and Moore, Eichendorff, Heine, Rückert—saturated still more with the emotional music of his predilection, Schubert, Beethoven, Chopin, he was often able to produce two or three songs in a single day. With him each song is the full musical utterance of the poem, without sacrifice of meaning and without repetition of words. The principal inflexions of the voice-part spring directly from the words, and every subtlety is emphasized by characteristic harmony or reiterated figures of accompaniment, or by some significant prelude, interlude, or coda. The balance between the voice and the instrument is well maintained, each factor makes for definite articulation and contributes towards a consistent and homogeneous whole. Thus the majority of Schumann's Lieder are

convincing as the direct utterance of his personal feeling [1].
Among the less well-known songs there is occasionally a touch
of weak ecstasy, as in *Du Rose meines Herzens*; or of pedantry,
as in *Räthsel*, where the singer is made to sing of ' Gottes-
gelehrtheit und Philosophie' (*Myrthen*, No. 16), or *Zahnweh*,
Op. 55, No. 2 ; or of sentimentality, as in *Frauenliebe und Leben*,
No. 6, where there is something artistically wrong that invites
parody. In certain other songs of a Spanish type, e. g. *Der
Hidalgo* (Op. 30, No. 3), *Der Contrabandista* (sequel to Op. 74),
as well as in the sets of songs, duets, and quartets, called
Spanische Liebeslieder, Op. 138, it is to be feared that Schumann
produced *de l'Andalou de Leipzig*.

Schumann, in his Lieder and choral pieces, was the first of
the Germans who troubled about correct declamation. Before
him, neither in opera nor in simple songs did any one take
offence at prosodical absurdities ; and it is significant that
Weber, Marschner, and Mendelssohn—educated men, and not
devoid of humour—should have allowed so many anomalies to
pass. The source of many a curious instance of obtuseness in
this respect—composers, singers, and the public are alike
implicated—may be sought in the fact that the tunes of German
popular songs and chorales, from Luther's time downwards,
were generally older, often much older, than the words.
Throughout the history of music, and not in Germany alone, it
has been a common practice to fit new words to old tunes—as,
for instance, Moore did in his *Irish Melodies*—and nobody seems
to have cared whether or not the words and the tune meet on
equal terms. To this, again, must be added the universal habit
of singing successive stanzas to the same tune, as in the German

---

[1] And, as he was the most German of contemporary musicians, and the most
intimately connected with his own language, it would seem to follow that they
had better not be sung in translation. Translations of German romantic songs, be
they ever so faithful, are heavily handicapped because the musical and verbal effects
belong together. Any translation of Schubert's *Du bist die Ruh, Sei mir
gegrüsst, Der Wanderer, Der Erlkönig*, Schumann's *Mondnacht*, Brahms' *Feldeinsamkeit*,
or Wagner's *Träume*, is foredoomed to failure.

Balladen of Zumsteeg and Zelter, or in many of the sea songs of Dibdin.

Compared with Schumann's method, the connexion of the melody with the verse in Mendelssohn's songs is rather lax. The melody reflects the mood of the poem well enough, but it rarely starts directly from the sound and sense of the words. Always facile, graceful, delicately refined, the music seems to stand aloof from the verse, and in many cases it appears as though either the words or the tune might be other than they are. This severance of verse and music marks Mendelssohn's songs as distinctly inferior to Schumann's; though the best of them show a mastery of their own which, from a vocalist's point of view, is supreme—as is the case, for instance, in the setting of Lenau's *Frühlingslied*, Goethe's Suleika I: *Ach, um deine feuchten Schwingen, West, wie sehr ich dich beneide,* and Suleika II: *Was bedeutet die Bewegung?* In like manner the setting of Heine's *Auf Flügeln des Gesanges* is above praise as a vocal expression of the mood of the poem. Yet nevertheless, cases where Mendelssohn's melody chimes perfectly with the words are all too infrequent. Perhaps *Frage*, Op. 9, No. 1, shows him at his best in this respect—and a prosodical blunder such as *Frühlingsmächtig* in Op. 47, No. 3, at his worst.

There is the same difference between the vocal duets of Schumann and Mendelssohn as between their songs. Schumann's melody, in the treatment of the vocal parts, is more emotional and more closely in connexion with the words, whilst Mendelssohn's is more effective from the singer's point of view. In the department of vocal quartets and part-songs without accompaniment, Mendelssohn's choral mastery shows to advantage; he proves himself superior in point of choral technique quite as clearly as in the choruses of the oratorios and cantatas [1]. Mendelssohn's productions in song form embrace eighty-three solo songs, thirteen duets, twenty-eight quartets for

---

[1] Some of the weaker songs of Op. 8 and 9 (Nos. 2, 3, 4, and 7, 10, 12, respectively) are by his elder sister, Fanny Hensel.

mixed voices, and seventeen quartets for male voices. *Wer hat dich, du schöner Wald*, one of his four-part songs for male voices, has become a folk-song in Germany.

Robert Franz's [1] *Lieder und Gesänge*, forty-four books in all, containing some 340 numbers, have compelled the admiration but failed to elicit the full sympathy of later musicians. Finished in structure and technique, they lack the human sympathy of Schumann, the fluency of Mendelssohn, the weight and power of Brahms. Apart from three or four spontaneous outbursts, such as the celebrated *Er ist gekommen* and the less well-known *Völker, spielt auf*, Op. 27, No. 1, Franz is subtle, delicate, contemplative; he often exhibits a note of resignation or of quietism—derived, it would seem, from the *Freylinghäuser Gesang-Buch*, the hymn-book of the later Protestant Pietists, so well known to J. S. Bach. Complete unity of expression was Franz's aim. A song, with him, is intended to be the reproduction of a single mood, simple or complex, and all the factors, voice and verse, melody, harmony, figures of accompaniment, are co-ordinated and made to contribute their share towards the end in view. Most of Franz's songs come and go like a gleam—they are nearly all too short and frail for performance in public. The matter is ingenious in weaving up the voice parts and the accompaniment without interfering with the flow of the words. ' I merely illustrate the words, and my music does not pretend to be much by itself. In this respect my Opus 1 is no better and no worse than my last ' (Opus 52). Franz is in fact generally content with the articulation of the poem, supplemented by a rather complex pianoforte part. Technically, he is a master in the fullest sense. But impulse is impulse, and he had little of it. Compared with Schubert, and still more with Schumann, he is impersonal and, in so far, weaker than they. He fails in personal charm, and his pathos at its most touching (e. g. *Verfehltes Lieben, verfehltes Leben*, Op. 20, No. 3) strikes the

---

' *Recte* Knauth, 1815–92.

hearer as somewhat factitious. A sense of weakness is almost
always present when Franz unites his music to verse by his
friend Osterwald. He is at his best when he sets Lenau's,
Heine's, or Goethe's verse; as in the following example:—

fan - den den Weg zur Trau - ten, doch kom - men sie wie - der und

kla - gen, und kla - gen und wol - len nicht sa - gen, was

sie im Her - zen schau - - - ten.

To understand Franz's ideal, his setting of Tieck's *Ruhe, Süss-liebchen, im Schatten der Matten*, Op. 10, may be compared with Brahms' treatment of the same words (*Romanzen aus Tiecks Magelone*, Op. 33, No. 9), or his setting of Lenau's *Durch den Wald, den dunklen, geht*, Op. 52, with Mendelssohn's in the *Frühlingslied* already mentioned. Franz usually expresses his sentiment in a rather complex and somewhat laboured manner, apparently natural to himself. His style is an amalgam of Bach, Handel, Schubert, Schumann, the German folk-song, and the Lutheran chorale,—all of which Franz, from time to time, absorbed and reproduced in his own way. Hence, the quasi-abstract, scholastic sound of so much of his work. He was, in fact, essentially a scholar, and much of his most congenial work is to be found in his textual commentary on the scores of Bach and Handel.

Of a very different character are the pieces written by Berlioz, Liszt, and Wagner for solo voice with the accompaniment of pianoforte or small orchestra. The songs of Schumann and Franz are effusions belonging more or less to the intimacy of private life, whereas the aim of Berlioz and Liszt was to meet the requirements of singers or actors in the concert-room. Berlioz offers the Chanson and the pathetic Arioso; Liszt both the Chanson and the German Lied, or the Lied expanded to a short scena; Wagner, by the side of his three Chansons, has a Ballade in French, a German Lied, and five pieces which he calls ' Poems set to music,' *Gedichte in Musik gesetzt*, and which, as reminiscences of the lyric stage, appear to form a link between the two categories. It is pleasant to find that the tendency to eccentricity rarely appears in Berlioz's Chansons. Ditties, such as *Chanson de Paysan, Petit oiseau, La Belle Voyageuse, Elle s'en va seulette*[1], or the Villanelle No. 1 of *Les Nuits d'été* (verses by Théophile Gautier), are gems with a real charm of their own. No. 2 of the Gautier set, *Le Spectre de la rose*, is a broad Arioso. *Connaissez-vous la tombe blanche?* No. 5, has a touch of the

---

[1] *Paroles imitées de l'anglais de Thomas Moore*, par Thomas Gounet.

same melancholy which is expressed in the introduction to the
Symphonie fantastique. No. 3, the so-called Lamento, *Sur les
Lagunes*, and No. 4, *Absence*, rank among the finest histrionic
examples of forlorn passion. For their due effect *Les Nuits
d'été* should be sung, not at the pianoforte, but with a small
orchestra as originally written. Berlioz himself pointed to *La
Captive*, Op. 12—the poem taken from Victor Hugo's *Les
Orientales*—as his supreme achievement in the way of solo song ;
and, from the musical impressionist's point of view, this
Rêverie, as he calls it, is truly a fascinating piece. The exotic
mood of the poem is well expressed in a compact and beautiful
tune, and the scoring for a small orchestra is a marvel of skill—
a treasury of novel and picturesque effects, all directly illustrating
the verse.

Liszt, when composing for solo voice (a total of about sixty
songs, published in nine books), took less account of the poem
as a whole than of its successive details. He tried to intensify
the effect of his lyrics by emphasizing the more important single
words or clauses, or by strongly contrasting one word or clause
with another, and was thus led to develop an exaggerated style
that tends towards the incoherence of melodrama. Brief and
unified expression is rare with him, though we meet with it in
his setting of Victor Hugo's *Comment, disaient-ils ? Oh, quand
je dors,* and *S'il est un charmant gazon,* as well as in *Es muss
ein wunderbares sein,* and in Goethe's *Kennst du das Land ?*
Once and again he approaches the Ballade, as in the most
picturesque of his songs, *Die drei Zigeuner,* or the Scena, as in
Lorelei. Frequently he appeals to that public taste which is
caught by over-emphasis, as in *Enfant, si j'étais roi* and
Vergiftet sind meine Lieder, or in *Es war ein König in Thule*
and *Wer nie sein Brod mit Thränen ass,* in which latter song

the words 'Der kennt euch nicht, ihr himmlischen Mächte,' are at first directed to be 'spoken softly,' and, when they recur, 'to be sung with full force.' Again, he is disposed to indulge in over-sentimentality, as in *Ich möchte hingehn* and *Tre Sonetti di Petrarca*, or in decorous platitudes, as in the two songs called *Mariensträusslein*, or in languorous sensuousness, as in *Liebesträume*, Nos. 1 and 3. In point of accent and declamation Liszt's French songs are admirable.

al - gua-zils?

un peu retenu

un peu retenu

ppp

mezza voce
p

Ra - mez,   ra -

dim. . . . .

- mez, ...

smorzando

The German ones leave much to be desired; an annoying discrepancy is felt to exist between the true sounds of the words and the musical accent—for example, the stress on *du* and *die* in Goethe's *Kennst du das Land?* is detestable; and there are other errors of declamation in the rest of the song.

Gold - o - ran - gen glüh'n.

Ped.

Musically considered, *Kennst du das Land?* is a song remarkable for its romantic colour and the exquisite touches of longing expressed in the refrain. The atmosphere of *Die drei Zigeuner*, too, is wonderfully characteristic.

Wagner's French Chansons, *Dors, mon enfant; Mignonne; Attente;* and the Ballade *Les Deux Grenadiers*—a translation of Heine's *Die beiden Grenadiere*—belong to the period of his first sojourn in Paris (1841-2), when he finished *Rienzi* and wrote *Der fliegende Holländer.* Another Ballade, *Der Tannenbaum*, words by Scheuerlin, was written at Riga in 1839, when only two acts of *Rienzi* were completed. Yet this piece has some connexion with the style of *Tannhäuser*, as the *Fünf Gedichte*, the verses of which were written by Frau Mathilde Wesendonck (1855-7), are closely connected with *Die Walküre* and *Tristan.* The earlier of Wagner's songs and vocal pieces differ as much in style from the later as his operas differ from the tone-dramas. The third and fifth of the *Fünf Gedichte*, 'Im Treibhaus' and 'Träume,' are offshoots or forerunners of *Tristan und Isolde*. 'Träume' prefigures the love-scene in the second act, 'Im Treibhaus' recalls the instrumental introduction to Act III. Again, 'Stehe still,' No. 2, is connected with the third act of *Tristan*, 'Schmerzen,' No. 4, and 'Der Engel,' No. 1, with *Die Walküre*. It is curious to watch Wagner listening to himself, as it were, in his own workshop. His personality is as perfectly revealed in these five songs as in the later *Siegfried-Idyll*, which belongs to *Siegfried*, Act III.

Wagner laid great stress on prosody. Compared with Schumann, Robert Franz, or Brahms, who each are occasionally lax in their ways, and more or less consciously take up a recalcitrant position in regard to declamation, Wagner is an uncompromising purist. In every case, he insisted, the spirit and sense of the language must be respected and the laws of prosody and of musical rhythm should form an equilibrium.

Lapses such as Robert Franz's *Ich stand gelehnet an den Mast*, or *Ihr Thränen, bleibt mir aus den Augen* (*Wasserfahrt*, Op. 48, No. 3), roused his ire. 'If Franz,' he said, 'did not care to sacrifice the characteristic figure or the tune, he might have found a better figure or a better tune.'

In connexion with the partially dramatic lyrics of Liszt and Berlioz mentioned above, it seems convenient here to touch upon certain earlier forms of Ballade and of Melodrama proper. Carl Loewe[1], who is practically the originator of the German Ballade as it now exists, relies on various means of artistic effect, justifiable it may be, but not entirely musical. Declamation, histrionic changes of voice, and even mimicry are called upon to bear their part. With the aid of the musical actor's art, some of Loewe's Balladen, such as *Edward*, are effective enough, but they need such external assistance to cover defects in the music. The poetry usually is allowed to tell its own story, but the music is subordinate. There is a sense of insecurity. Rarely does the musical mood embrace the entire poem, and almost invariably the stress is laid upon the externals of the story rather than upon the lyrical emotion which underlies it. The impression left is that of a partially musical recitation by an actor, not the consistent outpouring of a musician[2].

Excepting the pieces mentioned, to which may be added *Herr Oluf*, *Prinz Eugen*, *Der Pilger von St. Just*, and *Der Wirthin Töchterlein*, the musical ideas are neither new nor deep, and they

---

[1] 1796–1869.

[2] This may help to explain Wagner's inordinate fondness for Loewe's *Edward* and *Erlkönig*, as well as the fascination which these pieces had, and still have, with operatic singers.

occasionally approach the confines of bathos. Loewe's manner of writing for the pianoforte is a little in advance of the point reached by his predecessors Zumsteeg and Zelter, yet, like theirs, it is somewhat commonplace. There is abundant evidence of a gift for rapid improvisation, but little restraint or self-criticism. Hence the superiority of certain Balladen by later masters, such as Schumann's *Belsatzar*, *Die beiden Grenadiere*, and *Die Löwenbraut*. The early dates of Loewe's best work must not be overlooked; *Edward* and the *Erlkönig* belong to 1818, *Der Wirthin Töchterlein* to 1824; while, on the other hand, *Archibald Douglas* appeared in 1857, which was Loewe's sixty-second year—a date which may account for certain instances of apparently direct indebtedness to Wagner's *Der fliegende Holländer*.

Melodramatic music, such as that contained in Mendelssohn's *Midsummer Night's Dream* and Schumann's *Manfred*, is an offshoot of the great melodramas in Beethoven's *Fidelio*, or in Weber's *Freischütz* and *Preciosa*, or a combination of both styles, as in Marschner's *Vampyr*. Schumann, besides the three melodramatic fragments in the music to Byron's *Manfred* —the calling of the witch of the Alps, the invocation to Astarte, and Manfred's address to Astarte—published three pieces for declamation with pianoforte accompaniment, *Schön Hedwig* and *Vom Haidenknaben*, both by Hebbel, and *Die Flüchtlinge*, Op. 122, taken from Shelley's *Fugitives*. These pieces, again, prompted Liszt to write melodramatic music to illustrate a recitation of Bürger's *Lenore*, and a Ballade by Lenau called *Der traurige Mönch*[1]. As early as 1773 J. J. Rousseau, with his *Pygmalion*, set the example, and the amateurish character of this early instance appears to have tainted all its successors. There was the alternative of recitation and music, musical illustration or mere support of the reciter's voice—then again music, and again recitation, and so on. The unity of effect was difficult, if not

---

[1] Liszt's music to the latter poem is a curious experiment in ugliness—an entire piece built on a whole tone scale. Compare Verdi's *Scala enigmatica* quoted above, p. 223.

impossible to attain, because as the reciter's topic or his mood changes, the music must change—and, as music must recur to its beginning or remain inchoate, the two aspects rarely fit together.

In connexion with the stage, melodramatic music is acceptable in so far as it underlines the words; it supplies emphasis and descriptive touches and, in the intervals of speech, completes the expression of the emotion. How well it can serve in the latter capacity may be felt in the great prison scene, Act II of Beethoven's *Fidelio*, and the invocation and address to Astarte in Schumann's *Manfred*. Apart from the stage, however, a true fusion of the poetical text with the musical accompaniment seems impossible. The speaking voice and the music fail to blend. If the reciter is competent he will absorb the interest, or else the accompanist will disturb the reciter. Musically considered, melodramatic effects appear tolerable only in connexion with a poem that contains a certain proportion of definitely musical elements, such as Tennyson's *Enoch Arden*, for instance, to which Richard Strauss has recently added illustrative music; but even in this case the result is of doubtful value.

CHAPTER XIII

REFERENCE to the followers of those Romantic masters who founded a school, as the phrase goes, has hitherto been avoided. We may now turn to the adherents of Mendelssohn—such as Niels Gade, Sterndale Bennett, Rubinstein, Stephen Heller, Sullivan; of Schumann—such as Volkmann, Kiel, Goetz, Theodor Kirchner, Jensen; of Liszt and Berlioz—such as Peter Cornelius, Hans v. Bülow, and the eclectic Joachim Raff. It is pleasant to record that most of these men were independent enough to indulge their personal note and guard their spontaneity, though they frankly adopted the methods and even some of the mannerisms of their leaders.

But before going into details we may consider the case of two composers who are not followers at all, and whose claim to recognition rests entirely on its own merits: the twin masters of English church and organ music (they happen to be father and son), Samuel Wesley (1766–1837), and Samuel Sebastian Wesley (1810–76). And in connexion with their productions we may also touch upon certain specifically English forms of vocal music—the glee, the round, and the catch.

In the musical history of the nineteenth century the work of the two Wesleys is of real importance. They are by far the weightiest composers who wrote for the Anglican Church Service at a period when English music in general was at a low ebb. They tower above their English contemporaries, laymen or churchmen; and in their particular department—in which they are by no means imitators—need not shun comparison with continental celebrities such as Spohr, or even with a master such as Mendelssohn. The fine eight-part antiphon for double chorus and organ in *In exitu Israel*, the motets *Dixit Dominus* and *Exultate Deo*, the bold motet for two altos, tenor, and bass in B♭, *Levate capita vestra*, and the noble *Ecce Panis* in D minor for soprano, alto, tenor, and bass, the ' Carmen funebre ' for five voices, *Omnia vanitas*, by Samuel Wesley[1], together with S. Sebastian Wesley's eight-part anthems, *Let us lift up our hearts*, and *O Lord, thou art my God*; his Morning and Evening Service in E; his masterly five-part anthem *The Wilderness*; his four-part anthem *Man that is born of a woman*, with its direct expression and fine pathos; his beautiful setting of the Nicene Creed, which forms a part of the Morning Service just mentioned; and the poignantly expressive *Wash me throughly from my wickedness* are the most valuable of their pieces. There is nothing in the range of modern religious music more sincerely felt and expressed than, for example, the anthem last mentioned, *Wash me throughly*—neither in Spohr, with whose practice certain chromatic progressions seem to coincide, nor in Mendelssohn, with whose oratorio style there is a certain resemblance in phraseology. S. S. Wesley's way of expressing religious emotion appears more individual than either Spohr's or Mendelssohn's, and it is for that very reason better worth hearing. Always in close connexion with the traditions of English vocal music, the choral technique in the work of both masters is of a high order—witness the elder Wesley's five-part madrigal *O sing unto my roundelay*, and Samuel Sebastian's five-part glee *I wish to tune my quivering Lyre*. The sheer musical invention in S. S. Wesley's *O Lord, thou art my God*, in the Credo belonging to the Morning Service, and in *Wash me throughly*, is that of a virile genius, who knows his J. S. Bach not only contrapuntally but emotionally, and loves him[2]. The quotation subjoined may appear inordinately long, but it is not possible to convey in a few bars an adequate idea of the persistent strength of this contrapuntal music, that ought to be studied and recognized as masterly wherever the English language is spoken.

[1] A complete list of S. Wesley's pieces will be found at p. 446 of Grove's *Dictionary*, vol. iv.

[2] The elder Wesley's enthusiasm for Bach's organ works and the 48 preludes and fugues, which the son fully shared (S. Wesley, together with C. E. Horn, brought out the first English edition of *Das wohltemperirte Clavier* in 1110), is well shown in the familiar epistles known as the 'Bach letters' written to Benjamin Jacob in 1808, which were not published till 1875.

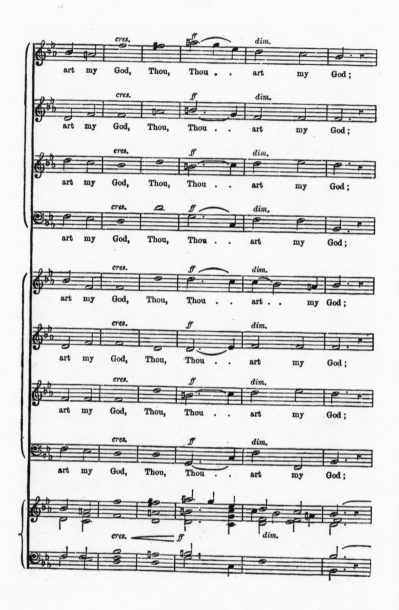

Not less magnificent is the closing chorus of the same anthem. Indeed, the best examples of S. S. Wesley contain an expression of the highest point up to that time reached by the combination of Hebrew and Christian sentiment in music. They are well worthy of comparison with Mendelssohn's psalms, with the best things in Spohr, and with the *Beatitudes* of Liszt and of César Franck, to which their relation may be illustrated by the following excerpt from the anthem *Wash me throughly.*

In the wake of these masterpieces (*longo intervallo*) certain contemporary compositions written for the Anglican Service, and for Societies of Glee-singers, merit a passing notice. Thomas Attwood Walmisley's (1814–56) *Magnificat* and *Nunc Dimittis* in D minor are sincerely felt; his Thanksgiving Anthem in G minor, *If the Lord Himself had not been on our side*, shows individuality, is strong at the beginning and the end, but has an unfortunate touch of sentimentality in the middle (G major ¾). A dainty five-part madrigal, *Sweete Floweres, ye were too faire*, also deserves mention. S. Webbe senior's (1740–1816) *Discord, dire sister of the slaught'ring power*, a glee for alto, two tenors, and bass, F minor ³⁄₂, is concise and powerful with a suave close in F major[1]. Sir John

---

[1] Dr. Callcott's (1766–1806) rather saccharine *With sighs, sweet rose, I mark the faded form* is a homophonous four-part glee in E ♭, for alto, two tenors, and bass, R. Spofforth's (1768–1827) five-part glee for two altos, tenor, two basses, *Come, bounteous May*, and William Horsley's (1774–1858) *By Celia's Arbour*, a four-part glee, are both well contrived for the voices. Thomas Moore's verse is reproduced

Goss's anthems, *If we believe that Jesus died and rose again,* and *O Saviour of the World,* are sincere and beautiful, and the part-writing is masterly. His *Ossian's Hymn to the Sun,* as well as the anthem *Praise the Lord,* lacks the personal note. Finally, we may mention J. L. Hatton's lively four-part song, *King Witlaf's Drinking-horn,* and R. L. de Pearsall's *Sir Patrick Spens*—a ballad-dialogue in ten real parts, as he is careful to note. Pearsall's glee for four voices, *When Allan-a-dale went a hunting,* is spirited and deservedly popular[1].

This would seem to be the right place to call attention to a species of concerted music for solo male voices unaccompanied, which is worthy of note as peculiarly English, intrinsically genuine, and in its peculiar way good. Setting aside the madrigal, it may be said that from about the fourth quarter of the eighteenth century to the end of the first quarter of the nineteenth, the round, the catch, and the glee held the field now occupied by the part-song for mixed voices. From Cromwell's time onwards, and especially before and during the Napoleonic wars, a truculent male element was conspicuous in English society, and was reflected in a manner which needs no further particularization, in the 'tavern-catches' on which a good deal of current musical invention was employed. The glees are mostly sober, gently bucolic, or sentimental; but with a large proportion of the rounds, and with most catches, there is only one sentiment—*ergo bibamus.* Yet, whether emotional or lively or boisterous, many rounds and catches are distinctly effective both from the musical and from the histrionic point of view[2]. The quotation of a catch by Purcell,

---

in the music, and, as in Moore's, there is a curious air of sensuousness obviously at second hand.

[1] Other well-known productions of Pearsall's, such as *There is a Paradise on earth,* from the German of Hölty, *Lay a garland on my hearse,* also an eight-part madrigal, *Great God of Love,* though nobly sonorous, are rather dry, and the music hardly chimes with the spirit of the words.

[2] It appears that certain catches were not only sung but *acted.*

though it belongs to the seventeenth century, may perhaps be condoned, since it serves to exhibit the social function of such *jeux d'esprit* [1].

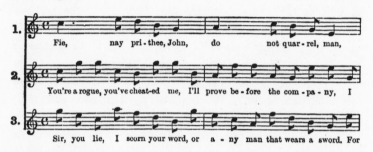

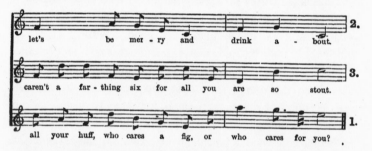

The first voice starts, the second enters after the fourth bar, the third after the eighth bar. Thereafter the first starts again at the point where the second entered, and finally at the point where the third entered. The process consists in giving out, first a solo, then a duet, finally a complete harmonic trio which, with successive changes and histrionic exaggeration, may go on for ever. 'The catch in music,' says Dr. Hayes, the editor of several sets of catches, 'answers to the epigram in poetry, where much is expressed within a very small compass, and unless the turn is neat and well pointed it is of little value.' Like the round, the catch is a short *Canone infinito* in the unison or the octave, and the 'epigrammatical touch' is sought in the connexion of pointed words with the musical sounds.

---

[1] Compare also Purcell's catch in G minor, *If all be true that I do think*, reprinted in Samuel Webbe junior's *Convito Armonico*, p. 423.

A glee may be described as a sort of harmonic madrigal for three, four, five, or more *male* voices—i. e. combinations of alto, tenor, bass (with the occasional addition of a boy's treble), depending on the deft interweaving of vocal parts—in which the contrapuntal element is usually more or less present[1]. Points are started and taken up, much as in the madrigal proper; indeed, though less persistently developed, they are more frequent than in the madrigal, and they are generally *poetical* points. The musical structure is always strictly harmonic (there is no trace of the modes), and the total appeal is rather to the poetical perception of the auditor—that is to say, attention is drawn to the drift of the verse as emphasized by means of harmonic music. Of course the specifically musical charm is never entirely absent. Frequently a glee consists of various movements in succession, suggested by the course of a poem; and this again differentiates the glee from the madrigal, in which the same words are repeated to support contrapuntal points. Many a glee, round, or catch is remarkable for good craftsmanship and delicate knowledge of vocal effect. In a number of rounds, catches, glees, something like a democratic note may be felt: each voice seems to represent an individual holding his own, yet harmonically co-operating with the others. This applies, for instance, to a fine work by a recent master of contrapuntal and vocal effect, Sir John Goss's[2] five-part glee, *Hark! heard ye not that strange tumultuous sound?*

[1] It is entirely absent from the fine homophonic glees of R. G. S. Stevens.
[2] 1800–80.

sound, that grates, that grates dis - cor - dant on the star - tled

sound, that grates, that grates dis - cor - dant on the star - tled

sound, that grates, that grates dis - cor - dant on the star - tled

sound, that grates, that grates dis - cor - dant on the star - tled

sound, that grates, that grates dis - cor - dant on the star - tled

ear? Too .. faith - ful e - cho, too .. faith - ful e - cho of a

ear? Too faithful e - cho of a

ear? Too faithful e - cho, too faithful e - cho of a

ear? Too faithful e - cho, too faithful e - cho of a

ear? Too faithful e - cho of a

The best glees deal with poetry in a sympathetic, often very human and manly way. The composers are generally mindful of their poets, and their music keeps closely in touch with the language. No doubt, in the case of many a favourite glee—e. g. Stevens' *The cloud-capped towers* or *Ye spotted snakes with double tongue*—the words *far* outshine the musical expression; yet it must be conceded that correct declamation, as here represented, is a feature worth having and accentuating, inasmuch as it makes for conciseness and sincerity in musical diction, and leads to effects which chime with the modern feeling for elasticity in point of *Tempo*. Too frequently in this curious by-way of vocal art—an ill-tilled wheat-field, where tares predominate—the musical expression is cheap, dull, narrowly provincial, yet it is sometimes novel, ingenious, beautifully contrived for the voices and delightful to sing. The admixtures of the so-called alto voice, i. e. a bass or baritone in *falsetto*, brings about variety, and if the singing is well done there is sure to be beauty of tone-colour in the ensemble. And though the total effect may be a trifle sensuous, it need not be sickly. Incidentally too, the use of the alto voice—which, as an artificial product, is useless unless it is well trained and well managed—makes for artistic vocal style [1].

Among the followers of Mendelssohn, Niels Gade and Sterndale Bennett were the most conspicuous. Gade (1817–90), Mendelssohn's successor in the conductorship at Leipzig, subsequently held a leading position in Copenhagen akin to that of Sterndale Bennett (1816–75) in London. Both men were friends and disciples of Mendelssohn, and in some sense, particularly in their later days, disciples of Schumann as well, yet their style, far from appearing as a mere reflex of the greater masters, exhibits a distinct physiognomy of its own. Gade, who was more of an expert in instrumental

---

[1] In the matter of vocal ensemble, just intonation, and correct phrasing, lovers of English music have always had a good example in the performances of the trained vocalists belonging to the cathedral choirs.

colour than a master of design, in such pieces as his overtures, *Reminiscences of Ossian* (1841), and *In the Highlands*, shows a fine vein of imagination, recalling the spirit of Scandinavian folk-song and Northern scenery. His themes, though rarely passionate, are spontaneous, and never without some special grace of colour or sentiment, or a tinge of Norse melancholy. The fascination usually lies in the prevailing sense of beauty and poetical suggestion conveyed by the entire piece, rather than in any prominent feature of tune or harmony or rhythm, and the details are always apt to the particular instrument concerned. His cantatas, *Comala* and *Erlkönigs Tochter*, met with well-merited success. He published eight symphonies, two violin concertos, Novelletten for orchestra, and a mass of chamber music, amongst which an octet for strings and a sonata in D minor for piano and pianoforte are the most conspicuous.

With less pathos than the best effusions of Gade, Sterndale Bennett's dainty pieces leave a less definite impression. Yet Bennett (1816–75) accomplished the work of a high, though but a secondary master. His style was distinguished by fluency, as well as fineness and delicacy of fancy. There is grace and natural beauty in much of his work. His attitude towards Schumann's musical poems with suggestive titles was at first one of hesitating assent. Later in life he made some compromise with programme music—as in his last publication, the sonata called *The Maid of Orleans*, Op. 46 (the themes of which are labelled as they occur, like the themes in Lizst's *Ideale*), and the 'Phantasie-Overture' to Mooie's *Paradise and the Peri*, Op. 42. His cantata *The May Queen* (1858), which suffers from a weak libretto, and his oratorio *The Woman of Samaria* (1867), fell flat, as did the Symphony in G minor, Op. 43, produced three years earlier—the only one of his symphonies that was published. His best overtures are *Parisina* (1835), Op. 31, *The Naiads*, Op. 15, and *The Wood Nymph* (1836), Op. 20. The passage work of Bennett's piano-

forte pieces, like that of Mendelssohn's, is derived to a large
extent from the methods of the older harpsichord players, and
from Clementi; but his treatment of the instrument is neither
vigorous nor various. The Toccata in C minor, the exquisite
sketches entitled *The Lake, The Millstream, The Fountain,* the
Barcarolle belonging to the Concerto in F minor, and the Rondo
piacevole are good examples of his individuality and style[1].
His Chamber Trio for pianoforte, violin, and violoncello, in
A, is really good chamber music of a delicately reticent sort.

George Onslow (1784–1852), a composer of English origin,
though born and chiefly resident in France, gained an ephemeral
reputation with a comic opera, *Le Colporteur,* and enjoyed a
wide popularity in amateur circles, both in France and in
England, chiefly by reason of his string quintets with double
bass, which have no inconsiderable merit.

Like Liszt, Anton Rubinstein[2], in some respects incompar-
able as a pianist, was given to rapid improvisation as a composer. But, unlike Liszt, he chose to ignore the *labor limae*—
with the unfortunate result that many an ambitious piece, fine
in impulse, remained sketchy, flimsy, and diffused. He wrote
many operas, of which the least unsuccessful is *The Demon,*
after a Caucasian legend versified by Lermontov; 'sacred
operas,' i.e. oratorios contrived with a view to stage performance; symphonies, concertos, quintets, quartets, trios,
sonatas, preludes, études, smaller pieces for the pianoforte, and
something like two hundred miscellaneous songs for one or two
voices. The larger works—operas, both secular and sacred,
symphonies, &c.—were for the most part stillborn, though it
is true that some were received with acclamation when the
composer personally introduced them. But in a few instances
has there been a success other than ephemeral. The Symphony
in C entitled *Ocean,* six movements, the Symphonie dramati-

---

[1] Felix Moscheles' *Autobiography*: 'It sounds like Mendelssohn, it must be
Sterndale Bennett.'

[2] 1830–94.

que in D minor, the Pianoforte concertos in G major and D minor, the Trio in B♭, the 'Cello sonata in D, are the most likely to survive. Certain trifling improvisations, little pianoforte pieces, like the Barcarolles in G major and F minor, and especially a few little songs, have a singularly oriental charm. The best of the songs, *Gelb rollt mir zu Füssen der rauschende Kur*, belongs to a set of so-called Persian Lieder[1]. With a minimum of elaboration, and in spite of two glaring faults in declamation, this Lied is both novel and charming; and, somehow, with its Eastern melismata, haunts the memory. Other such Lieder, though on a lower level, are No. 1 of the Persian songs, *Nicht mit Engeln im blauen Himmelszelt mein Mädchen vergleich ich*, and a fine setting of one of Heine's most original poems, *Und der Slave sprach : Ich heisse Mahomet, ich bin aus Jemen, und mein Stamm sind jene Asra, welche sterben wenn sie lieben*. As in the poem there is considerable originality in the music.

In contrast to the diffuseness of Rubinstein's pianoforte concertos, études, &c., we may note the graceful futility of Stephen Heller's pieces (1815–88). Heller, in spite of his conspicuous mannerisms and constant production for the market, was a conscientious worker in the field of solo pianoforte music and free from affectation. His études, Op. 16, 47, 46, 45, his preludes, Op. 81, *Promenades d'un Solitaire*, Op. 78, may be taken to represent his delicate talent. His pianoforte technique is sufficiently effective and refined, though he rarely gets full value out of the instrument.

Arthur Sullivan, apart from his true domain, the operetta, comes into view under other aspects. There was an English note already in his early music to Shakespeare's *Tempest* (1863), which ranks with his best productions; also in the duet from *The Merchant of Venice*, 'How sweet the moonlight sleeps upon this bank,' which forms part of the cantata *Kenilworth*, 1864; and particularly in the set of six Shakespearean songs

[1] *Lieder des Mirza Schaffy*, edited by Friedrich Bodenstedt.

written and published in 1865, one of which, *Orpheus with his lute*, with its genuine tunefulness, gained great popularity and deservedly retains it. There is something English too, though not so pronounced, in the effect of the overtures *In Memoriam* (1868), *Di Ballo, Macbeth* (1888), and, we may even add, in the so-called *Irish Symphony* (1866). Of Sullivan's quasi-oratorios, *The Martyr of Antioch*, a sacred music drama, has actually been performed on the stage. Other oratorios, *The Light of the World* (1873), Mendelssohnian in style and arrangement, and *The Prodigal Son* (1887), which shows a little more of his individuality, do not at the present day count for much. But the sincerely expressed *Golden Legend*, half cantata, half oratorio, proves as attractive as ever. A collection of the best modern English songs would as certainly exclude Sullivan's hypersentimental *The Lost Chord*, as it would include Hatton's *To Anthea*, and Sullivan's *Orpheus with his Lute*.

As equivalents to certain simple songs by Rubinstein and Sullivan, just mentioned, we may point to Luigi Gordigiani's *Canti populari Toscani*, which, with their artless charm, have found their way to the hearts of cultivated amateurs, as have Rossini's *Soirées musicales*, Gounod's *Quand tu chantes bercée le soir*, and certain German sentimentalities by Abt, Kücken, Lassen, and other Capellmeister. Taubert's naïve Kinderlieder deserve mention.

Robert Volkmann (1815–83), a German who lived in Hungary, and whose music contains many Hungarian traits, merits consideration as the composer of a good pianoforte trio, B♭ minor, Op. 5 (1852), and a fine set of solo pianoforte pieces, with characteristic titles after the manner of Schumann, called *Viségrad*. The trio, Op. 5, attracted the attention of Liszt and was frequently performed by him at Weimar. It is of elegiac import, a sort of forerunner to Tchaikovsky's trio *A la mémoire d'un grand Artiste*, and, technically, fully up to the mark of that interesting work. In *Viségrad* Volkmann appears as an illustrator, of power and originality and on consistently musical lines of his own. For the most part his pieces are like German translations of the Hungarian idiom—pomp and pride, a ponderous sort of grace, and some pathos —altogether well set for the instrument. Five string quartets, two symphonies, a violoncello concerto, and two serenades for strings, still belong to the staple concert repertoire in Germany. Volkmann also published two Masses for male voices and other choral music.

Schubert's friend Franz Lachner (1804–90), who made his name with an opera, *Catarina Cornaro,* and a number of orchestral suites, may be bracketed with Friedrich Kiel (1821–85), a North German composer of considerable attainment who is best remembered as a master of counterpoint. A Requiem Mass, Op. 20, appeared in 1862, a Missa Solennis in 1867; and these, with the two oratorios, *Der Stern von Bethlehem* (1866) and *Christus* (1872), and a second Requiem (Op. 80), produced shortly before his death, are the most conspicuous of his works for chorus and orchestra. Good in their way, there is nothing of real importance about them. Kiel also composed a large amount of chamber music—three pianoforte quintets, two pianoforte quartets, seven pianoforte trios, four violin sonatas, a viola and a violoncello sonata, two string quartets, and a set of waltzes for strings, of which the same estimate may be offered.

Goetz, as a composer of instrumental music, must be included on account of an overture entitled *Frühlingsouvertüre,* Op. 15, and a Symphony in F, Op. 9 (1876), both of which pieces, like the late and latest efforts of Gade and Bennett, were at first well received, but failed to make a definite mark. The one concerted piece by Goetz likely to survive is his *Nänie,* Op. 10, a poem by Schiller set for chorus, solo voices, and orchestra. Not particularly strong, but emotionally genuine and technically finished, it forms a sort of pendant to Brahms' *Gesang der Parzen über dem Wasser* and the *Schicksalslied.* Goetz' church music is insignificant.

About 1860 there was a ready sale for Theodor Kirchner's [1] smaller pianoforte pieces, and for Jensen's [2] pieces and songs—with the usual result that both men continued to compose for the market, with increased facility, but, as time went on, with decreasing freshness. This may not be entirely true of Jensen, whose songs show progress, but it is near the mark in both cases.

It was not until after his death that Peter Cornelius' verse and music began to attract attention. He wrote much and published little. Each carefully considered publication, however, represents something in the growth of his talent. His three operas, written to his own librettos, have already been mentioned. It remains to touch upon his remarkable choral music *a capella*, and his songs and duets with pianoforte accompaniment, which are also for the most part attempts to set his own verses to music. The songs, some fifty in all, are little more than an array of trifles—occasional pieces, akin to certain little lyrics of Goethe—each the expression of some particular emotional experience, many among them perfect in their delicately reticent way. Neither as a writer of lyrical verse or of lyrical music does Cornelius aspire very high. But what he has put forth in each department shows perfect sincerity, a rare sense of fitness, and considerable technical attainment. Everywhere one hears the voice of a man who is somebody, a man with a delicate ear for balanced beauty of verbal and musical expression. In a number of instances the verbal expression appears richer than the musical; but this applies to the solo songs, duets, and the operas more than to the choral pieces, *a capella*, which latter belong to the best modern work in that department. Here, especially in the unaccompanied choral pieces, Cornelius combines contrapuntal mastery on the traditional lines of canon and fugue, with the chromatic harmony of the later romantic development, in the manner of Berlioz, Liszt, and Wagner. The majority of these secular anthems are therefore difficult to

[1] 1823-93.   [2] 1837-79.

intone, but when the choristers have mastered the strange
intervals the result is good, and at times very impressive, as for
instance in the setting of Abbot Notker's (Balbulus) Sequence
Media vita in morte sumus (Mitten wir im Leben sind von
dem Tod umfangen), which perfectly represents the Neo-German
ideal of declamation, or the remarkable setting of Uhland's
Die Vätergruft ('The ancestors' tomb') for solo baritone and four-
part chorus of mixed voices, which is the most original piece of
vocal programme music in existence.   Of Cornelius' songs, one
at least deserves special mention—*Ein Ton*, Op. 3, No. 3, a
curiously speculative and original piece, in which the voice
reiterates one note (B natural) whilst the elaborated piano part
develops the poetic idea [1].   Among the duets the most remarkable is No. 3, Op. VI., a strict canon for baritone and soprano,
the voice parts a crotchet asunder.   This is a setting of the old
hymn attributed to Abbot Wernher of Tegernsee, *Ich bin dein,
du bist mein, dess sollst du gewiss sein.*

[1] Compare Chopin's Preludes, Op. 28, No. 15, in D ♭ and No. 6, in B minor;
Op. 4, No. 2, 'Komm, wir wandeln zusammen im Mondenschein, So zau-
berisch glänzt jedes Blatt,· Vielleicht steht auf einem geschrieben, Wie lieb
mein Herz dich hat'—the music to these lines, in D ♭ and in ¾ and ⅜ time, is as
simple and direct as the words.   Masterly too, are *Die Hirten*, and *Die Königin*,
Nos. 2 and 3 of Weinachtslieder, Op. 8, and Op. 5, No. 5, *Der Pelion sprach zum
Ossa*.

musst du e - wig, nun auf e - wig drin-nen sein.

e - wig, nun auf e - wig drin-nen sein.

E - - - - - - wig!

E - - - - - - wig!

Hans v. Bulow (1830–94) in his younger days was ambitious to excel as a composer. He wrote pianoforte pieces, songs and duets, a Poème symphonique, *Nirwana,* also an overture and incidental music to Shakespeare's *Julius Caesar,* an Orchestral Ballade, *Des Sängers Fluch,* after a poem by Uhland, &c. But the vein of his invention proved essentially jejune, and in spite of technical attainment and undeniable musical ability he failed to make a mark as a composer. The cleverest and least dry of his pianoforte pieces are a set of modern dances, entitled *Il Carnevale di Milano,* Ballabili ed Intermezzi, dedicated to an Italian opera dancer, as Op. 21. His editions of classical pianoforte music, particularly those of Beethoven's later Sonatas, beginning with the Waldstein Sonata, Op. 53, and of certain pieces which formed part of his concert repertoire, are very instructive, in spite of the fact that he is prone to indulge his personal whims.

Joachim Raff (1822–82) was the most curiously eclectic among the modern Germans, and, in so far as technical mastery and versatility of production are concerned, the most accomplished. His works exhibit traits belonging to a variety of contemporaries, from Mendelssohn to Liszt. He composed operas, oratorios, eleven symphonies, many concertos, quintets, quartets, trios, suites, sonatas, a host of solo pianoforte pieces, songs, &c., of very unequal value. Some of them are merely productions for the market, whilst others show artistic aim. Two symphonies still evince signs of vitality, *Leonore* (1869), and *Im Walde* (1872). Both have a full programme; thus, *Im Walde*: (1) Daytime, impressions and emotions; (2) Twilight, dreams, dance of Dryads; (3) Night-time, silence and darkness, coming and going of the 'Wild-chase' with Odin and Venus; (4) Break of day. In *Leonore* (after Bürger's well-known Ballade) Raff tries to depict the lovers' farewell, the war, the return of the dead lover and the spectre's ride. But in both cases an annoying discrepancy between the programme and the exigencies of musical logic impairs the value of the work. The composer, to satisfy his instinct for musical symmetry, finds himself compelled to violate the continuity and progress of his story; he falls between two incompatible ideals, and his music, in spite of its skilful instrumentation, strikes us as essentially dull and artificial. Next to these symphonies may be ranked his pianoforte quintet in A minor, the trio No. 1 in E minor, a suite in E flat, Op. 200, for pianoforte with orchestra, a solo suite for pianoforte in E minor, Op. 72, and a very effective set of variations on a Gigue belonging to the suite in D minor, Op. 91, also for pianoforte.

In this place mention may fitly perhaps be made of a remarkable set of quasi-amateurs who called themselves the 'Five Neo-

Russian innovators,' a coterie held together by friendly rivalry and patriotic ambition. It consisted of four men of uncommon talent, Balakirev the leader, Cui, Musorgsky, Rimsky-Korsakov, and a man of genius, Alexander Borodine, who was a son of a Prince of Imeretia in the Caucasus. Their cry was ' Russian music for the Russians.' Following the example of Glinka and Dargomijsky, they studied ecclesiastical melodies, folk-songs and dances, investigated the various oriental elements which are intermingled with Russian art, and strove for novelty in melody and harmonization, and for piquancy of orchestral effect. In the Liturgy of the Greek Church, together with the semi-oriental songs and dances of the peasantry, they found a vast amount of material that strikes Western ears with a strange sense of power and spontaneity. Balakirev (1836), a man of keen intelligence and an accomplished musician, collected Russian folk-songs, composed orchestral pieces in the manner of Berlioz and Liszt, and pianoforte pieces in a manner of his own—of which the oriental fantasia *Islamey* (variations on an Eastern tune) is the most ingenious. Rimsky-Korsakov, born in 1844, has written some twelve operas, many songs, a pianoforte concerto in E♭, two Poèmes symphoniques, *Antar* and *Sheherazade,* and published two valuable collections of folk-songs taken down from oral tradition [1]. Cui, born in 1835, a truculent critic, produced eight operas, over 160 songs, and a large number of small pianoforte pieces—many of which are but Schumann at second hand. Musorgsky (1839–81), the ' most Russian of the Russians,' in his vocal efforts appears wilfully eccentric. His style impresses the Western ear as barbarously ugly. Alexander Borodine (1834–87) composed two symphonies (two movements of a posthumous third have been published), an orchestral sketch *Eine Steppenskizze aus Mittel-Asien,* two string quartets, a Petite Suite in D minor for pianoforte, twelve songs, some to

---

[1] Korsakov is fond of reproducing the peculiar metrical structure of certain Russian folktunes, $\frac{5}{4}$, $\frac{7}{4}$ and the like, and so gets surprising effects of rhythm and colour. He is a master of orchestration.

his own words; and left unfinished one of the most original productions of modern times, *Prince Igor*, an opera on a Russian subject, which, after his death, was completed by Rimsky-Korsakov and Glasounov. The picturesque oriental elements upon which Balakirev laid so much stress, the use of chromatics, augmented seconds, and sequences of whole tones, frequent changes of rhythm and surprising modulations, abound in Borodine's works. His instrumental pieces, almost throughout, are programme music sincerely felt and expressed, and without a trace of affectation. The thematic material is novel, the workmanship careful, the sense of variety and beauty in instrumental colour striking. *Dans les steppes de l'Asie centrale* forms a good pendant to Berlioz' *Marche des Pèlerins*[1]. The second symphony in B minor, the two movements of a third, the Asiatic sketch just mentioned, the second quartet in D major, and the Petite Suite, have permanent value. For completeness' sake the name of Dargomijsky (1813–69) must be included. A disciple of Glinka, he wrote several operas—*Roussàlka* ('Water nymph') has been most frequently given—about 100 songs, a number of which are noteworthy by reason of a curious alternation of passion with oriental languor, and a grotesque ' Cossack-dance ' (*Kosatshòk*) for orchestra, that made the round of European concert-rooms, and is indeed very clever and characteristic.

Borodine is, however, the national genius after Glinka. So far as concerns sheer novelty in the scenes depicted and originality in the musical material and treatment, his *Prince Igor*, an opera in four acts with an overture and a prologue, published in 1889,

---

[1] The programme is as follows: ' Dans le silence des steppes sablonneuses de l'Asie centrale retentit le premier refrain d'une chanson paisible russe. On entend aussi les sons mélancoliques des chants de l'Orient ; on entend le pas des chevaux et des chameaux qui s'approchent. Une caravane, escortée par des soldats russes, traverse l'immense désert, continue son long voyage sans crainte, s'abandonnant avec confidence à la garde de la force guerrière russe. La caravane s'avance toujours. Les chants des Russes et ceux des indigènes se confondent dans la même harmonie, leurs refrains se font entendre longtemps dans le désert et finissent par se perdre dans le lointain.'

equals, perhaps surpasses, Bizet's *Carmen*. It is the strangest and the strongest production of the Neo-Russian school. Borodine, better than any other composer, represents the poetry of the manners and the sights and the sounds of the north and south-east. He does not consciously strive to produce characteristic Eastern music; with him it is true, spontaneous, and irresistible. Throughout his work Russian local colour is supreme—so much so that Rubinstein's and even Tchaikovsky's oriental tints fade before its vivid rays. Borodine's invention never flags—he is ever ready with something new, strange, and appropriate. In *Prince Igor* there are popular Russo-Asiatic motives of surprising delicacy and charm, as for instance in the dances, the songs, and the choruses for female voices. Certain virile movements again, such as the Introduction and the close of Act I, the Warriors' dance at the end of Act II, or the march at the beginning of Act III, are pieces of barbaric splendour, which, for all their colours, are as compact and logical in construction as they are subtle and penetrating in style. Better materials for a Russian opera could hardly have been found[1], yet *Prince Igor* is perhaps more of an epic pantomime than an opera proper. It consists of a series of scenes, choruses, ensembles, dances, songs—for the most part of startling originality, so vivid indeed that once heard they persistently linger in the memory. A professional librettist might denounce the book as inorganic—it is not weak or inept, but sketchy rather, and unfinished. It has only a semblance of a plot and is pervaded by a curious duality: two khans, two Vladimirs, two ladies in love, two fools, two outrages on the princely dignity, two captive princes, two victorious armies. It should be added that the composer's command of musical form and diction, of the treatment of solo and choral voices and the orchestra, is that of a bold, highly accomplished master—one who never rouses the suspicion that he may have intended one thing and by lucky

---

[1] Of course the work must be heard in Russian; for reading purposes the French translation may be called fairly good, the German is clumsy.

chance achieved another [1].   For delicacy and strange charm it
would be hard to surpass the following twenty-eight bars of
Kontchakovna's Cavatine (*Prince Igor*, No. 9):

Dans ton man-teau d'é toi - - - les,

Ô . . . nuit, Ô . . bel - - - - le

nuit: Le doux rê ve

dolce

Le doux rê - ve te

Doux mo - -

So exquisite a sample of the exotic element in artistic music has not been seen since Chopin's Mazurka, Op. 17, No. 4, and the Trio of his C minor Polonaise[1]. The idiom is not altogether

[1] One of the most extraordinary attempts at musical humour (musicians take their humour seriously at St. Petersburg) is a pianoforte composition for four hands entitled, 'Paraphrases sur le thème favori et obligé, dédiées aux petits

new : indeed it has been in some measure anticipated both by Dargomijsky and by Glinka, but no master has ever employed it to such admirable effect.

The total work of the Russian innovators is a distinct, though very late outcome of that development of the historical and critical sense which has been already discussed [1]. On the basis of the Russian language, coloured by ecclesiastical chants, most of which are modal, by peasants' songs and dances, by funeral laments and festive tunes, together with the quaint wail of Hebrew and other Semitic melismata, something has of late years been achieved in Russia that exhales 'le rude et viril parfum de la terre slave [2],' and offers one of the most important contributions to the history of romantic music. The composers, like their precursors and masters, Schumann, Berlioz, Liszt, looked at music through the lenses of literature. Hence their pronounced tendencies in favour of a programme, whether it be avowed or not. Hence also their leaning towards the further or nearer East—which, apart from oriental barbarisms deliberately chosen for barbaric ends, as in Musorgsky, has hitherto made for good. Kept within proper artistic bounds, the Russian movement now in full course may ultimately lead to illustrative instrumental music of the highest beauty and value. There is no need that the young Russian composers should hark back to partially exhausted formulas. The laws of musical design, the principles of good sense and proportion will make themselves

pianistes capables d'exécuter le thème avec un doigt de chaque main ! ' The theme is that known in England as the 'Chopsticks Waltz,' and is played continuously by one of the two performers, while the other accompanies it with galops, mazurkas, requiems, fugues on the name of Bach, and similar incongruities. Started by Borodine this curious jeu d'esprit was a joint production by himself, Cui, Liadow, Rimsky-Korsakow—and, later on, by Liszt and N. Stcherbacheff (who well replaces Musorgsky). Some of these very speculative variations rival those of Schumann's *Carneval* in point of beauty, and for variety and subtlety of invention may be said here and there to surpass them. A similar piece of still more serious fooling is the *Quatuor sur le nom de B-la-f* (Belaieff—the generous publisher's name), but this concoction, though enormously clever, is really too serious.

[1] See ch. i. pp. 3–5.

[2] Alfred Bruneau, *Musiques de Russie et Musiciens de France*, 1903.

felt, whatever be the material to which they are applied. With Tchaikovsky (1840–93) Russian music became cosmopolitan. His pianoforte concerto *The Russian*, in B♭ minor, has already been mentioned. The second and third concertos in G and E♭, and the Fantaisie de Concert in G, Op. 56, fell far below that high mark. Among his six symphonies, the fifth and sixth are the most important, and the latter of them (known as the *Pathétique*) is the most famous. Next to these symphonies, or rather beside them, we may place the Poèmes symphoniques, *Roméo et Juliette* and *Francesca da Rimini*. The plan of the latter pieces, it has been said by Mr. Ernest Newman, 'fulfils very happily one of the main requirements of good programme music—that the various points shall not be not only dramatic but musical, lending themselves naturally to musical treatment at the same time that they speak connectedly to the intellectual ear'.

Among Tchaikovsky's achievements may further be included an overture entitled *1812*, another overture, *Hamlet*, the Poème symphonique, *Manfred*, a symphonic Ballade, *Der Wojewode* (after Mickiewicz), three string quartets, and a pianoforte trio, *A la mémoire d'un grand artiste* (Nicholas Rubinstein). His lesser works of unequal merit—suites for stringed instruments, numerous small pianoforte pieces, 117 songs, many set to inferior verse [1]—have all, more or less, a fascination of their own. It seems to be the rule with the Slavs, 'that the power of creating intrinsic interest is considerable, but that the faculties which are needed for concentration and systematic mastery of balance of design are proportionately weak [2], and this applies to Tchaikovsky in almost the same degree as to all the rest. His operas, *Eugène Onégin* and *La Dame de Pique* excepted, met with little success outside Russia—they contain much graceful and at times interesting and original music—but the composer approached the theatre as a novice, and his stage instincts, if

---

[1] And generally sung to perfunctory German translations.
[2] C. Hubert H. Parry, *Summary of Musical History*, p. 89.

he ever had any worth cultivating, remained in an undeveloped condition.

Edvard Grieg, born 1843, a Romantic of the Romantics, had the good fortune to light upon topics of a fresh and fascinating nature, in the folk-songs and dances of his native Norway; and he had the instinct to treat them adequately, without disguising or unduly accentuating their characteristic features. His *Norwegische Volksweisen*, Op. 17 and 66, contain all the germs of his music : the tunes, plaintive or crude, as the people sing and play them—the drone bass (which is implied), the chromatic inner parts, which he supplies, the use of some quaint fragment of the tune by way of introduction or coda, the studied compactness and concentration, the sudden and unexpected contrasts. That he should have been able at all to weld these tiny phrases, and fuse them so as to serve for the thematic material of pieces in large form, such as his pianoforte concerto, already mentioned, his string quartet, and the sonatas for violin and for violoncello, speaks highly for his genius. We owe to Grieg a number of the most beautiful of modern songs, and a host of charming lyrical pieces for pianoforte solo. Mention must also be made of Max Bruch, born in 1838, a master of choral as well as instrumental effect, and the writer of some very effective violin concertos—and of Felix Draeseke, born in 1835, an accomplished theorist and critic, and a gifted composer whose music is full of original and romantic ideas.

Before we pass on to the consideration of organ music, mention must be made of the little-known pianoforte pieces, chiefly Études, by C. V. Alkan, who died in 1880, and of the clever transcriptions of certain movements from Beethoven's string quartets (in the manner of Liszt's partitions de piano) by Tausig and Saint-Saëns. Alkan's Études—the work of a speculative and eccentric rather than an essentially musical talent— are technically magnificent in so far as the treatment of the instrument is concerned ; the inventiveness in virtuosity is very considerable, though musically, that is to say, melodically and harmonically considered, they are somewhat barren. Alkan's most important Opus is marked 39. It is made up of twelve impressionist Études of inordinate length : I, is entitled, 'Comme le vent,' II, 'En rhythme molossique,' III, ' Scherzo diabolico ' ; Nos. IV to VII are meant for a symphony ; Nos. VIII to X for a concerto; No. XI for an overture. The twelfth Étude, called *Le Festin d'Ésope*, in E minor, is a veritable *tour de force*—it consists of a set of curiously characteristic variations on a theme of eight bars akin to that of No. 6 of Liszt's ' Paganini Caprices ' in A minor, and of Brahms' 'Paganini Variations' in the same key—remarkable for an almost farcical humour and for ingenuity of contrapuntal device. If well played the total effect of this grotesque piece is astonishing from the virtuoso's point of view—and almost, if not entirely, satisfactory from the musician's. There is no actual indication of a plot, but the comical effects tell their own tale. Other numbers worth attention are *Le Chemin de fer*, Op. 27, Trois Études pour les deux mains séparées et réunies, Op. 76, and twelve Études, Op. 35 [1].

The organ music of the nineteenth century owed much of its impetus to Mendelssohn, who infused new life into the forms of prelude and fugue. His so-called organ sonatas do not essentially belong to the sonata order, having little about them of its typical character or its principles of design ; still they rank among his best works and occupy an important place in the literature of the organ. Schumann's six fugues on the name B-A-C-H have already been mentioned ; Liszt's ambitious fantasia on *Ad nos, ad salutarem undam*, published in connexion with the ' Illustrations' to Meyerbeer's *Le Prophète*, and his B-A-C-H Fugue must also be mentioned. Finally there remains a mass of organ music by Joseph Rheinberger—which consists of two concertos with orchestra, twenty-two trios, twelve ' Méditations,' twenty solo sonatas, &c. Rheinberger's operas and his numerous

---

[1] *Huit prières pour orgue ou piano à clavier de pédales*, Op. 64, have been admirably transcribed for pianoforte solo by José Vianna da Motta.

symphonic and choral works have almost entirely disappeared. An early work, a deft and fresh pianoforte quartet in E♭, Op. 38, had some vogue, and is still welcomed in amateur circles.

Few of the elder Wesley's works for the organ are in print. The best of those contained in Vincent Novello's collection of Select Organ Pieces consist of a ' Slow Air in D,' ¾ , a Fugue in D, the transcription of a choral fugue for four voices, *Sicut erat*, in C, a Voluntary and Fugue in B♭, and a Fugue in C minor on a partially chromatic subject. Of these, the last two, especially the Fugue in C minor, show considerable skill and originality.

Of Sebastian Wesley's works for the organ, fourteen numbers have been edited by his pupil, the late Dr. Garrett, ' for modern Pedal organ.' They consist of single pieces—elegiac cantabile voluntaries, andante, or grave and andante, and produce their impression by persistence of mood and without any particular contrapuntal subtlety, somewhat after the manner of Spohr, though generally freer in treatment, broader in melody, and less cloying in harmonization. There are a few instances of incongruous pianoforte technique, as for instance the Andante in F (No. 5), and the fourth and fifth variations on the National Anthem (No. 10); but apart from these the workmanship is sound and musicianly, with bold sweeping melodic outlines and a strong and characteristic handling of the bass. Among the finest numbers may be cited the opening Andante in C (No. 1), the Introduction and Fugue in C♯ minor (No. 9), and the masterly settings of Psalm-tunes (Nos. 11 to 14) which close the volume.

CHAPTER XIV

THE ROMANTIC OPERAS OF WAGNER AND THE INCIPIENCY OF THE MUSIC-DRAMA

So far as the musical stage is concerned Wagner [1] sums up and completes the ideas and aspirations of Romanticism. He expresses them in *Tannhäuser* and *Lohengrin*, transcends them in *Tristan*, departs from them in *Der Ring* and *Die Meistersinger*, and returns to them in *Parsifal*. The gradual transformation of the *opera seria*, *semi-seria*, or *buffa* into the current modern equivalents, the development of German 'Singspiel' into 'Romantische Oper' and finally into the music-drama, both alike mark a change in the relative position of the two operatic factors to which nothing in artistic history supplies an exact parallel. By degrees the play asserts its full rights, operatic conventions recede, and the music becomes pliant; until at last dramatic illusion is attained by means of a compromise between the imitative arts on the one hand and music on the other.

Dramatic poet by instinct, by training supreme master of musical effect, Wagner was gradually led towards a new manner of blending music with the drama. Eight early operas or musical plays conceived between 1833 and 1848 saw the light in pairs, with an interval of about five years between each group of two—*Die Feen* and *Das Liebesverbot*, *Rienzi* and the *Flying Dutchman*, *Tannhäuser* and *Lohengrin*. *Siegfrieds Tod* and *Friedrich Rothbart* did not go beyond the stage of elaborated sketches for a musical drama (*Siegfried*), and a spoken tragedy

---

[1] Richard Wagner was born in 1813—thirteen years before Weber's death and fourteen years before the death of Beethoven. He died in 1883.

(*Rothbart*). In 1848-9 Wagner carried a number of dramatic
sketches with him, sketches for the tragedy *Rothbart*, for *Die
Franzosen vor Nizza* and *Wieland der Schmied*, the operas,
Jesus von Nazareth, the music-drama, as well as for other less-
matured dramatic ideas, such as *Achilleus*. The development
of his dramatic and musical capabilities took place with logical
consistency, even when the process was quite instinctive, from
one positive experience to another. There is nothing like this
in the history of any musician, and it can be explained only by
the extraordinary energy of Wagner's character, which kept him
isolated from the world and wholly surrounded by the atmosphere
of his own deeds and aspirations.

In the libretto to the *Holländer* Wagner begins to pay
attention to poetic qualities regardless of operatic considerations.
He had begun, he tells us, by trying to acquire the faculty of
musical expression in the way in which one learns a language.
A man speaking in a foreign tongue over which he has not yet
acquired complete control must consider its peculiarities in every
sentence that he utters ; if he wishes to be understood he must
always be thinking of the expression, and this will influence him
in the choice of what he shall say. Wagner, however, was an
apt pupil, and could soon declare : ' By this time I had finished
learning the language of music. I am now able to use it like
my own mother tongue.'

Again, Wagner maintains that legendary subjects are to be
preferred to historical ones, inasmuch as the substance of a
legendary story is so readily intelligible that there remains plenty
of space for the full expression of the inner motives of the
action. For instance, the story of *Der fliegende Holländer* is
set forth in the simplest way possible—details resembling the
intrigue of every-day life are excluded, whilst stress is laid
on those aspects which serve to accentuate the expression of
emotion. In *Tannhäuser* the action springs mainly from the
inner motives of the characters, and even the final catastrophe
is essentially lyrical. In *Lohengrin* the interest is concentrated

on a psychological process in the heart of Elsa. Thus the lyric spirit pervades the whole, and the total effect depends upon close connexion of the play with the music—each factor being modified in turn by the other.

Questions of aim and method arise here. If in an opera close and direct expression is desired, the use of formal musical design seems to stand in the way, for during the process of musical exposition the action is apt to be retarded, whereas it would seem to be a necessity that the music moves simultaneously with the action; and the difficulty from beginning to end consists in the proper adjustment of speed, the give and take between the motions of each collaborator. Every true melodic subject has its inner law of growth and expansion, and this musicians are loth to infringe for the sake of histrionic effect; on the other hand, operatic music must be true to the situation. It is, therefore, the principal convention in the Wagnerian drama that musical sounds may be accepted as symbolical. Music for the theatre must be regarded from a standpoint other than that of chamber or concert music; for as soon as dramatic presentation and stage effect are elements in the artistic whole, the appeal is not exclusively to the auditor's sense of musical balance and proportion, but it is also addressed to other forms of consciousness. It follows that the standard of absolute self-contained formal music cannot be fairly applied. Dramatic music is meant to arouse, stimulate, or exhaust emotion—it does not aim at delight in purely musical expression in just balance of statement and restatement. And because it illustrates or emphasizes, or fully expresses something more or less extraneous, it ought to be frankly accepted and judged as a kind of rhetoric.

To suppose that Wagner ever was guided by some abstract theory would be entirely erroneous. With him theory and practice advanced together, or rather his artistic instincts led the way and his theoretical opinions acted as support and rearguard. With his divine discontent and self-sufficing strength he, the great learner, was ever striving after something fresh and new.

Every work marks a step in the development of his genius, and the distance traversed from the first romantic opera, *Die Feen* (1833), to the last music-drama, *Parsifal* (1882), is perhaps greater than the distance ever before covered by any great artist. Wagner's individuality was first revealed in *Eine Faust-Ouvertüre* (1839-40) (pp. 106-10 *ante*), then in *Der fliegende Holländer* (1841), and so onwards. The three operas of earlier date, *Die Feen, Das Liebesverbot*, and *Rienzi*, do not demand close examination, though the third, *Rienzi, der letzte der Tribunen*, is of vast dimensions—a grand tragic opera in five acts in the manner of Spontini, and with sundry traces of Meyerbeer. All three resemble the types of opera which prevailed in their time, and were it not for their authorship, the first two, at least, might rest in oblivion. *Das Liebesverbot* was withdrawn from the stage after two performances: *Die Feen*, a weightier and more important work, was never heard until after the master's death. His first operatic victory was won with *Rienzi*, which contains some noble passages, such as the Introduction to Act IV, and particularly the Introduction and the Prayer in the fifth act. Its remarkable success at Dresden in 1842 was fully justified.

It is curious to note that these early pieces possess the stamp of theatrical rather than of musical originality. The grip of the dramatist is unmistakable; there is a keen instinct for general effect, there is frequent evidence of a practical acquaintance with the stage, but the musical details, both in the action and in the orchestra, are often raw and blatant. One point, however, stands forth · conspicuously : Wagner always succeeds in his fusion of dramatic and musical elements, and invariably contrives to get the result that he wants. And this gift remained with him throughout his wonderful career. As he approaches maturity the technique of the musician and the power of the dramatist is everywhere seen to expand with the complexity, the subtlety, and the intensity of his aims ; but from the first he approaches his hearers on every side and excites them with the cumulative appeal of all arts in combination.

The libretto of *Die Feen* is an arrangement of Gozzi's *La donna serpente*. *Das Liebesverbot* is based on Shakespeare's *Measure for Measure*. Bulwer's novel, *Rienzi, the last of the Tribunes*, suggested the characters and the plot of the third opera. The poem of *Der fliegende Holländer*—it must not be called a libretto—is derived from Heine's account[1] of the Ahasuerus of the ocean. The materials for *Tannhäuser* and for *Lohengrin* were collected from the wide field of German mediaeval ballads and epic poems, and from certain modern romantic stories by Tieck and Hoffmann[2].

Now and then the music of *Die Feen* is reminiscent of Weber and Marschner, as *Das Liebesverbot* contains echoes of Auber and Bellini. In *Die Feen* the composer's sudden change of aim and of style comes as a surprise. It is the only one of his works planned in two acts, and the only one that is tainted with what has been called ' an open championship of the rights of the senses.' In this matter it is difficult to criticize; but as, throughout the opera, the music is, on the whole, the predominating factor, its effects may be judged from a musical point of view ; and in that respect they appear just as little deserving of censure as anything of Auber or Bellini. As is the case in some of Marschner's less important operas, a certain lack of melodic distinction is noticeable in *Die Feen*—the musical phrases are effective and by no means weak or commonplace, yet they might be signed with a name other than Wagner's. The pianoforte score of *Die Feen* was published in 1888[3] ; but' of *Das Liebes-*

---

[1] *Memoiren des Herrn von Schnabelewopski* in Heine's Salon.

[2] Tieck's rhymed Erzählung ' Tannhäuser,' and Hoffmann's novel ' Der Kampf der Sänger' (*Serapionsbrüder*, ii. ı).

[3] The following pieces will be found fairly representative :—Act I. Ouverture and Ballet, in E major; a characteristic Tenor Aria in C minor ; Quartet in B b. Act II. Introduction and Chorus of Warriors, D minor (powerful and very effective) ; a touching Aria in F minor ; a capital comic duet in C for Soprano and Bass ; a fine Scena and Aria for Soprano in D, and a grand Finale. Act III. Terzett in C, and Finale in E minor and major, remarkable for its use of the trombones. Extensive and good use is made of Ritornellos before and after the principal arias and ensembles.

verbot only one complete number and certain slight fragments have hitherto appeared in print [1].

The imposing spectacular and musical pomp of Spontini's *Olympie* and of Meyerbeer's *Huguenots* is at least equalled in Wagner's *Rienzi*. The subject first attracted him by the superb opportunities that it offers for the display of operatic pageantry on a grand scale, and by the presence of certain lyrical elements, such as the chorus of the Messengers of Peace, the Battle Hymns, the Church's call, and the Excommunication. When Wagner wrote *Rienzi*, grand opera loomed large before him ; and it was the object of his ambition not merely to produce a copy, but to outvie the original on its own ground and in its every detail. Yet already in *Rienzi* stress is far more consistently laid on the drama than in the case of any contemporary grand opera.

Der fliegende Holländer was originally meant to be performed in one act, as a long dramatic Ballade, and not as a conglomerate of operatic pieces. Reference to the score will show that the division into three acts is made by means of crude cuts, and of new starts equally crude [2]. The music grew out of Senta's Ballade in the second act, which Ballade, as it were, forms the musical nucleus and contains the principal thematic germs (symbolical *Leitmotive*) which permeate the entire work. Far more distinctly than in *Rienzi* (1839), we may recognize in the *Holländer* (1841) the true incipiency of the music-drama. In the poem of *The Flying Dutchman* Wagner treats the legendary subject on its own merits, with the total effect in view, and with little regard to any operatic scheme of recitative, aria, and ensemble, though, to a considerable extent, their forms and even their cadenzas are still present. 'There are moments when the music rises to an extraordinary pitch of vivid picturesqueness and expressiveness. The whole of the overture is as masterly a

---

[1] They consist of a vivacious carnival song in D, $\frac{4}{4}$, specimen bars of which, together with two other short quotations, may be seen in Mr. Wm. Ashton Ellis' *English version of Glasenapp's Life*, vol. i. pp. 184–5.

[2] This has been set to rights at Bayreuth.

musical expression of omens and the wild hurly-burly of the elements as possible, and carries out Gluck's conception of an overture completely; Senta's ballad is one of the most characteristic things of its kind in existence, and hits the mood of the situation in a way that only a man born with high dramatic faculty could achieve; and the duet between Senta and the Holländer is as full of life, and as fine in respect of the exact expression of the moods, of the situation, and as broad in melody, as could well be desired[1].' The instrumentation of the entire score was twice retouched—in 1846 and in 1852—and the close of the overture completely rewritten.

Originally the legend of Tannhäuser and the Hill of Venus, and that of the contest of the Minnesingers at the Wartburg, were not connected. The fusing and welding of these materials is Wagner's own. *Tannhäuser* has undergone more change and transformation than any other of Wagner's productions. We can but touch upon a few salient points. At the close of the third act, both action and music were altered (1845–7) with the intention of making things clear to the sensuous perception of the audience in lieu of an appeal to their imagination; and the entire scene in the Venusberg, Act I, was completely transformed for performance at Paris in 1861. Wagner immediately realized the difficulty of adapting French verse to the prevailing square rhythms of the German music, and he seems to have felt no hesitation in making extensive changes to triple time, both in the scene in the Venusberg and the Ballet that frames it. In the course of revision both the Ballet and the scene came to be expanded to more than double their original dimensions. And, together with the great expansion, there came an equally great change of style—a change so great that one cannot help deploring the interval of fully sixteen years which intervenes between the old *Tannhäuser* and the new (1845–61). The new music was composed to French rhymed verse (by M. Nuitter), and all that remained of the old was

[1] C. H. H. Parry, *The Art of Music*, p. 350.

carefully revised so as to meet the exigencies of French accentuation [1].

The *Lohengrin* legend tells of a knight from oversea, who reached the banks of the Scheldt in a skiff drawn by a swan. There he fought for a noble maid and was wedded to her, but when she asked whence he came and desired to know his name he was forthwith obliged to depart. Wagner takes up this legend—one of the many mythical stories with a religious colouring that cluster round the traditions of the Holy Grail—at the point of its contact with History in the first half of the tenth century. He develops the historical aspect side by side with the supernatural, and thus contrives to present an unrivalled picture of Teutonic mediaeval manners and belief. *Lohengrin* presents the ideals of the later Middle Ages so completely that, for emotional essentials, it would seem idle to go back to documents, and we may add that this is the last of his pieces which Wagner called a *Romantische Oper*. The copiousness of resource displayed, the power and variety of dramatic and musical detail, are astounding. The whole work is a single organism, the soul of music clad in a body of dramatic action.

It may be stated here that for complete comprehension of Wagner's intentions in *Holländer*, *Tannhäuser*, *Lohengrin*, and especially in the later music-dramas, it ought always to be borne in mind that on the stage, the power to declaim and put dramatic meaning into the delivery is in the forefront, and the singer's task is little more than that of assisting and intensifying the expression of emotion. In other words, the hearer's attention is meant to be drawn and directed more to the dramatic whole than to the musical details [2]. If this be understood, it

---

[1] The Parisian version is of course adopted at Bayreuth as 'the sole authentic one'—in spite of the fact that translation back into German has inevitably brought about certain discrepancies between text and music. On the whole, however, the new *Tannhäuser* is superb and perfectly convincing. Wagner dropped the sub-title *Romantische Oper* and called the new version *Handlung*, i. e. action.

[2] But every singer ought to be able to sing—a fact overlooked by the majority of people who are allowed to take part in Wagnerian performances.

will be readily conceded that since the poetical subject is everywhere amenable to the governance of music, the latter, no
matter how complex, need not be cast in the mould of conventional operatic forms, the declamation need not spoil the vocal
melody, and the melody, vocal or orchestral, need not interfere
with the progress of the action. Thus, without consciously
striving to deepen the musical expression, Wagner, in accordance
with the peculiar nature of his subjects and of certain histrionic
details connected with their due presentation, did in point of fact
develop a new melodic idiom; and so step by step, particularly
with the inception of the music-drama, considerably enlarged
the scope and power of his music.

Lohengrin, already, shows great concentration in the scenic
arrangements. Its precursor, Weber's *Euryanthe*, was laid out
in three acts, with two changes of scene in each. *Lohengrin* also
has three acts, but each has only one set scene—an immense
gain in the direction of perspicuity and sustained interest. The
choruses, in their prodigious variety, from mere ejaculatory
utterance to the most expansive lyrical effusion, are very important
factors in the development of the dramatic action. To take but
one instance, the beautiful chorus in eight parts which precedes
and accompanies that miracle of scenic effect, Lohengrin's
arrival in the first act, is perhaps the finest example extant of a
dramatic chorus springing directly from and entirely belonging
to the plot. The instrumentation of *Lohengrin* exhibits the
highest instinct for beauty of tone. ' To any one who has
neither seen nor heard Wagner's scores, neither studied their
consummate workmanship nor felt their scenic power, it is not
so easy to convey a notion of his extraordinary doubling of the
great symphonist with the great dramatist. . . . The orchestra
is divided into three main constituent bodies, with subsidiary
groups of three. This ternary system has the advantage,
among other things, that the whole chord can be given and held
in the same scale of colour. . . . Wagner also makes frequent use
of the distribution of the strings into separate bodies. In a

word, instead of treating the orchestra as an almost homogeneous mass, he parts it into tributary streams and brooks; at times —to change the metaphor—he spins it out to the finest parti-coloured threads, and casts their spools first here then there, now weaving them together, now dividing, until their wondrous ravelling has formed a tissue of priceless lace [1].'

We have already mentioned the occasional touches of Weber, Marschner, Auber, and Bellini which are apparent in Wagner's earliest works. As he comes nearer to maturity Italian and French melody predominates—*Rienzi*, and even ten years later the Finale to the first act of *Lohengrin*, recall Spontini. In the *Holländer* the melody leans either towards the tersely rhythmical folk-song (e. g. the Ballade, the spinning chorus, and the sailors' choruses) or the broad cantilena in which emotion is paramount. In *Tannhäuser*, and still more in *Lohengrin*, the melodic ebb and flow is regulated by the action, which in turn is enforced by characteristic harmony and instrumentation. Finally, in the music-dramas *Tristan und Isolde, Der Ring des Nibelungen, Die Meistersinger, Parsifal*, the vocal melody often springs from the words; it is frequently independent of the orchestra, in some cases, indeed, it is but an intensified version of the actual sounds of the German language, and it becomes lyrical only when the situation demands lyrical ardour.

In the hands of the dramatist, music possesses an inestimable advantage in its capacity to convey the mood of an entire scene or act at once and in an unmistakable manner. A few bars suffice to indicate a mood, and, once established, the expression of such a mood can be sustained for as long a period as may be desirable. A series of scenes or an entire act can be so laid out as to be governed by one or more musical moods, each at will developed, focused, and brought to a climax. The greatest scenic contrasts may thus be risked without fear of failure—such as the sudden transformation in *Tannhäuser* from the lurid light of the Venusberg to sunshine and open air,

[1] Liszt, *Tannhäuser et Lohengrin à Weimar*, 1850.

the reappearance of Venus after Tannhäuser's recital of his
pilgrimage to Rome, the appearance of Elsa on the balcony
after the scene of the conspiracy in the second act of *Lohengrin*,
or the happy contrast between the two sections of the third act
of *Die Meistersinger*; while, for similar examples of homogeneous
development, we may take any of the three acts of *Tristan und
Isolde*, the first or third act of *Die Walküre*, or the first act of
Siegfried.   In all such cases music makes for simplicity in
dramatic construction, whilst it furnishes the fullest and deepest
expression.   Witness the opening of the second and third act
of *Tristan*, and the third act of *Die Meistersinger*.

Every medal has its reverse.   Wagner, whose work at the
dawn of the twentieth century is acclaimed with indiscriminate
admiration all the world over, was, in the third quarter of the
nineteenth, the best abused man in Europe.   Violent and
rancorous attacks upon him found admission into the columns
of German, French, and English journals.   Leading musical and
theatrical critics were bitterly hostile.   Musicians, the veteran
Spohr excepted, stood aside in the difficult position of Molière's
Bridoison : ' Ne sachant pas trop que dire pour exprimer sa
façon de penser.'   Playwrights, actors, singers, put forward
the most inept professional comments.   At best poets were
ready to admit Wagner's musical attainments, composers had
no objection to his dabbling in poetry, whilst sober-minded
people among the laity felt uneasy and held aloof.   Thus during
the greater part of his lifetime Wagner was placed in an
anomalous position ; that of an idealist, a passionate poet,
confronted with the journalists, the miscellaneous public, the
host of professionals connected with the opera and the operetta.
It requires a long period of cure to eradicate from the body
of art the poison of a bad tradition.   In his own words, ' It was
like having to walk against the wind with sand and grit and
foul odours blowing in one's face.'   But time has brought its
revenge.   The present generation of professional musicians is
making the most minute study of Wagner's scores, both from

the dramatic and the musical point of view; public performances of his work are still on the increase, and are steadily
improving in quality; while if we put aside sundry attempts to
find 'hidden meaning' in the dramas, it may be said that even
the futilities of an overgrown Wagner literature [1] appear to
have their use, inasmuch as they frequently arouse and stimulate
enthusiasm.

About the time of the composition of *Lohengrin* Wagner's
mind was agitated by the question whether he ought to
continue as dramatist or musician or both. As has already
been said, he tried historical subjects, *Friedrich Rothbart*
and *Jesus von Nazareth*—the latter a tentative effort in the
direction of *Parsifal*, for which a vast number of notes were
taken and elaborate sketches made [2]. Both of these subjects
were conceived as spoken plays. Ultimately his musical
instincts gained the upper hand, and he came to the conclusion
that, in his own case at least, perfect emotional expression was
possible only when the idea occurs simultaneously to the poet
and the musician. Accordingly he discarded *Barbarossa* and
Jesus von Nazareth, and went on with the story of Siegfried's
death—which ultimately grew into *Der Ring des Nibelungen*.
So by degrees he approached the music-drama. Before it was
reached, however, an immense amount of mental fermentation
was at work—as may be traced in the mass of theoretical
writing which he put forth between 1849 and 1852. His great
problem, 'the problem of the art-work of the future' as he
called it—somewhat like the social problem of Comte—was to
inquire, first how the scattered elements of modern existence
generally, and of modern art in particular, could be united so as
to form an adequate expression of the whole; and secondly,
what hope of a reaction in favour of higher forms of life, than
our present industrialism, would the creation and acceptance of

---

[1] 'Lorsque celui qui parle ne comprend pas et celui à qui l'on parle ne comprend
non plus, alors c'est de la métaphysique' (*Mémoires de Voltaire*, p. 151).

[2] They have now been published.

such a work of art hold out ?   His views of artistic possibilities
being thus ultimately connected with those of social regenera-
tion—art reform with social reform—he might well venture to
take a plunge 'dans l'improvisation risquée des théories
sublimes,' if only to clear his own mind of doubts and
cobwebs [1].

There is many an utterance in Wagner's writings of 1849-
53, which appears but as a comment upon certain experiments
in the execution of *Tannhäuser* and *Lohengrin*.   His writings
at that important period of transition are little more than a
forcible reaction against obstacles in the way of his impulse to
produce—he admits [2] some obscurity, some want of definiteness
in the use of philosophical categories—he rightly calls it
confusion.   In quite early days, and even later up to the end,
his writings represent the extreme sensitiveness of the modern
man—occasional lassitude alternating with crudely vigorous
effort.   In consequence his utterances are at times fanatical in
tone, at times needlessly protracted.   If we take his prose
works as a whole, and appraise them with regard to style, we
must admit that Nietzsche's words are final.   'These products of
Wagner's genius excite, produce unrest; there is an irregularity
of rhythm in them, which makes them, as prose, confusing.
The discourse is frequently broken ; a sort of aversion on the part
of the writer lies like a shadow over them, as if the artist were
ashamed of conceptual demonstration.   What perhaps most
offends those who are not quite at home in them, is an expression
of authoritative dignity, which is quite peculiar to them, and
difficult to describe.   It seems as if Wagner often felt he was
talking before enemies—for all those writings are in a talking, not
a writing style, and they will be found to be such when they are
read aloud—before enemies to whom he refuses familiarity, and

---

[1] Letter to Uhlig, May 1852.   'Nur insofern kann ich mit einiger Befriedigung
auf meine in den letzten Jahren gespielte Litteratenrolle zurückblicken, als ich
fühle, dass ich *mir selbst* dabei vollkommen klar geworden bin.'

[2] Introduction to vols. iii and iv of his collected writings.

for this reason he shows himself reserved and supercilious. But not unfrequently the violent passion of his feelings breaks through the assumed impassibility; then the heavy artificial periods, loaded with qualifying words, disappear, and sentences and whole pages escape him which are amongst the most beautiful that German prose possesses [1].'

The main object Wagner had in view was, as he put it, 'to reconcile the claims of poetry and music with the claims of that most contestable, most equivocal institution of our day, the opera.' Or in other words, and broadly stated, it was his aim to reform the opera from Beethoven's point of vantage. Can the modern spirit produce a theatre that shall stand in relation to modern culture as the theatre of Athens stood to the culture of Greece? This is the complex problem that he set himself to solve. Whether he touches upon minor points connected with it; speaks of the performance of a play or an opera; proposes measures of reform in the organization of existing theatres; discusses the growth of operatic music up to Mozart and Weber, or of instrumental music up to Beethoven; treats of the efforts of Schiller and Goethe to discover an ideal form for their dramatic poems; whether he sweeps round the problem in wide circles; comparing modern social and religious institutions with ancient, and seeking free breathing space for his aspirations, he arrives by either method at the same ultimate result—his final answer is in the affirmative. Starting from the vantage ground of symphonic music, he asserts that we may hope to rise to the level of Greek tragedy; our theatre can be made to embody the modern ideal of life. From the opera at its best a drama can be evolved that shall be capable of expressing the complex relations of modern life and thought. In the first of his speculative, semi-prophetic books, *Die Kunst und die Revolution* (1849), he points to the theatre of Aeschylus and Sophocles, searches for the causes of its decline, and finds them identical with the causes that led to the decline of the ancient

---

[1] G. A. Hight's translation.

state itself. An attempt is then made to discover the principles of a new social organization that might bring about a condition of things in which proper relations between art and public life might be expected to revive. These and similar ideas are further developed in *Das Kunstwerk der Zukunft*, which followed in 1850—a book which, despite its difficulty, is well worth attention. The main argument is as follows: Poetry, imitation, and music were united in the drama of the Greeks; the drama disappeared with the downfall of the Athenian State; the union of the arts was dissolved, each had an existence of its own, and at times sank to the level of a mere pastime. Attempts made, during and since the Renaissance, to reunite the arts, have been more or less abortive, though most of them have made some advance in technique or in width of range. In our day each ' separate branch of art' has reached its limits of growth, and cannot overstep its limits without incurring the risk of becoming incomprehensible, fantastic, absurd. At this point each art demands to be joined to a sister art—poetry to music, imitation to both; each will be ready to forgo its special pretensions for the sake of an ' artistic whole,' and the musical drama may become for future generations what the drama of Greece was to the Greeks.

Wagner's next work, *Oper und Drama* (by far his largest critical and theoretical treatise), contains little of this revolutionary and philosophical ferment. It is set forth in three divisions, of which the first contains an historical criticism of the opera, the second consists of a survey of the spoken drama, and the third is an attempt to unite the results obtained and so construct a theory of the musical drama. In the opera, Wagner asserts, the means of expression (music) have been taken for the sole aim and end, while the true aim (the drama) has been neglected for the sake of particular musical forms. Mythical subjects are best, and Beethoven's music indicates the ideal language in which they are to find expression.

These and other assertions of Wagner's tending in the same direction have already been discussed. One further point, however, requires elucidation—his use of alliterative verse in *Der Ring*, and of a combination of alliteration, assonance, and rhyme in *Tristan* and *Parsifal*. Poets of the Middle Ages, to attain regularity of rhythm, constructed their verses according to some semi-melodious chant or fixed melody; the great variety of Greek metres arose under mimetic influence, springing from the pantomimic action of a dance combined with the choral song. German poets have imitated, as well as their language permits, every possible metre, but no one can deny that the complex rhythms, upon which they pride themselves, exist far more for the eye than for the ear. Take the most common form of verse in modern German plays—accentual iambics—is it not torture to hear the sense of the language forced and twisted to suit the purpose of this metre? Sensible actors, when iambics first came into use, were afraid of sing-song, and recited the lines as prose [1].

French poets, who do not base their rhythms upon recurrences of stress, and who measure their verse by the number of syllables that it contains, believe rhyme to be indispensable. Now if we examine the relation of music to verse, we find the curious fact that musicians declaim iambics, and indeed every species of verse, in every sort of time; as for the rhyme at the end of a line, music usually engulfs it! and the cases wherein the musical rhyme actually corresponds to the rhyme in the verse are for the most part accidental or at any rate few and far between. A musician can do more with iambics than the actors did: he must treat them as prose and stretch or compress them to fit his melody. Seeing that modern versification offers such small attraction, Wagner was led to ask himself what sort of rhythmical speech it might be that would best admit of musical diction, and the answer was not far to seek. When we speak under the

---

[1] 'Talma, in remarking to me that a French actor has difficulties to surmount which an English has not, began with pointing out the necessity he lies under of breaking the joints and claws of every verse, as of pigeons for a pie, and of pronouncing it as if it were none at all; thus undoing what the writer had taken the greater part of his pains to accomplish' (Landor, *Imaginary Conversations, The Abbé Delille and Walter Landor*).

pressure of some strong emotion, we drop conventional phraseology ; we enforce accents with a raised voice ; our words become
strongly rhythmical. In the early days of the Teutonic
languages, such a manner of speech was in use for artistic
purposes ; it is the alliterative verse of the Eddas and of
Beowulf. The condensed form and the close relative position of
the accented vowels in alliterative verse give to it an emotional
intensity, which renders it peculiarly musical : while, in like
manner, assonance and rhyme can be contrived so as to suit the
musician's requirements. The verse, then, with Wagner, is
conceived and executed in the spirit of musical sound, and there
is neither place nor scope for subtleties of diction ; music can
supply all that is needed. Firm and concise, abounding in
strong accents, the alliterative lines of his verse, notably in *Der
Ring*, seem to demand music ; indeed musical emphasis and
prolongation of sound render them more readily intelligible and
more impressive.

The entire music-drama is *musical* in spirit and in detail.
The mythical subject, chosen because of its essentially emotional
nature, the division into scenes, and their sequence ; verse,
declamation, the orchestra, preparing, supporting, commenting,
enforcing, recalling ; all these factors are imbued with the spirit
of music. The pathos of dramatic speech is positively fixed by
the musician's technique, and their interrelation is a direct appeal
through the senses to the emotions.

Artists connected with the opera—scene painters and stage
managers, dancers, choristers, actors, the members of the orchestra
and the Capellmeisters, have been roundly scolded by Wagner
for this or that reason, but all owe a debt of gratitude to him.
He has made their task more difficult, but infinitely more
interesting. Even apart from the stage, at every good performance of music on a large scale, Wagner's spirit is present. The
leading conductors, whether they care to acknowledge the fact
or not, are under his spell : and who can name a composer
(Brahms perhaps excepted) who has not to some extent felt his
weight and in some measure submitted to his influence ?

CHAPTER XV

MUSICIANS AS WRITERS ON MUSIC

IT remains to trace the Romantic masters' efforts in criticism and to mention some of the good work which they have done in musical philology, historical research, the editing of classics and the like. The most significant feature in the mental activity of nineteenth-century musicians is the fact that the spirit of J. S. Bach has become a living influence. The Romantic element in Bach, already pointed out in Chapter I, found response in the mind and heart of Schumann, Mendelssohn, Chopin, Brahms, and Wagner. Bach's earnestness and consistency became the ideal of all serious-minded composers, and his contrapuntal technique gave a fresh impulse to polyphonic treatment in choral and orchestral composition. The study of his works, with their solidity, their variety, and their elasticity of form, acted as a steadying and staying power, and it may be hoped that it will ultimately serve as an antidote to the incoherence and laxness of structure which came as the attendant disease of programme music.

E. T. A. Hoffmann, a writer of imagination and poetical insight, was the first to recognize Beethoven's genius. His reviews of Beethoven's fifth and sixth Symphonies, of the Trios, Op. 70, the Fantasia, Op. 80, together with his so-called Phantasiestücke *Ritter Glück* and *Don Juan*, all of which belong to the early decades of the nineteenth century, are still worth reading. 'When we speak of self-dependent music,' says Hoffmann in an article on Beethoven [1], 'do we not intend

---

[1] *Kreisleriana*, 4.

instrumental music exclusively? Is not instrumental music the most romantic of arts, the one truly romantic art? Is not the infinite its sole object? There are secrets which only sounds can reveal, and under whose weight words break down.' His estimate of the C minor symphony is broad, sympathetic, and tersely expressed: 'Critics have often complained of a lack of unity in Shakespeare, and failed to realize that a fine tree, with its leaves, blossoms and fruit, may spring from a single seed. So they might fail to comprehend the clearness of vision, the high seriousness and complete self-possession [1] which mark the genius of Beethoven and stamp his art.' Valuable remarks on music occur incidentally in Hoffmann's tales; and it is well known that several of the tales and many a stray aphorism made a strong impression on both Schumann and Wagner. For instance—'A fantastic description of a piece of music is admissible only in so far as it is understood to be metaphorical.' Certain titles adopted by Schumann are borrowed from Hoffmann's works: Nachtstücke, Kreisleriana, Phantasiestücke; Hoffmann's Serapionsbrüder and Schumann's Davidsbündler are closely akin. Wagner's indebtedness to Hoffmann's story Der Krieg der Sänger has already been pointed out; and, in like manner, the influence of Hoffmann's Meister Martin der Küfer is perceptible in Die Meistersinger von Nürnberg. Moreover, Hoffmann's opinions on the subject of Poetry and Opera, as set forth at length in a brilliant article entitled 'Der Dichter und der Komponist [2],' are the immediate precursors of Wagner's article 'Ueber das Operndichten und Komponiren.' The very language strikes one as Wagnerian: 'Ja, in jenem fernen Reiche, das uns oft in seltsamen Ahnungen umfängt—da sind Dichter und Musiker die innigst verwandten Glieder einer Kirche: denn das Geheimniss des Worts und des Tons ist ein und dasselbe, das ihnen die höchste Weihe erschlossen.' And again: 'Eine wahrhafte Oper scheint mir nur die zu sein, in

---

[1] 'Die hohe Besonnenheit.'   [2] Serapionsbrüder, i.

welcher die Musik unmittelbar aus der Dichtung als nothwendiges Erzeugniss derselben entspringt [1].'

Weber did not aim at literature when he wrote his ' Dramatisch-musicalische Notizen '—little articles on new operas. His object was to attract attention and induce sympathy with the works which he was about to conduct for the first time at Prague or Dresden. Marschner (*Heinrich IV. und D'Aubigné*), Meyerbeer (*Abimelek*), Hoffmann (*Undine*), Fesca, and other composers of operas, profited by his generous advocacy. Examples of Weber's technical strictures have already been given in the extracts from the review of Hoffmann's *Undine* [2]. That they are always apt and to the point goes without saying; yet there is little of enduring value in Weber's literary remains, except in his last publication—a small pamphlet that accompanied his directions as to the tempi in *Euryanthe* : ' On Tempo in music and on its metronomic indications.' This is a little masterpiece, a landmark in the history of style. Weber's views regarding ' modification of tempo ' are exactly those of Wagner, as set forth in the latter's essay on Conducting. There is another curious and highly significant point of agreement between the two masters : ' I look upon any one,' says Weber, ' who performs a piece from one of my operas at a concert as my personal enemy ' (Letter from London, 1826).

Schumann was proprietor, editor, and chief writer in *Die neue Zeitschrift für Musik* from its foundation in 1834 to 1853, when he took leave of his readers with the prophetic article on Johannes Brahms. Shortly before his death he revised a number of the essays, reviews, and reports, and in 1852 republished them in four small volumes. The *Zeitschrift* was issued to a few hundred subscribers. But in book-form, since

---

[1] ' Yes, in that far-off land which we often reach in dreams, poet and musician are closely related members of one church : and in their highest moods the secret of word and tone is revealed to them as an identity.' And again : ' It appears to me a true opera is one in which the music emanates from the poem as an inevitable product.'

[2] See p. 25.

about 1860, Schumann's writings have been widely read and have had great influence. It is the rare union of literary gifts with the insight of a composer of genius that renders Schumann's writings unique. At once enthusiastic and humorous, bold in imagery, and whimsical in phrase, the style is redolent of Jean Paul Richter and E. T. A. Hoffmann—not involved like Jean Paul's, however, but made up of short vivid sentences, always fresh and breezy. Like his forerunners, the brothers Schlegel, Tieck, Jean Paul, Hoffmann, Schumann protested against all kinds of pedantry and formalism ; like them, he was ever ready to hail anything that showed a touch of individuality and of genuine human nature. His weightier reviews, such as those of Berlioz' Symphonie fantastique, Meyerbeer's *Huguenots*, Mendelssohn's choral works and overtures, Liszt's études, and a large number of Chopin's pieces, are of permanent value. A note of perfect sincerity pervades them, and the style has a rare charm, even when it deals with mere technicalities. In some of the earliest articles (1834–6) Jean Paul and Hoffmann are closely imitated. Later on, the quaint ironical devices, disguises, and *noms de guerre* are dropped, and Schumann writes like a serious artist addressing his equals. Everywhere, even when he laughs or plays tricks, his earnestness is felt to be present. He was a perfect hater of shams. And though he dealt gently and kindly with all manner of ephemeral productions he never lost sight of a high standard of excellence. The essay on Brahms, with which he closed his career as a journalist, is written with the same care as the essay on Chopin with which he began it [1].

Mendelssohn's letters, many of which were apparently written to be read outside the family circle, demand some notice. They are full of facts and precepts valuable to practical musicians and to students of contemporary musical history ; they show a delicate gift for reproducing impressions received from nature

---

[1] A good English translation of his works would be a boon. Madame Raymond-Ritter's version is incomplete and miserably inadequate.

and art, and are expressed in a tone of genial good humour. Mendelssohn always expresses himself with the crispness and precision of a man who thoroughly knows what he is talking about.

There is no such thing as a Wagnerian system of aesthetics. *Das Kunstwerk der Zukunft* and *Oper und Drama* excepted, Wagner's writings are occasional pieces without any calculated continuity. The earliest Romantic pieces, i. e. the Parisian feuilletons[1], recall the manner of E. T. A. Hoffmann. Then came the books which reflect the revolutionary ferment of 1848–52 and show a leaning towards Hellenism ; next follow the mature pieces written at Munich and Triebschen (1864–70), *Ueber Staat und Religion, Deutsche Kunst und deutsche Politik, Ueber das Dirigiren* (1866), and *Beethoven* (1870). These are the result of insight, wide culture, and wide experience. Finally we may mention the occasional contributions to the Bayreuther Blätter, such as *Ueber das Dichten und Komponiren, Ueber die Anwendung der Musik auf das Drama, Wollen wir hoffen ?*, in which the master talks leisurely and confidentially to his friends. They are singularly charming and instructive.

Wagner's criticism is always valuable, even if it is but a side-light or indirect comment on his own practice. Now and then his judgement seems somewhat strained and beside the mark— as when he maintained that in Beethoven's 9th Symphony instrumental music has burst its confines and said the last word possible, when he denounced the oratorio as a feeble hybrid without proper *raison d'être*, or when he refused to credit Jews with creative ability. But his width of view and his absolute sincerity are everywhere apparent. Next to the valuable essay on Conducting—a treatise on style in the execution of classical music—we must rank *Beethoven*, an exposition of the author's thoughts on the significance of Beethoven's music. This work contains his contributions towards the metaphysic of music, if indeed such a metaphysic can be said to exist. It is based on

[1] See W. A. Ellis' translation of the prose works, vol. viii.

Schopenhauer's famous theory; which that philosopher candidly admitted to be incapable of proof, though it satisfied him. Wagner accepts it, and supplements it, by way of analogy, with quotations from Schopenhauer's *Essay on Visions*, the doctrine of which is at least equally problematic [1].

The history of music in Paris from 1835 to 1863 might be traced in the feuilletons which Berlioz wrote for the *Journal des Débats*. Though he was a journalist of genius and well aware of the fact, Berlioz all along protested against his weekly task, and eloquently complained of it as downright slavery [2]. The celebrated *Mémoires* are a brilliant *plaidoyer*, but not a record of fact. 'Ma vie est un roman qui m'intéresse beaucoup,' he says in his letters [3]. Indeed his own standard seems to have been *Désordre et Génie* in literature as in music. The fantastic child of a fantastic time, he never passed beyond the period of storm and stress belonging to his youth and early manhood. His critical remarks, often penetrating, do not spring from a consistent principle, but strike or retort as the occasion suggests. The famous attack on Wagner (*Journal des Débats*, Feb. 8, 1860) and Wagner's dignified reply (Feb. 22) only serve to accentuate the fact that Berlioz could not be just to Wagner without disavowing part of his own work. Comparatively few articles can be classed as literature. The enthusiasm expressed in the more elaborate—the essays on Spontini, on Beethoven's symphonies and sonatas, on Gluck's *Alceste* and *Orphée*, Weber's *Oberon* and *Freischütz*—was doubtless genuine; but now and then, notably in the essay on Spontini, it seems as though Berlioz was writing *de parti pris* with more fervour than penetration. Many of the smaller pieces, brilliant fireworks for

---

[1] See the writer's translation of *Ueber das Dirigiren*, 1887, and *Beethoven* with a supplement from Schopenhauer, London, 1880.

[2] 'Il faut pourtant m'obstiner à écrire pour gagner mes misérables cent francs et garder ma position armée contre tant de drôles qui m'anéantiraient s'ils n'avaient pas tant peur. La violence que je me fais 'pour louer certains ouvrages, est telle que la vérité suinte à travers mes lignes, comme dans les efforts extraordinaires de la presse hydraulique l'eau suinte à travers le fer de l'instrument.'

[3] *Lettres intimes*, p. 127.

the most part—biting, satirical, ironical—were issued in book form as *Les Soirées d'orchestre*, *A travers chants*, and *Les Grotesques de la musique*[1]. A number of *Éloges de complaisance arrachées à sa lassitude* were not reprinted, but the rancorous attack on *Wagner et la musique de l'avenir* was included in *A travers chants*. A series of letters describing his tours in Germany and visits to England and Russia are incorporated in the *Mémoires*. Taken altogether there is not much beyond amusement to be gained from Berlioz' feuilletons. He had little to teach[2]; and his teaching was too often phrased in terms of contempt. The two following sentences will convey some idea of his position and his attitude : 'La musique pure est un art libre, grand et fort par lui-même.' 'Les théâtres lyriques sont des maisons de commerce, où cet art est seulement toléré, et contraint d'ailleurs à des associations dont la fierté a trop souvent lieu de se révolter.' In point of style the *démon romantique* occasionally led him to bizarre exaggeration, and to a confusion between the grandiose and the great. He seemed to consider Beethoven as older Berlioz. But many pages are full of wit and charm; and this is particularly the case with a large portion of the *Mémoires*. There is something musical about the tempo, the rhythm, and the cadence of Berlioz' best sentences. Like his own music his prose is always rhetorical, sometimes eloquent, sometimes violent, sometimes even grotesque. His humour occasionally degenerates into buffoonery, his wit too often takes the form of parody or sarcasm. One only of his literary efforts is really a landmark in the History of Music: the *Grand traité d'instrumentation*, Op. 10, with its sequel *Le Chef d'orchestre*, which, taken all round, is an exhaustive, and in the full sense of the word, masterly work. Thus, Berlioz on Instrumentation, Weber on Tempo, and Wagner on Conducting, are the three practical treatises (classics in their way) that

---

[1] A volume of his miscellaneous articles has recently been collected under the title of *Musique et Musiciens*.

[2] 'Esthétique! Je voudrais bien voir fusiller le cuistre qui a inventé ce mot-là!'

represent the refined sense of style and instrumental colour prevalent in the nineteenth century.

Liszt habitually wrote in French[1]. His enthusiastic admiration for Wagner is recorded in the best of his literary works, a short pamphlet entitled *Lohengrin et Tannhäuser à Weimar*. It made a great stir and was very helpful in the furtherance of Wagner's aims. Next to this masterpiece of sympathetic criticism, we may rank a delightful little essay on John Field, written to serve as an introduction to an edition of Field's nocturnes. The more ambitious efforts, *Frédéric Chopin*, and *Les Bohémiens et leur musique en Hongrie*—improvised contributions to the *Gazette musicale*—were rewritten with the collaboration of Princess Sayn-Wittgenstein, and spoilt in the process. Both contain much irrelevant detail couched in hyperbolical language. *Les Bohémiens*, in book form, was published together with the revised edition of the *Rhapsodies hongroises*. In the main it consists of a laboured attempt to prove the existence of something like a gipsy epic in terms of music—an attempt which was met with ridicule in Hungary itself—the fact being that Hungarian gipsies merely play Hungarian popular tunes in a fantastic and exciting manner peculiar to themselves, but have no music that can properly be called their own. Liszt's book on Chopin contains much that is delicately appreciative and valuable as a record at first hand of Chopin's methods as a player and composer; unfortunately, it also contains many mis-statements of fact, and a good deal of verbiage. Other pieces of interest are the articles on Robert Franz' songs, on Wagner's *Fliegende Holländer*, and on Berlioz' Symphony, *Harold en Italie*. German critics, not without good reason, have spoken of the correspondence between Liszt and Wagner as worthy to rank with that between Goethe and Schiller. These letters, Wagner's especially, are full of interesting passages on problems of music and literature. Liszt's literary efforts, whatever their short-

---

[1] The complete collection of his writings is to be found in a German version by Lina Ramann, six volumes.

comings, proved a stimulating force, the effect of which is
still felt.

The manner of Hoffmann's imaginative criticism was success-
fully imitated by Ambros, the historian of music, whose *Culturhistorische Bilder aus dem Musikleben der Gegenwart*, a collection of admirable essays, 1860–5, stands forth conspicuously
among the doings of the lesser men. Ambros was well equipped
as a musician and gifted with some of Hoffmann's insight and
felicity of speech, which he further qualified with Jean Paul's
fantastic imagery and verbal wit. Even in comparison with
Schumann his articles hold their own, and in point of detail he
occasionally surpasses his master. Bülow's analysis of Wagner's
Eine Faust-Ouvertüre and Draeseke's articles on Liszt's 'poèmes
symphoniques' deserve mention as models in their way [1].

With advancing years the historical tendency gained in strength
and widened in scope. The success of the Bach revival prepared
the way for editions of the works of Palestrina, Lasso, Purcell,
Handel, Gluck, Mozart, Beethoven, Schubert, and also of a
number of Bach's immediate precursors, such as Schütz,
Sweelink, Frescobaldi, Frohberger, Buxtehude, Reinken, Kerl,
George and Theophilus Muffat, Fux, Couperin, Rameau, and
both Alessandro and Domenico Scarlatti.

Antiquarian research brought to light the splendid collection
of early English music for the Virginals known as the Fitzwilliam
collection, Denys Gaultier's *La Rhétorique des dieux*, and a vast
number of miscellaneous Italian, Spanish, and German pieces
for the lute. Extensive collections of folk-songs and dances
were made; and good historical and biographical work was
done.

Among the leading books of antiquarian research, history, and
biography may be mentioned :–Kiesewetter's *Geschichte der euro-
päisch-abendländischen oder unsrer heutigen Musik* (1834–46);

---

[1] Ferdinand Hiller's lucubrations were characterized by Wagner as ' Literatur'
—meaning waste paper. And the same holds good of Riehl's once celebrated
Characterköpfe, 1853, and La Mara's *Musikalische Studienköpfe*.

Coussemaker's *Les Harmonies des* XIIe *et* XIIIe *siècles,* and *L'Art harmonique aux* XIIe *et* XIIIe *siècles* (1865); Ambros, *Geschichte der Musik,* of which vols. ii and iii are the most valuable (the third volume of Ambros' History, extending down to Palestrina, appeared 1868, and the work was completed, in rather perfunctory manner, by W. Langhans); Ritter's *Geschichte des Orgelspiels* (1884); Weitzmann's *Geschichte des Clavierspiels* (1863)[1]; Wasielewski's *Die Violine und ihre Meister* (1869). The standard biographies are Pohl's *Haydn,* Jahn's *Mozart,* Thayer's *Beethoven* (to be read in Deiter's much augmented German edition); F. W. Jähns' *C. M. von Weber in seinen Werken* (a thematic catalogue, chronologically arranged, the comments on which form the most trustworthy treatise on Weber's works), 1871; Chrysander's *Händel,* Spitta's *J. S. Bach,* and Glasenapp's *Life of Wagner* as rewritten by Mr. W. Ashton Ellis. Among technical treatises Helmholtz' *Die Lehre von den Tonempfindungen,* and Riemann's researches into the nature of rhythm, and his ingenious solutions of difficult rhythmical problems, are important. In Russia much energy has been devoted to the history and theory of ecclesiastical music. Dimitri Rasumovsky —author of *Der Kirchengesang in Russland, Die patriarchalischen Sänger, Diakone und Unterdiakone* (1868), and *Untersuchungen über die Lesung der Znamja-Notation* (1884)—began to lecture at the Conservatoire of Moscow on the music of the Orthodox Church in 1866. Yurij v. Arnold published *Die alten Kirchenmodi, historisch und akustisch entwickelt,* 1879; *Theorie des altrussischen Kirchen- und Volksgesanges,* 1881; *Die Harmonisierung des altrussischen Kirchengesangs,* 1886. Smolensky, Rasumovsky's successor as lecturer at Moscow, wrote a *Kursus des kirchlichen Chorgesangs* (1887), and *ABC-Buch des Gesanges nach der Znamja-Notation des Alexander Minez* (1868), which is said to be an important work with regard to the history of the melodies belonging to the Russian Church.

---

[1] See third edition, edited and enlarged by Max Seiffert and Oskar Fleischer, 1899. An admirable piece of work in course of publication.

Instrumental music does not form part of the Greek orthodox service, which is exclusively choral. And in this connexion the ten volumes of sacred music *a capella* by Dimitri Bortniansky, which have been edited by Tchaikovsky, deserve mention. Bortniansky (1779–1828) was a pupil of Galuppi, and to his vapid Italianisms, quite as much as to the Italian opera, may be traced many of those curious southern idioms which so often and so incongruously occur in the melody of later Russian masters.

CHAPTER XVI

SUMMARY AND CONCLUSION

A BRIEF summary will be sufficient to recall to the reader's mind the salient points in this survey of the Romantic movement. In Weber's time musicians came under the spell of Romantic literature and learnt to look at their art from the Romantic standpoint. Increased facility of international intercourse was a powerful source of change. Thus it has come about that at the present day exotic rhythms, harmonics, and even melodies are found to be admissible and sometimes welcome elements in the musical speech of Western Europe. Indeed, if a lexicon of musical diction were compiled, it would have to include many curious rhythms as well as melodic and harmonic deviations from the normal language. In opera as well as in instrumental music poetical suggestion by musical means became one of the chief aims. In music for the orchestra and the pianoforte characteristic titles, mottoes, superscriptions, were employed. Gradually 'poetical intentions' took the lead ; and composers began to accept relaxations of the laws of structure. In symphonic music design on purely musical lines was gradually set aside to make room for a kind of impressionism, wherein unity was sought not so much in well-balanced musical development as in extraneous considerations, such as the sequence of ideas in a poem, the incidents in a story, or the variety of colours in a landscape. After a time illustration became the ideal and symphonic music was transformed into programme music. At first the aim seemed to be freedom in matters of form only. But with this freedom the door was opened to sheer eccentricity and ugliness of theme. Yet in the long run the common sense of musical art showed that these extravagances were mere incidents which did not prevent the attainment of more pliant and varied forms, together with increased power and beauty of emotional expression.

The entire process, in instrumental music, was a change from the formal to the characteristic—a movement away from the precise symmetry of the sonata and the symphony and tending towards the Characterstück and the Poème symphonique. In dramatic music, it was a movement away from the conventions of the older opera and a tendency towards the freedom of the music-drama. Expressive consistency, at times of a very subtle sort, was retained and depended in songs, chansons, Lieder ohne Worte, nocturnes, and other short characteristic pieces. A taste for excessive emotionalism was developed, and composers took pains to attain the clearest articulation of details. Everywhere in the short lyrics of the time there is the charm of novelty, 'the magic touch of Romanticism, the addition of strangeness to beauty.' Technically the principle of tonality was expanded, and new departures in key distribution and an increasing use of chromatic harmonies and complicated discords became prevalent, especially in Chopin, Berlioz, and Wagner. Liszt, in particular, endeavoured to find new cadences to serve for the close of his pieces.

Weber's *Freischütz* marks the triumph of early Romanticism, his *Euryanthe* the transition to the continuous music of later times. Characterization, subtle devices of instrumentation, and local colour, played an important part in his work. In France the storm and stress of Romantic literature found an echo in the opera, and in Berlioz' orchestral pieces. Italy began with sentimental cantilena and ended with a marked increase in dramatic effect. The tendency towards closeness of characterization affected the oratorio and the cantata, which were rejuvenated, and somewhat secularized in the process. Instrumental music in the concert-overture and the symphony endeavoured to reproduce moods and impressions derived from literature or from natural phenomena. The beginnings of illustration proper, apart from the ostensible writers of programme music, appeared in Mendelssohn's octet and the cantata *Die erste Walpurgisnacht*. Attempts at direct alliance of music with poetry and painting were made by Berlioz and Liszt, who frankly employed the means of musical expression for purposes of illustration. The programme, suppressed or implied, made its appearance in the concertos of Spohr and Weber. The instinct for concentrated expression produced Schumann's string quartets. Weber in the ball-room and Chopin in the salon infused the Romantic spirit into the dance. The growth of instrumental technique is exemplified in Paganini, Chopin, and Liszt; the last of whom invented the 'Dramatic Fantasia' and produced faithful transcriptions of symphonies, overtures, and songs for the pianoforte. Berlioz and Wagner extended the technique of orchestration. National elements, Polish, Hungarian, Norwegian, Spanish, Russian, came into play. Schumann was successful in obtaining a perfect equipoise between verse and music in the Lied. Impressionism and word-painting made their appearance in Liszt's Lieder and Berlioz' chansons; the dramatic and histrionic element prevailed in the vocal ballade; and music, even apart from the stage, was pressed into the service of melodrama.

One result which followed from this attempt to make music representative was the development of a new kind of comedy, its lighter form in Offenbach and Sullivan, its more elaborate in Wagner's *Meistersinger* and Verdi's *Falstaff*. At the same time national opera, based on folk-tunes and dances, appeared in Poland, Bohemia, and Russia. Finally Wagner gathered together the various Romantic tendencies; tested them through a period of experiment, speculation and theory, and ultimately reached the music-drama.

The main problem set before us by the Romantic movement is that of an alternative between programme music, with concomitant laxness of structure, and self-dependent music, it may be in conformity with an unwritten programme, but firmly and consistently designed on musical lines. The case for self-contained instrumental music cannot be better stated than in the words of Schopenhauer: 'If we look at pure instrumental music, we shall see that in the symphony of Beethoven there reigns the greatest confusion, beneath which nevertheless there is the most perfect order: the most violent strife, that in the next moment grows into loveliest concord: it is *rerum concordia discors*, a true and complete image of the essential nature of the world, that rolls on in the immeasurable complication of countless shapes, and supports itself by constant destruction. At the same time all human passions and emotions speak from this symphony: joy and sorrow, love and hate, fear and hope, in countless gradations; all however in the abstract only, and without any particularity; it is merely the form of emotion, a spirit world, without matter. It is true, however, that we are inclined to *realize* it while listening, to clothe it in our fancy with flesh and blood, and to see in it the various scenes of life and nature. Yet on the whole, this neither facilitates its comprehension, nor enhances its delight, giving rather a heterogeneous and arbitrary alloy: it is therefore better to receive it directly and in its purity [1].'

Perhaps the following considerations may be taken to represent fairly what can be said of music with an implied or an avowed programme. In characteristic overtures such as Mozart's *Don Giovanni*, Beethoven's *Coriolan*, *Leonora*, *Egmont*, and the overtures of Weber, the feeling for musical symmetry and proportion is completely in accord with the tendency to express the particular mood or moods indicated by the titles. But in the poème symphonique, symmetry and proportion are made to depend, not on purely musical, but on more or less extraneous considerations. Under such circumstances, so long as the composer develops his subjects and figures on musical lines and makes no attempt to deal with concrete facts of any kind,

[1] Schopenhauer, *Die Welt als Wille und Vorstellung*, ii. chap. 39.

musical design may still be direct and definite. Conversely the question may be asked: if a poem or a picture forms the programme, can the music be actually identical with the material contents of the verse or with the scene upon the canvas? It can be *analogous*, but that is all. Yet so long as the moods of a poem or picture are truly rendered in terms of music, this very analogy will illuminate the musical form with its own beauty and suggestiveness. Programme music, at its best, means symbolism—that is to say, expression gained by the use of symbolical phrases which are treated by some intellectual process necessarily logical. But the genius of symphonic music cannot rest satisfied with signification. Beethoven's musical design is complete in itself; it appeals to us not by what it signifies, but by what it is, and its fullest expression never obscures or weakens its architectonic structure. On the dramatic side, Wagner's method is at present the most completely organized system for purposes of musical expression. On the instrumental side illustration, apart from design, is in pursuit of a false ideal: it is the satyr Marsyas, imitating on his flute the music of his native uplands, and doomed to destruction if he challenges the golden lyre of Apollo.

INDEX

70820